DATE DUE

Creative Management

Shigeru Kobayashi

Creative Management

English-language edition planned and translated from the Japanese under the auspices of the Japan Management Center Inc.

American Management Association, Inc.

Library of Congress catalog card number: 71-130916
International standard book number: 0-8144-5241-8

FIRST PRINTING

Preface

FROM the summer of 1961, when I entered Sony as Atsugi Plant manager, until the summer of 1969, when I was relieved of that position, my life there was a stretch of pretty hard work on the one hand and, on the other, a series of the most solidly rewarding, joy-filled experiences. Sony's unique environment, which is characterized by both freedom and vitality, called forth all my ability and made me deliver my best. My years at Atsugi, in short, developed in me beliefs which can be summarized into the following three major points:

1. All human beings, deep down, have the desire to devote themselves to work as the central element in their lives and even to lose themselves completely in their work.

2. Traditional management is creating all sorts of "people" problems by habitually treating human beings as if they were machines or domestic animals.

3. The task of achieving innovation in management becomes harder as organizations grow larger. Perhaps it is simply the infinite process of evolution that is concerned here. In any case, I believe such innovation is not only possible but also inevitable.

The experience and thinking which led me to these beliefs eventually became known to a publishing firm. As a result of its persuasive encouragement, my first book, *Sony Makes People Live,* was published in 1966. My second—*Creative Management* —followed in 1967.

By definition, however, I am a "doer" and not an expert who specializes in thinking or writing, and therefore my two books were written naively. But the reaction of Japanese readers to these two books has been astounding. Indeed, it still is, even at this date. The fact that the response has been so overwhelming makes me realize how many people—regardless of what company, plant, government agency, or school they belong to and what their social status, age, or sex may be—are struggling for solutions to the same kinds of problems with the same kind of awareness. A number of readers have written to me saying that, thanks to my books, they have been encouraged to hope that their efforts will bring success. This vote of confidence, in turn, has proved to be a source of further encouragement to me.

The English version of *Creative Management* has been produced by combining my two books in Japanese through careful editing and translation. Substantial differences exist between East and West from the standpoint of language characteristics, institutions, manners, and customs. I believe, however, that no difference exists between East and West in regard to the three major points with which I began this preface. It is my sincere hope that Western readers, overcoming the many differences that, as I have said, do tend to separate us, will respond favorably to these essentially universal points.

Sony's present-day Atsugi Plant has grown much bigger than it was when my original books were written. Various systems have since changed and been developed further, but in this English version I have made no particular effort to update the facts.

Then, too, since assuming a new post at Sony in the area of management and personnel development, I have changed parts of my thinking to some extent. Here again, however, I have made no revisions or corrections in the present volume; rather, I wanted to convey to my readers the true facts of Atsugi Plant's situation, as I saw it, up to 1966—together with what I believed was the right direction to move in exploring a new management philosophy as part of the ever evolving development of Sony.

Shigeru Kobayashi

小 林 茂

Tokyo
September 1970

Contents

Prologue

Embarking on a Dignified Management Style

1

A Company Named Sony

IT was in August 1961 that, having worked in several companies, I joined Sony, Inc. Although I had had some contact with the firm during the previous year, it will be obvious that the relationship between us was relatively new and not especially deep. Therefore, I was in a position to observe the company named Sony with relative objectivity even as I became an "insider," a working member of the organization.

By 1961, Sony was already well known throughout the world. However, it had—and still has—many elements of immaturity. In that sense it is a company with many shortcomings. In particular, when I had my first experiences with it, the so-called "15th anniversary strike" was in progress. There were rumors at the time that while Sony was a good, fast-growing company, both its personnel management and its management in general were average or below average and were up against substantial problems.

Such criticism is to some extent accurate. What, then, are the factors behind Sony's sustained growth as a superior company despite its shortcomings? This is an interesting question.

Youthful Energy Both Strength and Weakness

My own explanation is that, first of all, the company's short-comings are indeed a manifestation of immaturity—one that is inseparably linked with its rapid growth. These shortcomings, like those so often attributed to the United States of America, are the expression of the courage and energy—and lack of experience—that characterize young men and organizations in the process of growing.

Sony's shortcomings certainly must be corrected. Indeed, an aggressive effort is now being made to overcome them. But this effort should not result in the mature but lifeless nondefects of an old man—and, as a matter of fact, no such possibility exists in Sony at the present moment. Rather, these signs of immaturity that I have cited will be a source of strength as long as those in the company are aware of them and waging a battle against them with all the resources of youth. The fact that we are not vexed with problems is not important. What must be valued here is our capacity for solving problems when we do have problems. Conflict is the very source of creation; thus what is most to be feared by the company that wants its management to remain creative is loss of the sense of conflict through the resolution of conflict by an old man's methods.

The Philosophy of *Mu* [1]

Secondly, Sony has an incomparable philosophy of management excellence. This is well embodied in the attitudes of Masaru Ibuka, president, and Akio Morita, executive vice-president. These two men are different from each other in many respects, yet their strengths and weaknesses combine as in a symphony to

[1] *Mu* is one of the tenets of Buddhism. The word is normally translated as "nothingness" or "a void."

make up Sony's guiding force. Behind this guiding force, and implicit in the thinking of both men, lie the concepts and principles—the philosophy—which resulted in the development of Sony.

What is this philosophy? It might almost be termed one of *mu*—that is, nothingness. For instance, asked by a journalist, "What are your company's principles and policies?" Mr. Ibuka emphatically answered, "We have no such thing." And Mr. Morita, in the epilogue of his book *No Diplomas Required,* declares: "What I have said so far reflects my way of thinking only up to the present moment. I cannot tell how it may change in the future."

"Nothingness" does not mean that the company is to be managed on the basis of whim from day to day or that no fundamental principles are involved. It does mean that without being hampered by our own and others' fixed ideas, we are to observe honestly both the subjective and the objective aspects of conditions as they appear to be at various times, set our goals accordingly, and establish means of achieving those goals in a spirit of complete open-mindedness. It means that even if the conclusions reached in this manner should prove to diverge widely from generally accepted thinking—or our own thinking up to that point—we will still implement them with courage and fervor.

The process of implementation may often tend to produce results that are different from the ones anticipated, thus indicating the existence of facts unsuspected in the past. This means that any such newly determined facts must be incorporated in our data for additional consideration and that subsequently established goals or methods will have to be revised or even abolished—again with complete open-mindedness. It means, possibly, issuing an order in the morning and rescinding it in the evening without prejudice. It does not emphasize the subjectivity of individual judgment; rather, it is faithful to the ever changing objective facts of a given situation. Hence "there is no such thing" as a company principle or policy.

This type of management attitude has no parallel among Japanese industrial circles today. In the majority of companies, when staff personnel recommend a certain policy to top man-

agement, they try to make their advice authoritative by saying
that the policy in question is being implemented successfully or
that good results are being obtained with it in many Japanese
firms. Top management, listening to this kind of argument, tends
to accept the advice lest it fail to get aboard the bandwagon.

The first thing I learned after I joined Sony is that such a
modus operandi does not hold good here. Should anyone try to
sell a proposal in that manner, top management would merely
listen to it and brush it aside. Selling a proposal to top management at Sony requires a clear, detailed presentation of the subjective or objective data from which it is derived. In addition, the
seller must communicate his own position, thought out dispas-
sionately on the basis of such data, and impress his listeners with
the zeal with which he argues his points. As long as the position
he assumes is right and his thinking is logical, top management
will bravely adopt the recommended policy—however contrary
it may be to generally prevailing ideas of common sense—unless
facts unknown to the man making the proposal negate it alto-
gether.

This open-mindedness is Sony's unique characteristic—the
very root of the management attitude which created the company
of today. Its shortcomings notwithstanding, Sony will continue
to grow in the future so long as this open-mindedness does not
vanish. I believe that creative management *should* be open-
minded and that this is precisely the philosophy that is needed by
any company which, like Sony, is oriented toward technological
development.

The Rejection of Pseudo-Learning

The majority of Japanese companies either have been imita-
tors or have depended on imported technology both in management and in the physical sciences. Every sign clearly indicates,
however, that both types are facing a dead end. Imitation is effective in catching up with perfect, stable models; but Japanese
industry, having attained its current level of growth, can no
longer find such advanced models to copy. It has available to it

nothing but fluid models in the process of development, and no one can imitate a fluid model. Therefore, mere imitation can only fail from now on.

In contrast, what we at Sony have been doing since 1961 in the area of plant management is, in a nutshell, the faithful implementation of Sony's traditional creative or pioneering spirit. This, paraphrased, means that we are making management more scientific and more democratic. And, in the final analysis, "more scientific" and "more democratic" are one and the same thing. It all goes back to Sony's management: that is, encouraging everyone, at all levels, to face facts without prejudice; implementing what the facts teach us courageously; and making immediate corrections if we are in the wrong—all of which is the very essence of scientific management.

When we talk about scientific management in Japan, we immediately associate it with such concepts and functions as quality control and industrial engineering. Making something scientific tends to be regarded as systematization of methods or as mechanization. This can be explained in part by the fact that Japan imported its science. Importation of accepted academic theory from foreign countries "as is" immediately establishes a new branch of learning, and this was true in Japan with regard to both management and other sciences. In short, importation of refined methods or systems is regarded as the act of making something scientific. Should those responsible meet with strong resistance from reality or should they fail to produce any remarkable effects, they try to vindicate themselves by remarking humorously that such-and-such an academic discipline is too advanced or that misguided Japanese practices are beyond any relief.

I, for one, am entirely opposed to this practice of making something pseudo-scientific. As Dr. Hideki Yukawa, the Nobel Prize-winning physicist, once said: "In science one cannot arrive at an absolute truth. Many Japanese scientists are convinced that they have already searched for truth during the preparatory phase in the search for truth." (Dr. Yukawa's words apply to management science in Japan as well as any other.) I dare say, at the risk of incurring misunderstanding, that nothing can be regarded as true science unless it is something which is continually changing, unless it is something which has not yet been perfected, and unless the search for it calls for self-sacrificing courage like that of Copernicus. The cautious yet bold and open-minded attitude which persistently searches for something unknown with the full knowledge that something unknown exists may be the really scientific attitude. To regard a certain system as supreme represents a fixed and dogmatic attitude that is surely the most unscientific.

To quote Dr. Yukawa once more: "Learning without the wisdom of life is no learning." And again: "Learning starts from intuitive recognition in the place of living." These statements have profound implications for us here.

Every Royal Road Was Once Abnormal

I have so far described what this business of making management scientific should be. Now let us see what it so often is said to be but is not—as, for example, when a certain management scholar reportedly asserted, "Sony is different. It is abnormal." And when he continued by saying, "Even in the area of management there is an orthodox, 'royal' road. Truly successful, long-lasting companies belong to the school that follows this road. Abnormal companies, when all is said and done, may not last. Therein lies a problem for Sony."

This remark indicates a common type of thinking on the part of many so-called management scholars in Japan. What are this "royal road" and this "orthodoxy," anyway? According to these scholars, they seem to mean generally accepted ways of doing things or ways indicated in the American literature or ways which are theoretically (so they think) logical. But every royal road was an "abnormal" one at the time of its birth regardless of where it was born. So were all scientific discoveries and so was the Ford system. When the Ford system became fixed and rigidly adhered to—that is, when it became the "royal road," as our Sony critic puts it—Ford faced a crisis.[2]

---

[2] The system introduced by Henry Ford, which resulted in his golden era, was based on the idea of higher wages for greater efficiency. But, as time went on and

If there be a problem for Sony, it is the always-present possibility of losing its "abnormality" and becoming orthodox. Avoiding this danger and maintaining this abnormality require Sony to be constantly on the move and to continue its process of self-innovation. And, in order to make all this possible, management must exclude any but the truly scientific spirit to which I have just alluded.

The uniqueness of our plant management is continually being publicized nowadays. And, indeed, the plant is *not* managed in accordance with any specific, preconceived ideologies or theories of management science. In fact, I am against all kinds of ideologies. In our progress we have simply let reality be our tutor—in other words, been guided by what the facts taught us.

That is the point I want to underscore right here at the beginning of this book.

---

the system became firmly established, it began to lose its flexibility and its ability to adapt to an ever changing environment. The organization began to suffer from a sort of "arteriosclerosis," and dissatisfaction among the workers grew—a dissatisfaction that Ford interpreted as indicating the presence of agitators among his employees. Granted that extraneous factors may or may not have had something to do with the so-called crisis in the plant, I believe that the real, *inner* crisis was brought on by Ford's philosophy about the management of an enterprise. The alienation of human beings by the concept of meaningless labor, plus the emphasis on more work for more pay, was the true cause of the dissatisfaction. Ford failed to understand this because of his preconceptions about management.

2

The Start of the Revolution at Atsugi Plant

OUR plant specializes in the manufacture of transistors. Its total employment in 1961, when I first joined the company, was about 500 to 600, and 85 percent of the employees were girls—graduates of junior high schools who were recruited in groups from agrarian areas. The majority of these girls lived in company dormitories and were working on a two-shift basis. Their reputation at that time was anything but good. For instance, the strike staged on our 15th anniversary involved mostly women workers who, at the instigation of the union, were herded into buses and picketed in front of company headquarters. The citizens of Atsugi City, which used to be a mere pastoral area, frowned at the workers' red flags. Also, eyebrows were raised in disapproval of these women's morals as evidenced in their daily conduct.

With this advance information in mind, I went alone to assume my post as plant manager. Originally in the printing business, I was completely unfamiliar with transistors. No one in the plant knew me well then, nor have I tried since that time to bring in personal friends from outside. So, as I took over my duties, I was a bit worried. "I would like to study a little about transistors," I told Mr. Ibuka. "I wonder if you could recommend any good books on the subject." "There is no need for such study," he shot back. "You wouldn't understand the books even if you did read them." And he continued by saying, "Mr. Kobayashi, I shall not mind if this plant has to be shut down. You are free to do what you like." This was a singular expression of confidence in me on Mr. Ibuka's part, and I thought I had an accurate idea of what he meant by it. I felt pleased. I had the best possible superior for the first time in my life.

I Like Human Beings

On the day of the ceremony that marked my assumption of authority, I stood in front of the workers, my mind refreshingly empty and receptive. Glancing at the girls, I found all of them irresistibly young. They were so cheerful, so smiling and cute—at least, they really looked that way to me then. So, without thinking, I blurted out something to this effect: "I don't know anything about transistors, but I like human beings very much. Let us do our best together." This was the start of my first encounter with my lovable people.

Even to this day, those who were present still remember this remark of mine. They tell me that they were taken aback at hearing me say, "I like human beings." But this experience and others which followed set me to thinking about labor unrest at Sony.

Under Sony's management philosophy, employees were expected to engage spontaneously in creative activity; therefore, the defects of imitative, pseudo-scientific management that I mentioned earlier simply could not exist. As a matter of fact, it was because these defects did not exist that Sony has been able to achieve such phenomenal growth. However, while the company was small, the entire workforce was under the personal direction of top management. Later, when Sony grew into a large-scale enterprise, this personal sort of operation was not possible any more. The outstanding Sony management philosophy then failed to reach the majority of company employees. The only way of making sure that it permeated all organizational levels was to make a fresh start at developing high-quality new managers and new management systems, yet the rapid expansion of the company scarcely left those responsible any time for that. Seizing this opportunity, mundane management principles which were a far cry from the philosophy of Sony began to spread in immature forms throughout the company. I felt intuitively that, although the resulting damage was still minor, it might very well be the real cause of our labor troubles.

Now that I was the manager of Atsugi Plant—I became convinced—it was my duty to establish in the expanded organization a new type of management based on the spirit of Sony's founding days. This was something nobody had yet tried. It would be an arduous task, but it must be attempted. It might be painful, but it would be worth the effort.

That was my state of mind on approaching what I now saw as my responsibility as plant manager. Thus I took my first step.

Revival of Cafeteria Service Without Attendants

Most of the plant employees, as I have said, lived in the dormitories provided for them and so ate three meals in the plant cafeteria. Soon after I took over, the matter of this cafeteria came up for discussion. The problem was overcrowding. There were long lines, and the employees needed so much time for meals that a great part of each "break" was necessarily eroded away.

The problem could be solved by enlarging the service counters or by increasing the number of attendants considerably— either of which would mean extra cost. With a specific purpose in mind, I proposed to the management personnel then in charge that service counters without any attendants be introduced, so that each person would get his meals in exchange for meal coupons [3] without being watched.

I drew a parallel with the business of making transistors. The tasks involved here demand extreme precision, and acceptable quantity of output has always posed problems. To increase the output, as well as the reliability of the finished product, calls for improvement not only in technical processes but also in the conscientiousness with which the individual employee does his job. No one could expect an employee who made a habit of enjoying free meals to produce a quality transistor—unless he were watched. Therefore, my plan for a cafeteria without attendants should by all means be adopted. Should we be unable to abolish the watchers, I pointed out, then there would be no reason for the existence of Atsugi Plant.

Every member of plant management opposed this plan strongly. "When the plant was built," they said, "we had no alternative but to resort to a cafeteria without attendants because of the shortage of labor. And we could not collect a third of the meal tickets." In other words, a third of the meals were obtained fraudulently. In addition, I was told, toilet paper was taken home, and so were the company-supplied slippers worn in the plant.

"So you see," declared my colleagues, "these are people with no morals. Your view of human nature as being fundamentally good will mean nothing to them. It is certain that your trust will be betrayed. Since it would embarrass us to see you let down, please don't take the risk."

Realizing that they all were opposing me with the best of intentions, I made the following rebuttal: "I don't know about the philosophical basis for the ethical doctrine that man's inborn nature is good, but I don't think my feeling is based on this doctrine. I agree with you completely about the untrustworthiness of human behavior. I cannot even trust my own.

"For example, I am a heavy smoker. On many occasions, I have resolved that I would quit smoking, but I have never been

[3] Meal coupons are a form of private "money" honored only at Sony cafeterias. They are issued in units of one to 40 yen, and one book of meal coupons is worth 1,000 yen. The coupons are used just like cash. Employees choose whatever dishes they like on a self-service basis, figure out how much they owe, and voluntarily pay for each meal by depositing the necessary coupons in the receiving box.

able to stick to any such resolution. Your opinions as to the trust-worthiness of our employees are the same as mine, but there is a fundamental difference between us on an important point. It has to do with your statement that 'these are people with no morals.' When you brand them as lacking in morals, you assume that you yourselves do have morals. And I simply cannot agree with you. Are these workers immoral and we managers beyond reproach? I think we should think about this for a while.

"I had a bitter experience during the war, toward whose end I was drafted as a mere Category IIB soldier.[4] Moved arbi-trarily from the Yokosuka to the Ohminato Marine Corps, I led a more pitiful life than many a prisoner. At that time, both com-missioned and noncommissioned officers were preaching patrio-tism to soldiers whenever they opened their mouths, yet they also kept saying that we soldiers were expendable and could be con-scripted by one sheet of draft paper. In short, they failed to treat us like human beings. How did we feel, under the circum-stances, and how did we behave? To this day I remember vividly the resentment I felt. I cannot forget it.

"We soldiers were well aware of the fact that these officers were diverting meat and sugar intended for the troops into other channels. So we were sure that we at least loved our country more than they did. Listening to them, I for one felt nothing but utter mockery in their preaching of patriotism, no matter how hard they tried. Meanwhile, for our part we were practically living the life of thieves. Meals were scarce, and we stole. We stole—and kept on stealing—many issued items.

"The following incident is something I still cannot wipe from my mind. This episode occurred when our company in the Ohminato Marine Corps was ordered to pick up firewood on a nearby mountain. We marched in a file, listlessly. This was actually more tiring than brisk walking; nonetheless, we soldiers never tried to walk in a normal way. The firewood had been cut in one-foot lengths. Everybody grabbed a piece, and we started back. It would have been easy for us to carry two pieces, one in

---

[4] A Category IIB soldier is so classified by physical examination at the time he is drafted. Draftees classed as Category IIB are those without prior military service who are relatively old in years. They are placed in the reserve forces.

each hand—even four or five pieces would hardly have been regarded as any form of strenuous labor. But to a man, deliberately, each of us took with him only one piece of wood.

"We could not have said then that we had any feeling of patriotism. Nor were we at all pleased with our behavior. We were just reacting to the deep gloom and weariness of our present mood. Why did we behave as we did? Because it was the only way in which we could keep up our morale. It was, so to speak, a pitiful kind of resistance. Denied humanity, we sadly committed the offenses of stealing and walking listlessly. These were the only channels left open to us. Only by such means could we express our feelings of anger.

"The commissioned and noncommissioned officers undoubtedly pointed their fingers at us and swore that we were unpatriotic. They most certainly thought that we were a bunch of immoral good-for-nothings. Yet how did I, then a soldier, differ from the man who is now a plant manager? I do not think there has been any improvement in my morals since then. I would not cheat in a cafeteria without attendants; however, that is not because I have morals but because my situation has changed. I cannot help feeling, therefore, that those of you who say our employees are immoral share the kind of feeling harbored by the wartime officers I remember with such bitterness.

"Suppose I resigned from this post of mine as plant manager and you resigned from your jobs and all of us here started again as workers in this plant—which then proceeded to deny us our humanity. We would be essentially the same people we are now, yet we would probably begin to do things which others would immediately brand as immoral—even though it would be highly unlikely for us to feel at all happy while doing so. My experience as a soldier convinced me of this.

"I do not trust the behavior of human beings, but at the same time I know that human beings cannot be happy while doing wrong. Human beings want to behave correctly. It is because of their own frailty and the treatment they receive from others that they grow rebellious and, unfortunately, lose their sense of moral values. To say it another way—I do not trust the behavior of human beings, yet I know *I can trust human beings as such*. This is not my mere personal belief but a universal truth, and it is in my perception of this truth that I differ from all of you."

Finally, I succeeded in persuading plant management to accept my proposal on two conditions: I must consult with the employees, and they must be willing to go along with the plan. I then summoned all hands together, saying, "For such-and-such reasons, I should like to eliminate the attendants in the cafeteria. We have only 500 to 600 people here now; yet, if we can successfully establish our cafeteria on this basis in a small way, we will be preparing the ground for continuing it without attendants in the future, when this plant may employ 2,000 or 3,000 people. If we can do that, the Atsugi Plant cafeteria will become a rare example of its kind in the world. It will be our pride and joy. I am sure we have what it takes, so why not give it a try?" As I anticipated, everybody agreed. The plan was implemented immediately.

This cafeteria without attendants has been doing well since then, and very few mishaps have occurred so far. Total employment in the plant now stands at 3,000; the amount of food handled in the cafeteria has increased considerably; yet the service counter is still able to cope with the load. We have many visitors to the plant who, when told how the cafeteria functions, marvel at the system's success. Generally they account for their surprise by saying that morality must be very high in the plant.

Because I cannot regard myself as a moralist, I do not view the matter so simply. True, our cafeteria continues without any attendants; but the reason for its success, I tell myself, is that—human frailty notwithstanding—everybody tries to live up to the trust placed in him. This, in short, makes operation of the plant cafeteria without attendants "barely possible."

Indeed, the trust we have come to place in our people in many such ways, the confidence growing out of their efforts to live up to this trust, and the universal satisfaction that has resulted comprise the backbone of the employer-employee relationship in our plant. Many management personnel who were with us in those early days are still here and probably will not take kindly to having the cafeteria problem brought up again after so long a time. I have ventured to review it only by way of indicating that its solution signaled a major change in our management style. This episode was the starting point for all the innovations that took place later on.

Why is it that managers always tend to misjudge people? Isn't it because they think the manager's job is to get the work done by *using* people? In their eyes, workers are merely tools— tools for the employer, tools for the manager. So their employees, treated in this inhuman way, revolt against management, seemingly, by indulging in behavior that is obviously beneath them. Or—to put it differently—managers sometimes feel that they have earned their position through their years of formal education, the degrees they hold, and their superior intelligence and personal characteristics. This gives them a sense of status which naturally makes them look down on the workers under them.

However, such preconceptions about people are clearly illusions which bear no resemblance to actual facts. And management today is being frustrated throughout the world by our failure to be aware of these illusions—or, rather, by our failure to take countervailing measures once we have been alerted to the dangers of self-deception.

What do we mean by "countervailing measures"? We mean management innovations which recognize that human beings are not to be used as tools. We mean switching to management based on trust in human beings and centered about the needs and desires of human beings. And, finally, we mean a conscious decision on the part of managers to discard their petty preoccupation with their own status as employers and abolish, once and for all, the ugly connotations of authority and power.

Part One

Humanity Revived

1

Dormitories Are Not Mere Containers

THE first thing that struck me when I came to Atsugi Plant was the fact that the juvenile workers who make up the majority of our employees were severely handicapped by a "small pebble" complex and that this was the crux of almost all their problems.

This sense of being just one small pebble on the beach can also be called an inferiority complex. I prefer my own term, however, in that it expresses the situation much more concretely and vividly. The small-pebble complex gives young people a feeling of despair as they look at what life has to offer. It is the root of such maladies as juvenile delinquency, lack of drive and interest in working, money worship, excessive labor turnover, the young Communist movement, and the abnormal rate at which students advance to schools of higher learning at the cost of too great a sacrifice on the part of many parents.

The Disillusionment of Youth

How is this small-pebble complex caused? It is never the fault of the juvenile workers themselves. It is implanted in their consciousness by society—in particular, by adults such as teachers and employers. For instance, during their middle-school days pupils are divided into those who will continue their education and those who will seek employment. The latter group, in comparison with the former, will be given proportionately less attention.

A profound sense of inferiority emerges even at this time in the young minds of the boys and girls who must go to work. In the process of job seeking through employment offices they are treated as though they were just another commodity to be distributed. No one can deny that deep-seated attitudes and prejudices are reflected here. The situation may vary from school to school and from teacher to teacher, but how much kindness and humane guidance are being given to each of these youngsters? How much accurate information are they getting about the companies they will work for? Nowadays, there are few pre-employment interviews, so it is only after the new recruits arrive at the station in Tokyo in a chartered train for group-employment personnel that they see the faces of their would-be employers for the first time.

For the moment they are immature, ignorant, unspoiled, and —in spite of it all—admirably hopeful. They have a burning desire to improve themselves. But after employment their expectations are mercilessly crushed, one after another. Why? Because the employers who receive them simply want them to do as they are told, obediently and without question. As I have said, they are considered mere tools—in traditional terms, cheap labor. Our current system of education may have its deficiencies, but it does have the merit that pupils are encouraged to think and act independently. The workplace has exactly the opposite effect—because there is no opportunity for independent thinking and action, the newcomers are betrayed with such severity that their disappointment becomes doubly keen.

A pattern of job organization that is essentially authoritarian;

control through surveillance based on the "carrot and stick" philosophy; simple, meaningless tasks endlessly repeated; and a grim outlook for the future—these are the facts of life awaiting middle-school graduates at their place of employment. Current manpower shortages and labor unrest are forcing employers to raise wages, to provide adequate facilities and benefits, and to speak to their employees in calmer, almost "coddling" tones instead of continually reprimanding them in front of their fellow workers. Some of these measures are not necessarily bad in themselves, but they will tend to do more harm than good so long as they are used for purposes of "softening"—or, to put it more bluntly, as hocus-pocus which leaves untouched the basic attitude of regarding workers as tools. They will only result in spoiling young people, who, deprived of humanity and troubled by their small-pebble complex, are being driven further and further toward delinquency.

My initial efforts therefore concentrated on eliminating this very real and formidable small-pebble complex. To this end I did everything possible—introducing the cafeteria service counter without attendants was only one of the important steps I took. In addition, to brighten up the atmosphere of the cafeteria, tables that had formerly been placed in long rows, giving the impression of a mess hall, were rearranged as in a restaurant and flowers were placed on each one. And all the vacant space around the factory was planted with grass and flowers.

Complete Autonomy for the Dormitories

The next important point to which I turned my attention was the fact that our juvenile workers did not have any feeling of "home" in their daily life. Employees who commute to work go reinforced by the warmth of real homes and return at the end of the day to recover from their fatigue and revive their "humanity." But those who lived in our Sony dormitories did not have this satisfaction.

The more one thinks about this problem, the sadder one becomes and the more serious it appears. Dormitories are not homes; they are merely containers for workers. The concrete buildings provided by Sony were cold and unattractive, and so were the dormitory "mothers"—who must have been regarded by the girls as an extension of the plant hierarchy. In any event, there was virtually no rapport between the residents and the mothers, and it can safely be said that the latter knew nothing about the actual life of their charges.

It was relatively easy for us to improve the dormitory buildings so that they could impart an atmosphere of warmth and affection. What proved to be an extremely arduous task, on the other hand, was improving the management of the dormitories so that they could become a real home for the workers. The main thing we did was to sever completely any connection between the management of the dormitories and the plant organization. That was the essential point. To the family of an employee, the company is not important. What *is* important is the members of the family—husbands, sons, daughters—who work there. That's why the fundamental change of policy we made with regard to dormitory management was our determination to create dormitories that would exist solely for the benefit of those living in them and not be just containers of workers for the benefit of the company.

Without any hesitation I proceeded with this plan. I did, however, encounter great difficulty in changing the thinking of people who had old-fashioned ideas.

First of all, our Dormitory Control Section was separated from the General Affairs Section. Others in the plant were forbidden to have any direct contact with dormitory-management personnel. This was, perhaps, carrying things a little too far, but it was inevitable. Because the dormitory mothers now had no place on the organization chart, they were instructed to report to the office of the plant manager.

Although it was possible to discard the old system with no trouble, specific measures like encouraging a change in the mentality of the dormitory mothers and rehabilitating life in the dormitories so that it would come closer to fine family life proved to be really difficult. Moreover, I as the plant manager was not able to devote full time to such matters. That we succeeded in implementing our plan at all was due solely to the fact that we had been able to obtain an outstanding organizer from outside the company. He was a layman and, naturally, far from perfect. He struggled continually, lost his confidence on many occasions, and more than once thought about quitting. However, by mustering all the resources at his command, he solved the many problems that faced him and was instrumental in building the superb dormitories to be seen at Atsugi Plant today. The road ahead, of course, is endless; we will always have problems. But it is with no hesitation whatsoever that I confess that I take the utmost pride in our present dormitories.

It is not too much to say that we have been able to provide living conditions for our dormitory residents that are finer than the homes from which our other workers commute. In fact, I feel that any young person might be well advised to leave home sweet home for once in his or her life so as to experience group living in such an outstanding environment. Why? Because these dormitories have become a place in which we do our best to develop independent, autonomous human beings. The old high schools which required in-house residence of all students must have been established with the same purpose in mind, and our Sony dormitories are the equivalent of "students' dormitories." The workers there are not small pebbles any more. There is no longer any trace of the old small-pebble complex; every one of our young men and women residents keeps his mind wide open to new knowledge and experience and is eager for self-improvement.

Since 1966, moreover, we have had a new "home dormitory" for high-school graduates. They make quasi homes in individually built, prefabricated houses and do their own housekeeping, with the result that—as intended—they learn to handle a higher degree of autonomy.

I have already described the fundamental spirit underlying this improvement in dormitory life at Sony. The crucial point in the implementation of this spirit was the fact that it was carried out through the autonomous efforts of the resident workers themselves. The managers of the dormitories were not directly responsible; more important, they found themselves becoming advisers to the workers as these autonomous activities developed. Indeed, I am convinced that no dormitories will ever be improved without this approach, which Sony initiated on a full-scale basis in 1963.

It was during this period that the coaching system which is still being used to this date was devised. A coach (one for every five new recruits) is appointed from among the senior workers in the dormitories two months before the next newcomers are to be enrolled in the company—which generally happens at the end of March. Study meetings are held for these coaches during the two intervening months. Occasionally guest speakers are invited to attend; however, the meetings are intended to provide a forum for discussion among the coaches, enabling them to identify areas where improvement in the dormitories may be needed and to spell out possible means for achieving that improvement.

On the basis of the conclusions reached in the first of these meetings, a manual was prepared so that the coaches, with no other assistance, could instruct the new recruits entrusted to their care. It was a simple text printed on pink paper, but it was very much alive. To me, this manual or textbook is the constitution created by the dormitory workers themselves to guide their life together. We are justly proud of it—as we are of the fact that there are no company-imposed rules and regulations in our dormitories. (See Exhibit 1.)

EXHIBIT 1

A GUIDE TO DORMITORY LIFE FOR HEALTH AND HAPPINESS

[Excerpts from a Manual Compiled by the Residents Themselves]

PREFACE

You who have rosy cheeks and are full of health and life, You who entered Sony with great high hopes, We are very happy that we now have such charming little sisters.

We want you always to be as lively, straightforward, and full of hope as you are now.

This *Guide to Dormitory Life* was prepared with the sincere wish that it may help you to grow further in physical energy, spiritual strength, and integrity of mind.

We hope that you will regard it as a close friend.

We hope, too, that you will benefit siginficantly from spending these important days of your youth here at Sony's Atsugi Plant and participate in the life of the dormitories in such a way that you will be able to reminisce when, several years from now, you leave to be a pretty, wise bride, "I spent my girlhood days in those dorms and, oh, how pleasant a life it was!"

And, finally, we hope you will open this *Guide* once in a while!

A DAY'S ROUTINE

Waking up (omitted)
Going to work (omitted)
Taking leave from the job:

- When you don't feel well, please contact your roommates, your coach/sister, or your dormitory mother. See a doctor or get medicine from the first-aid room and get well as soon as possible.
- If you aren't recovering from an illness properly, please ask your coach/sister or your dorm mother to go through the formalities required to obtain leave for you.
- Because it's lonesome and sad to be sick away from home, be considerate when one of your roommates is sick and try to comfort her.
- Whenever you want to leave for one reason or another, please contact your coach/sister, your dorm mother, or the people at your work station. Comply with the necessary formalities and try to avoid making trouble for anyone.
- By any means avoid absenteeism without notice or absenteeism caused by off-duty accidents.
- Prepare a notebook in which you can record your own attendance.

Taking meals (omitted)
Washing (omitted)
Taking a bath (omitted)
Putting out lights:

- Observe the lights-out hour and try to get enough sleep.
- Exchange "good night" greetings and go to bed quietly with gratitude for another day well spent. *Good night!*

DISCRETION IN DAILY LIFE

Dressing appropriately:

- Wear simple clothing. Elaborate, "fussy" dress seldom impresses people; on the contrary, it tends to give a false picture of the wearer. Simple clothes, neat and well laundered, reflect womanly discretion.
- Wear clean, pleasing clothes that match your personality.
- Dress your mind as well as your body. Thick paint will never show off your prettiness, but a little cultivation of your mental equipment in

EXHIBIT 1 (*Continued*)

place of cosmetics applied externally will, by a sort of radiation, enhance your appearance naturally.

• A pretty girl who is liked by everybody—that's YOU.

Speaking courteously:

• Remember that the manner in which you speak also expresses your
personality. Edgy words full of raw emotion not only hurt other people
but also hurt you.
• Use sincere, quiet, courteous words, always putting yourself in the
other person's position. That's the only way to make the other person
understand your thinking or feeling.

Greeting one another:

• Have you ever noticed that some people never fail to smile, whoever
you are, whenever and wherever you happen to meet? No other form
of greeting will show your personality to better advantage.
• Try to be a person who can sincerely say "good morning," "thank
you," "good afternoon," "good evening," and "good night."
• Greet visitors to Sony without fail. You are a representative of Sony.
Please smile at our guests regardless of how many of them you may
meet.

Thinking things through:

• You have a mind and are used to doing your own thinking, but you
are surrounded by devils of temptation who disguise their voices and
their faces and beckon to you slyly. Don't let them tempt you to buy
unnecessary things or do things that are wrong.
• Practice sound, independent thinking that will let you ignore this kind
of devilish temptation. Aim at responsible conduct that will cause
others no trouble.

Solving problems:

• When you can't get along with one of your roommates or somebody at
your work station, first ask yourself whether there may not be something in your own conduct or attitude upon which you ought to reflect.
• Don't brood over your problems. Consult with your roommates,
coach/sister, or dorm mother. If you keep a problem to yourself, it
may never be solved. Let's all work to solve it as soon as possible so
that we can lead a happy life together.

Writing letters home:

• Isn't one of your happiest moments—one you await impatiently every
day, now that you are away from home for the first time in your life—
the one when you hope to get letters from your family and friends?

Your father and mother have the same sort of feeling, remember. They let you go, but they worry about whether "my daughter is working hard every day."

- Even though you have no particular news, send a word to say just, "Hello! I'm fine!" How delighted and relieved your family will be!
- Once in a while, send an impromptu "round robin" to your family from everybody in the room. That will be fun for you and please those at home.

Keeping public places beautiful (omitted)
Keeping facilities, utensils, and private property in good condition (omitted)
Going out or staying out (omitted)
Meeting someone (omitted)

When the expected 200-odd new recruits came in, the first generation of coaches lived by the manual. Each one shared a room with her five charges and made every effort to create an entirely new life for them. For some of the coaches this process was indeed a bitter struggle with their innermost selves. I personally am moved to tears whenever I read the random thoughts jotted down by some boy or girl at the end of his three months' tenure as a coach. (See Exhibit 2.)

EXHIBIT 2

LOOKING BACK AT FOUR MONTHS OF COACHING

[Excerpts from Random Notes]

Coach wanted, the poster read. Ever since, my mind had been radiating excitement the way the sun radiates light and warmth. I promised myself that I would be a kind, gentle sister just as my own coach/sister had been when I entered this company for the first time.

About the study meetings for coaches: I am a member of an autonomous body, yet there is this lamentable person inside me who won't try to understand its significance. I can't help feeling I should not be where I am now. I hear many themes presented and many questions asked. Sometimes the panel discusses human relations. . . ; sometimes we consider whether the present way of life in the dorms can be improved or not.

There can never be any such thing as "having it made." We must keep on growing—or so they say. Some of us seem to think we're doing well as we are now. "No, we're not," others declare. All these opinions of ours are expressed freely and vigorously, and I learn a lot about things I did not understand before. I sincerely believe that these study meetings for coaches are very helpful.

EXHIBIT 2 (*Continued*)

There can be no "I've got it made" attitude no matter how much progress we make. Once we reach a particular goal, I want to go a step further—and another and another. I want to march ahead with my eyes on the future.

As the new recruits from Niigata, Yamagata, Iwate, and Akita came in, my 19-year-old heart kept pounding and pounding. I felt that everybody must feel like this the first time she does anything important, yet, as I faced these darling innocent girls, I got all excited and I blushed. It was not until the next day that I started to calm down and was able to speak to them quite freely. I only had to show them through Dormitory IA, but I kept going through the same place over and over again. . . . Everybody looked dazed but curious, and I was very pleased that they nodded gently as they listened to my explanation.

About the education of the new recruits: . . . There were girls who felt everything was new to them and were already worrying about whether they could do what was expected of them. There were girls who said they were fed up with this thing called education; they weren't sure how much of it they understood, and they claimed they got a pain in the back from being kept sitting all the time. To me, every word these girls spoke seemed to strike a familiar chord. I answered them carefully and sincerely. "Yes, yes, you are right," I said. Or: "And then? Really?"

A problem in human relations came up after a while. One girl, no more than a year older or younger than the rest, did not get along with everybody. The other girls in her room came to be afraid of her, and they asked me to stay in the room with them. I told myself that I was a coach and decided to have a talk with them that very day. I was on the morning shift, and I kept wondering all along what I should say to these girls and how I was ever going to make them understand me. So I jotted down some notes in a memo to myself and went through it time after time. . . . When I got back to the dorm and we sat down around a table, my tongue suddenly loosened up and I spoke eloquently. No human beings were perfect, I said. We would get nowhere by picking away at other people's faults. We all agreed that we should look for strengths, rather than weaknesses, in people. Needless to say, by pulling together we were able to re-establish relationships with the problem girl on an entirely new basis.

I also had the following experience: One Sunday, as I was working on some point lace, three girls came by. "Why did you become a coach?" they asked me. Without thinking, I answered, "Because I like it." "That's not true!" they said. Taken aback, I rested my hands on the lace. "Well, when I entered the company, I felt extremely grateful to the girl who was then my sister/coach. So I not only wanted to be of some help to inexperienced new recruits but I also wanted to help myself—although this may sound like a bit too much." By this time everybody was crying, so I cried too without any reason. "I want to be like you." This one sentence struck home in my mind.

Whenever anyone says kind words about me, I immediately begin to take them seriously; in fact, I become highly impressed with myself—in this case, with my influence over these girls. I was convinced that I could do anything for them. And, as they were initiated into the life of the plant, I felt they were so eager to listen to me and the other coaches that we could teach them anything, bad or good depending on our discretion. What with all the responsibility, it seemed to me that I was growing thinner day after day—until I looked at myself in a mirror. Then I grinned. . . . Frankly, it was a relief each time to know that I was expanding horizontally. . . .

The mottoes of our room are two:

1. "Don't forget that you're not the only person who is living in this room." This was handed down to me by my coach/sister when I was her subcoach, and it became mine.
2. "Face everything with a smile. Lead a pleasant life every day."

Each girl has her own goals and is trying to realize them. Whenever they interfere with one another, though, and are quarrelsome or just plain noisy, I am on the scene immediately, knocking on the door and scolding them. "You should sit down quietly," I tell them, "and consider how badly you have behaved." One day, as I returned to my own room, a girl followed me impulsively to say, "Sister, I'm sorry. I did such-and-such, and ever since I've been telling myself how wrong it was." I was delighted that she "confessed" in this way, even though she could perfectly well have kept everything to herself without anyone's knowing the difference.

I want to say out loud, as I begin my fourth month, that I'm glad I became a coach. There were mountains of small problems, as I've said, yet each of us promised that she would try to become a person who could help others and herself too.

Now, at the end of my tenure as a coach, I cannot help feeling somewhat unhappy about having to give up my duties.

FUKUKO OHRUI (19 years old)
Room 303
Dormitory IA

The days are long since past when, with all the innocence of youth, these first coaches labored to overcome the difficulties that beset them on every hand—yet always with high hopes in their hearts. But out of this hard experience the coaches themselves—not to mention the new recruits—emerged as full-fledged adults. By their efforts the new autonomous life of the Sony dormitories was firmly established; they were the central force behind its success. Furthermore, this method of operation has proved itself repeatedly over the years and is now applied to all dormitories for men and women workers alike.

To sum up—there are two facts that I should like to emphasize strongly: First, if plant management had been directly involved in improving the dormitories, we should not have the dormitories we have today. Second, we have these fine dormitories thanks only to the workers themselves and their dedicated advisers.

Autonomy in Recreation

The principle of autonomy also was applied to the improvement of recreational activities. These had formerly been the responsibility of the Welfare Section of the General Affairs Department—a fact which naturally guaranteed that there would be a paternalistic tendency to "coddle" the employees (who, after all, were merely "tools" for the company's use). In other words, the motive behind the recreation was suspect from the beginning. For example, famous singers are invited in and paid big money to perform at an entertainment only to show off the admirable benevolence of the company toward its employees. Since it is free of charge, everyone goes to the show—yet the result is nil. The company has not demonstrated its avowed goodwill, and the audience has not benefited in any way.

Recreation should be "for the people and by the people." Plant management should only offer a helping hand. All that is required is sufficient guidance, sincerely and competently offered, so that recreational activities can be properly autonomous. It was not easy for me—the new plant manager—to introduce this particular improvement. To start with, the recreation function had to be taken away from the old Welfare Section, and then we had somehow to encourage the spontaneous development of new types of recreation. Since no one in the Welfare Section had been motivated by actual ill will toward the employees, it proved rather painful to take the responsibility for recreation from the group; moreover, it was a long time before people who had become mere "pebbles" took the initiative. Patience, encouragement, and—here, again—an excellent organizer were needed in the end to realize the desired improvement. Of course we had endless problems, but we can say now that the plant's recreational activities are finally established on an autonomous basis.

Looking back, I have come to feel that autonomy has resulted in much healthier recreational activities than those that were formerly offered by the company. Why is this so? It is because the company—that is, the Welfare Section—in its efforts to mobilize passive, placid employees tends to incorporate in its programs only those activities that are certain to entertain, to give pleasure. Autonomy, on the other hand, deters employees from being mere pleasure seekers; of their own free will, they tend to choose activities that will give them lasting benefits. I believe this is important. The mind of youth is basically healthy and sound; what distorts it is the thinking of adults—especially that of businessmen trying to take advantage of the vulnerability of the young.

Nowadays, employers who are trying to recruit juvenile workers complain constantly that there are no candidates and that the people they do succeed in hiring are inferior, lacking in morale, and interested only in monetary rewards. Workers, they declare, change jobs all too readily in search of better benefits, however minor the improvement may be; moreover, even the slightest reprimand will make an employee dissatisfied enough to quit. All this, they further complain, is due to poor discipline at home and at school and to a bad social environment—just as if the employers themselves were in no way responsible. They are entirely wrong, however; my whole experience testifies to the erroneousness of such complaints. I recognize, of course, that a variety of situations are at fault here, yet what can an employer gain by blaming others? Complaining will not solve his problem. What should be improved are his own attitudes and actions.

I believe that the early innovations I succeeded in making at Sony tell us clearly how employers should improve themselves. If we can register enough improvement, things will show an astounding change for the better; and the only conceivable reason for our not being able to improve sufficiently is not the shortcomings of juvenile workers but the fact that we as employers have not been able to do the thorough job of soul searching that might lead to a change in our posture. This inability and failure on our part can only lead to self-destruction. Thus it is the employers who must be pitied, not the workers.

Autonomy in Recording Attendance

It was toward the end of 1961, immediately following my take-over at the Sony plant, that the following incident occurred.

In those days our plant inevitably used time clocks. Employees who were classed as section chief or above were not required to have their time cards punched; those below this rank had to have their cards punched on arriving or leaving.

Discussions were then going on between management and the union as to the location of the time clocks. They had been installed at the entrance of the plant building, but the union insisted that they should be at the gate. The reasoning behind this demand, I suspect, had to do with the distance between the gate and entrance door. This was considerable because of our spacious plant grounds; therefore, relocation of the time clocks at the gate would give the workers a substantial advantage. Once past the gate, they would be on company time, and their actual working hours would be shortened accordingly. The company, needless to say, objected to the move.

In a meeting of plant management held at this juncture, the manager of industrial relations made a proposal. Recently, he reminded us, there had been considerable dishonesty in the handling of time cards. For instance, some employees would punch not only their own cards but those of friends who expected to be late. Or, as quitting time approached, some would start getting ready to go home and, at the sound of the bell, rush to the door so that they could punch their cards right on the dot. Such cheating, said the manager of industrial relations, could not be tolerated; therefore, we should place watchmen at the time clocks to control the situation.

I had already given some thought to this time-clock problem, and hearing this proposal was enough to make up my mind once and for all. "Let's abolish the time clocks," I said. "All they've done is to bring about the war of offense and defense that's now going on between management and labor. And what in the world is a time clock? It has nothing to do with the existence of this plant. Our plant is one which produces transistors. We come here to work for that purpose. We do not come to punch time cards, nor do we manage the plant in order to let people punch time cards.

"To put it in a nutshell—we are being used by the time clock. The time clock is not responsible, of course, but both labor and management have become slaves to it. To be sure, it's a handy machine, but we who are in a position to use it have not grown up to be human beings just so that we would be capable of using it. So, I repeat, let's abolish the time clocks."

I gathered all the employees together and appealed to them. "When we say work starts at 8:40 A.M., we mean work starts at 8:40 A.M. When we say work finishes at 4:40 P.M., we mean work finishes at 4:40 P.M. There is no other logical way to operate. When we measure out a *sho* [1] of rice, we have no choice but to fill the *masu* evenly up to its top edge. When we start arguing that overfilling or underfilling the *masu* slightly should give us one *sho*, we are putting ourselves in the same class as a dubious banana peddler. How far the rice should be above or below the edge of the *masu* is simply not a matter for discussion.

"Obviously, we are here to make transistors. The only reason we joined this company is that we wanted this kind of job. I don't doubt at all that everybody comes to work here because he wants to and that everybody is trying to do his job right. Therefore, let's decide that beginning tomorrow we will work according to the time schedule without any time clocks. Your own reporting of your absences will be sufficient. So will your own reporting of lateness or early leaving. The company will trust you. No one really wants to lose time; no one really wants to be absent when he ought to be working. What is important in this world is honesty. Let us try to be honest, then, from now on."

[1] A *sho* is one of the ancient units used for measuring in Japan; it is roughly equivalent to 0.47 gallons. A *masu* is a wooden box to measure one *sho*.

This practice of doing without time clocks is still in force. However, we have observed no laxness in the reporting of time worked. On the contrary! The plant manager and the department managers who once used to start work late because they were excused from having to punch the time clock can no longer be late. Even overtime is now covered by our voluntary reporting system. In fact, there is no chance that time clocks will ever be installed again in our plant. Only once, when a certain amount of cheating occurred, I commented on it by suggesting that we might have no alternative but to reinstall the machines. Everybody, including management personnel, was opposed to taking this step.

Nothing makes us feel better than the fact that we can come and go without punching any time clocks and that department managers and everyone else are treated exactly alike. We might perhaps explain logically why we feel like this, but why bother? We know, at any rate, that this good feeling of ours is just as satisfying as the way we feel about having no attendants at the cafeteria service counters.

Situation Saved by Autonomy

As I have stated repeatedly, I trust human beings through and through, but I do not trust the behavior of human beings, my own included, simply because of our frailty. Therefore, in the case of the cafeteria service counters without attendants, the number of meal coupons turned in was rigidly checked against the total consumption of meals: bread, milk, and what-not. The results had been consistently good. However, about a year after the initiation of the new practice, there was an occasion when the value of the coupons received for milk and bread dropped to about 90 percent of "sales."

This was a crisis of major proportions. The house paper called *Atsugi Topics* (published every other day) was about to carry an article on the subject, admonishing the employees for betraying the trust placed in them. Fortunately, I came to know about this article before publication, and it made me so indignant and angry that I actually trembled. The attitude it assumed could ruin all the management improvements I was trying so hard to introduce. I demanded that the reporter who was responsible for the article withdraw it. I ordered him to report simply that there had been a sudden drop in the number of coupons handed in and that, should this situation persist, it would not be possible for us to continue the cafeteria without attendants in which we took such pride. And how sad that would be! After that, I could only pray that people would react exactly as I believed they would. My plan might not work, though—in which case, I told myself, it couldn't be helped; we simply would have been doomed to fail.

A week or so passed, after the appearance of this particular issue of *Atsugi Topics,* without any visible change. To me, this was indeed a long period. Then there was a sudden change. It was initiated by the residents of the dormitories themselves, who stood up voluntarily to defend the cafeteria without attendants— this autonomous body became the driving force in the battle to save the day. Many posters were displayed in the dorms, and the campaign soon spread to the work areas, appealing for honesty as the best means of protecting our pride against invisible enemies. The rate of coupon receipt returned to normal, and to this day I still cannot forget the thrill I felt at that time. Our joint efforts and the resulting success—transformed into solid confidence in one another—reduced to a minimum any possibility that such a danger might strike again.

Under the principle of trust in human beings, the checking that takes place is not meant to be surveillance. It is and can only be intended as encouragement—a fact that can never be overemphasized. Should we check for purposes of surveillance even slightly, our trust in human beings would become mere lip service and we would then be contradicting ourselves.

2

Management That Needs Neither Power nor Authority

JUST as is the case in setting up a cafeteria without attendants, the use of time clocks can never be abolished satisfactorily without a preconceived plan. How, then, could we implement checking based on trust in this particular instance? Urgent necessity again led to still further innovation.

Organization with Interconnecting Cells

Our plant is a composite of vertically and horizontally interconnecting teams (cells), each having from two to twenty members. The smallest cell is the *han* (crew), and its head is called the leader. *Han* leaders have three to four years' seniority; most of them are girls 18 to 19 years of age; and it is never too much to say that they make up the core of our organization structure. (See Figure 1.)

Each *han* handles one process, and several such crews together handle the complete flow of processes necessary to turn out a product. This single integrated line is the *kumi* (group), and its head is called the chief. A chief is normally a male worker who is assisted by a female worker called the subchief. The chief

FIGURE 1

ORGANIZATION OF ATSUGI PLANT

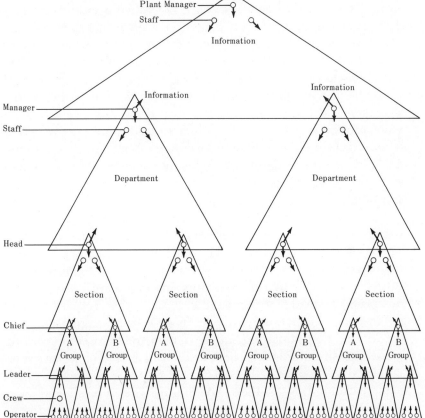

The minimum number of team members in department, section, or crew is three.

———▶ indicates flow of information, though *not* the so-called flow of orders, reports, suggestions, and approvals.

and the subchief, together with the several *han* leaders within the group, comprise a cell at the next higher level. The head of a section, his staff, and his chiefs and subchiefs constitute a further cell—as, at an even higher level, do the head of a department, his staff, and his section heads. Finally, the plant manager, his staff, and his department heads are members of a cell. In other words, each cell is linked to the next in such a way that there is a continuous chain from the bottom to the top of the organization. (In addition, the cells are horizontally connected, as will be discussed on page 106.)

We call this our cell type of organization. Its significance lies in the fact that the head of a cell is not called a vice-president, a section manager, a group manager, or a crew manager.

In the normal industrial organization structure, top management is of course in the highest position. It gives orders and instructions to each department manager or section manager. Each department manager in turn gets the work done by using section managers; each section manager uses group chiefs; each group chief uses crew leaders; and each crew leader uses workers. This is a perfect example of the authoritarian organization (see Figure 2), in which the authority of each superior depends on how high in the structure he is located. It is not what we call a cell organization.

In order to indicate clearly in a psychic way that our type of organization is completely different from the traditional authoritarian variety, we deliberately changed the way a manager is addressed. Now, whenever a team member speaks to his manager, he is encouraged to call him quite naturally by name, as Mr. So-and-So, instead of using his title.

Insisting on such unwieldy terms as "Mr. Managing Director" or "Mr. Section Manager" simply demonstrates to employees the authoritarian nature of an organization. It is one of Japan's more undesirable practices. In the United States, people use family names, calling one another "Mr. Smith," "Mr. Jones," and so on in most cases. This, I feel, is more reasonable. (In large progressive organizations like Texas Instruments, I am given to understand, they go a step further in that they call one another by their first names—"Jack," "Richard," or whatever—regardless of hier-

FIGURE 2

NORMAL AUTHORITARIAN ORGANIZATION

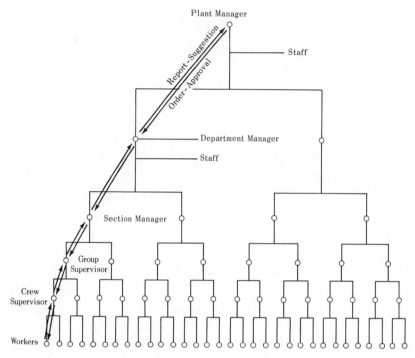

denotes order-report and suggestion-approval relationships.

archical position.) "Earned status is its own reward, the flaunting of symbols or other reminders of inequality is symptomatic of immaturity which serves only to undermine feelings of dignity and worth of those of lesser status on whom higher-status individuals depend for their continued success." * This comment by a Texas Instruments staff member is indeed a sophisticated one, to which I heartily subscribe. We must all realize today that respect for human dignity is the antithesis of power-consciousness.

The cell-type organization in our plant is not authoritarian by nature, nor is it individually directive. Each cell, from the bottom to the top of the organization, holds a meeting—we avoid using

---

* M. Scott Myers, "Conditions for Manager Motivation," *Harvard Business Review,* Vol. 44, No. 1 (January/February 1966), p. 67.

the word "conference"—once a week. At this session, each member exchanges information with his fellows and discusses possible courses of action on the basis of such information. The leader guides the meeting; however, he is not a power center but, rather, one of the team members.

Each cell is a living body which cannot be split further. In this, it resembles the Nichibo-Kaizuka volleyball team.[2] The difference lies in the fact that the cell is not an isolated body and that it interrelates with other cells to form a large grouping. Captain Kasai and Manager Daimatsu were never power holders. They were simply colleagues who assisted the group in establishing common goals and, as members of the team, encouraged and led the others in attaining those goals. No team member is just a cogwheel in the organization. Each is an independent human being with a personality that has its own internal-combustion engine.

Checking of Attendance Is Not Surveillance

It may seem that I have deviated here from this matter of abolishing the time clocks. It was, however, impossible for us to check the attendance on a basis of mutual trust without setting up some such organization as I have described. In other words, the action taken to abolish the time clocks forced us to create and implement a new type of organization.

What kind of checking, then, was initiated by the groups we call cells? Established concepts may make this rather difficult to understand, since attendance traditionally constitutes just one aspect of employee behavior with which management is concerned. The company desires—in fact, demands—regular at-

[2] In 1959, a nine-member volleyball team was organized by Nichibo Co., Ltd. (a fiber concern), drawing members from its factories. The nine selected were placed in one factory, and the team then began training to win the world championship. Miss Kasai was the captain, and Mr. Daimatsu was the team manager. In 1961, the group won the Japanese championship in a nine-member category; then it reorganized to compete as a team of six. In 1962, it won the world championship for the first time, becoming internationally famous as the "Witches of the Orient"; and, in 1964, it won the Olympic championship, after which five of the original members retired and Manager Daimatsu resigned. But the team is still doing well under the present name of Unichika.

tendance. At the same time, attendance is prescribed as an area in which data are to be collected—data on work performance and data for use in the calculation of wages (purchased labor).

Attendance, however, is basically something quite different. No one feels pleased—psychologically speaking—at being absent on a day when he should be working or at failing to arrive at the required hour. Absence does occur, though, in spite of this universal feeling because serious problems do arise in the individual employee's life: for example, sickness, personal emergencies, and other private matters—in short, all the blood, sweat, and tears of daily living. Therefore, checking of attendance in the true sense should be handled in such a way as to console and encourage the individual, to create understanding and compassion for him—that is, to benefit the individual and not just the company. This is the kind of checking done in our cells. Such checking can never be carried out by means of time clocks which are directly connected with a personnel department; it can be carried out, in our case, only in these cells, which, as I have said, are composite bodies—teams—clusters of colleagues.

Thus the abolition of the time clocks led to a succession of important changes. Personnel management at Sony is no longer a function performed chiefly by a cold personnel or industrial relations section. Instead, it has become the function of each cell—to be handled at the workplace in close contact with the very heart and soul of each individual. The worker has come to be understood, not as a mere laborer, but as a total man. In a normal authoritarian organization, the manager of a line department invariably tends to concern himself solely with the control of production and to delegate personnel management to the industrial relations department, assuming that the latter is "none of my business." It is in an environment such as this that a human being becomes just a tool for getting the work out; juvenile workers especially are likely to nurse the small-pebble complex deep in their hearts.

The establishment of cafeteria service counters without attendants, the improvements made in dormitories and in recreational activities, the abolition of time clocks, and the ensuing changes in organization patterns all were implemented in parallel and gained increasingly in sophistication. Together they eradicated the small-pebble complex almost completely. As the negative elements in the environment were eliminated, their removal naturally speeded up the progress we were able to make in encouraging people to develop into positive, determined, creative human beings untroubled by even the slightest feeling of insignificance.

I shall have more to say about this in later chapters; first, however, I want to touch upon two important subjects: power-consciousness and bureaucracy within the industrial organization and, in the chapter that follows, education at our plant.

Foiling the Bureaucrats

The major bottleneck in Japanese companies, especially in relatively large corporations, is their strong tendency toward bureaucracy. Staff departments are indeed gigantic beyond any comparison with their Western counterparts.

Characteristically, these behemoths are likely not to produce much of any value, and the bureaucrats in charge often become a burden to their companies, proposing rules, regulations, and policies one after the other and forcing them upon low-level departments with the authority of top management. Their proposals do not constitute a response to company needs; rather, they represent pseudo-scholarly imitation of rules, regulations, and policies prevailing in the advanced nations of the Western world. In other words, they originate in the backwardness of our industry and its orientation toward imported knowledge and procedures, and they pose a great threat in this day and age when we need creativeness and true democracy in our industrial concerns.

Therefore, I would like to suggest, first of all, that staff departments should be reduced. It is my feeling that personnel management, cost control, and production control should become chiefly line-oriented functions.

As a matter of fact, we at Sony have been moving in exactly that direction. Staff departments have been deprived of substantial authority and have become administrative centers. We find

that professional knowledge and skills are more and more required in our business, and we believe that these should be dis-
persed throughout the line organizations at various levels which
comprise the core of management control. We strongly discour-
age staff personnel from being overly conscious of any leadership
role or professional status and from taking the initiative in whatever action is indicated. Thus we require no great numbers of
staff people—and large staff organizations are not only wasteful
of good money but quite harmful. As for myself, I can't help
thinking that the majority of staff departments in Japanese industrial firms are trying hard—and with the best of intentions—to
destroy their companies.

Many concrete instances where it has proved possible to eliminate staff are described in this book, and many other such cases
could be cited. Take, for example, the recruitment of personnel.
Here we are rapidly changing the old system in which the personnel department used to take the initiative. This department
now is just the administrative center for the employment of personnel; it simply sets the stage, and each line manager is encouraged to do the actual screening (the personnel department
in this case provides sufficient opportunity for the line manager
to learn about screening). This change met with some resistance;
men in the personnel department said they were "not at all sure"
that each line manager would be able to handle the screening job
properly. But this is sheer nonsense. Essentially, an effective manager should be better able to size people up than anyone in the
personnel department. The personnel-department mentality of
feeling "not at all sure" about others' competence in itself indicates an unwarranted assumption of professional superiority, and
this is the root of the whole problem.

I can't help but feel, too, that this tendency toward bureaucracy is closely related to the prevalence of power-consciousness.
Hence it encourages an inclination on the part of top management
to defend the existence of a company bureaucracy. Indeed, one
might even say that the distrust with which the average top management looks at its employees promotes the growth of bureaucracy. Human beings do have a desire for power, and occasionally
I subject myself to a little soul searching lest I find traces of emerg-

ing power-consciousness in my thinking. Sometimes, in absent-minded moments, I suddenly realize that it is I who, by wrongly saying this or that to people because I distrust them, have thus contributed to the further growth of bureaucracy. Hurriedly, I shake my head in an effort to rid myself of such false notions and resolve to advance in management skill, along with my colleagues, through self-development and new knowledge and not through bureaucratic control.

How can we protect ourselves from this kind of inherent danger? I have devised several methods. For instance, there is our practice of not calling people by their titles ("Mr. Managing Director" or "Mr. Chief") and simply using each others' last names. This may seem to be a very trivial matter, yet it is not that at all. The desire to be addressed by one's title or to call someone else by his title indicates clearly, though perhaps not universally, a predisposition to power-consciousness or obsequiousness. As I have said before, at Texas Instruments in the United States, where everyone is on a first-name basis, management has abolished all kinds of discrimination by hierarchical position; such matters as size of room, size of desk, lunchroom privileges, and parking space are all determined by the extent to which they will serve a given purpose.

At our plant we recently implemented a so-called "interviewer" system. An interviewer is appointed at each place of work and is assigned the task of listening to the "silent majority." We can, I feel, pride ourselves on our relatively effective plant communication. It is not enough, though; incessantly, this consciousness of power on the one hand and the consciousness of being a mere employee on the other rear their ugly heads if only because they are a part of human nature. We want to defend ourselves against this sort of ugliness; therefore, we decided to introduce our interviewer system so that the plant manager and other management personnel would be able to correct themselves by listening to voices which might not be raised during meetings or otherwise brought to the attention of leaders at various echelons. All such personnel are asked to practice listening to others selflessly and to refrain from taking any measures which might prove disadvantageous to people who express candid, straightforward opinions.

Since we have just implemented this system, it has produced no sizable results as yet. We are very hopeful about the outcome, however.

3

A Place of Learning for Human Beings

WHEN I came to Sony, education in the form of high-school and general-arts courses was already available. Both were directed at the graduates of middle schools; the former offered a regular two-year curriculum at the high-school level and the latter so-called general arts for brides-to-be that included such subjects as flower arrangement and cooking. Working hours in the plant were divided into two shifts: one in the morning and one in the afternoon. Pupils studied in the afternoon when they were assigned to the morning shift and vice versa.

Both types of courses were established upon the initiative of Sony's top management and were the direct responsibility of company headquarters rather than plant management. The intent and purpose behind the instruction offered were indeed commendable. In his greetings at the time the courses were established, Mr. Ibuka, our president, said: "They are not being offered to you for the benefit of Sony or for the sake of molding people who will be compatible with Sony. I only want you to study to be fine human beings." Mr. Michiji Tajima, our board chairman, who was ex-Minister of the Imperial Household, offered himself as a sort of principal ex officio and also as a lecturer on ethics. Thus, unlike the administration of the dormitories, instruction from the very beginning was independent of the company hierarchy and was endowed with a spirit of idealism that aimed solely at benefiting the pupils. I heartily concurred in this spirit. When, presently, the courses came under the control of our plant, the separation from the plant hierarchy was retained; as in the case of the new dormitory setup, responsibility was placed directly with the plant manager. Since then, all I have had to do is to make the curricula more complete.

The Development of Sony Atsugi High School

I am convinced that true education consists in educating the whole man, which includes work. Therefore, I feel it is indeed lamentable that everybody nowadays wants to be enrolled in day high schools. In Germany, 75 percent of those boys and girls who complete their compulsory education go to work at the age of 15, and I believe they are right in doing so. A thoroughgoing change, however, must take place in the thinking of the Japanese public in general as to juvenile workers before we can implement a combination of work and study on any broad basis. We must see to it that work is what it ought to be; and then, too, industrial plants must be made to accept young people, not as workers, but as pupils, the way the Germans do.

I made up my mind that this type of work/study system should be established in our plant without delay. I also resolved that our plant school must be the best school in Japan, where a finer education than that obtainable in any day high school would be offered. Realizing this goal precluded the use of any part-time teachers and, in addition, required that we acquire official accreditation under the present-day educational system in Japan so that our graduates could advance into schools of higher learning.

Specific steps toward this end started in 1962. First of all, taking advantage of high-school education by correspondence, we registered our high-school course as a joint self-improvement organization designed to offer schooling by correspondence and thus became eligible to award a high-school diploma after four years of study.

However, it soon became clear to us that this system imposed a double burden on the pupils and did not permit a desirable curriculum. We therefore began in 1963 to try and establish the school as a legal body with the intention of turning it into an officially certified, private, part-time high school. This proved to be a difficult task. First, Sony had to put up 200 million yen out of its precious profits for the establishment of this legal body and had to pay an exorbitant amount of gift tax on its donation in accordance with the Japanese tax system. What an evil law this is! After all, we were only helping to do what the country should be doing.

Fortunately, the solution of this problem was relatively easy. The ideals expressed by top management on the occasion of the establishment of the high-school course were not given mere lip service. Both President Ibuka and Vice-President Morita bore witness to this fact, seeing to it that the donation was made in spite of the difficulty arising from the inherent rationality that is demanded of an industrial company. I was indeed pleased.

The next difficulty was the fact that we could not easily acquire the permit for the establishment of the legal body and, therefore, the high school. This was something which, in some ways, could not be helped. The trouble lay in the suspicion, prevailing in certain quarters, that the public interest might not be

served by a school within a company. The school we were proposing to establish was intended for the benefit of the pupils, not
for the benefit of Sony. To us, this was obvious, yet people's
"common sense" would not let them persuade themselves that a
company existed which was willing to "waste" its money in this
way.

Some officials said that they could not possibly encourage
what they claimed was a scheme for recruiting workers by issuing
a certificate for our high school. But nothing could have been
further from our minds. As far as the plant was concerned, we
always had then—and still have now—four to five applicants for
each vacancy. Therefore, recruiting workers was no problem for us.

I lost weight during this fight to obtain our certificate. We
asked not only teachers but pupils to write to the newspapers, we
appealed to the general public for help—in short, we exerted
every conceivable effort toward this one goal.

The breakthrough might have come earlier if we had taken
some sort of political action. At the time, though, we did not
know how, nor did we have any intention whatsoever of engaging
in politics. Looking back, I realize that we were inexperienced
and that we sometimes made mistakes. But Governor Uchiyama
of Kanagawa Prefecture and higher management personnel in the
prefectural office were understanding and progressive and sincerely tried to help us realize our plan. I am most grateful to
them—in fact, this was the first time I ever felt truly grateful
and appreciative toward politicians and governmental agencies.
Come to think of it, these people sometimes were more sincere
and earnest than I was!

Strenuous efforts, then, resulted in the establishment of the
legal entity known as Sony Atsugi High School in 1964, one year
behind schedule. I could not hold back my tears as I stood on the
platform during the ceremony that marked the occasion. All the
pupils who were taking the correspondence course at the time
were admitted to the school. Having started in the days of the
unofficial high-school course, the first graduates (who were to
finish in March 1966) in some cases repeated the first grade over
and over again without dropping out; they persisted for as long
as five or six years in their determination to earn the coveted
diploma. With the pupils still in school, I took my hat off to these

boys and girls for their perseverance. I was speechless with emotion at the time of their commencement exercises. What magnificent specimens of youth they were! This story of their bitter struggle should never fade from our memories.

Though far from being the best high school in Japan, Atsugi, I am convinced, will attain this status without fail. We have no youngster in this school with the slightest inclination toward delinquency—and I am given to understand that this is indeed a rare thing in Japan. Pupils here are never bothered with the problem of cutthroat competition for admission to schools of higher learning, and their conduct during annual field trips is the object of admiration everywhere they go. And, now that the dorms have become students' dormitories, Sony Atsugi High School is beyond any doubt a "high school requiring in-house residence of all students."

The school is operated on a self-paying basis and financed through tuition payments received from pupils with some subsidy from the company. Because it is a policy to de-emphasize academic degrees, a diploma from a particular school makes no difference in salary or wages. Sony workers, therefore, are never forced to enter into our high school, yet the majority of middle-school graduates who come to us enroll themselves in it. They are free to take any course of action after graduation, and guidance for the future is offered them as it would be at any other high school.

This guidance is intended solely for the benefit of the pupils and has nothing at all to do with the needs or convenience of the plant. This is the way it should be; Sony loses nothing here. If we felt we were losing anything, Sony would then have deteriorated. So long as these young people grow into fine, solid men and women who approach life with no sense of despair and in a frame of mind that is affirmative and positive, rather than negative, Sony will have a treasure that no money in the world will be able to buy.

Other Schools, Courses, and Activities

Education at Sony Atsugi plant next faced the second phase in its rapid development. With the number of workers who had earned high-school diplomas increasing, we felt we had reached the point at which we must further increase the sophistication of the curriculum and offer more advanced education. Thus, in 1966, our professional School of Technology was established as the first step toward education in basic technology for the benefit of top-notch students who were to be admitted without any restrictions and be educated in an individual rather than a mass-production way. Then, in 1967, we established a two-year college for women. All these schools collect sizable amounts of tuition, which we require because of our basic attitude that schooling is provided essentially for the benefit of the students and therefore should not be a burden on the company.

I am sure that some readers will argue in favor of our utilizing the public schools. However, our plant is operated on a two-shift basis, so that it is quite difficult for workers to take advantage of publicly offered opportunities for instruction. Also, we oppose to-day's knowledge-oriented, commercially slanted, mass-production education. It has been our belief from the start that we had no other alternative but to establish our own school—one that would be capable of molding a truly creative human being.

Educational activities at Sony beyond those related to our work are being offered in the form of periodic, one-shot lecture meetings. These are held once a month for each group of single girls, young married women, and boys. They provide a general-arts type of education in politics, economics, literature, philosophy of human life, science and technology, and the like.

Courses in such subjects as flower arrangement, the tea cere-mony, literature, and religion are offered continuously at a semi-nar house connected with the home dormitory I alluded to earlier. It is our plan to develop this into something like Denmark's na-tional high school. A basic principle, of course, is that expenses will be borne by the pupils.

Mistaken Philosophy of Education

We are deeply interested at Sony in the problem of school education in Japan in relation to the question of diploma-oriented personnel placement and the reinforcement of education within industry. My thinking in this regard has much in common with the ideas held by Mr. Masunori Hiratsuka, director of the National Institute of Education, who says, "The modern era is the era of education explosion throughout the world, and the universal trend is toward the democratization of education. It goes without saying that the less-developed nations are passionately involved in this trend, and that they and the advanced nations alike are exerting great effort in this direction.

"For instance, in the United States 95 percent of students continue into the latter half of their secondary education in the 15-to-18-year age bracket, while 35 percent go on to higher education in the 18-and-over bracket. The rate of enrollment in schools offering advanced education is the highest in the world, so why is it that U.S. educators are now having second thoughts about it? Herein lies a problem. The biggest mistake the United States has made in the area of education has been to consider only volume. Democratization does not simply mean that everybody is entitled to a complete secondary education plus advanced education. Democratization in its true sense should also give consideration to quality, and that is the direction along which the United States is now innovating its educational system.

"In Japan, 72 percent of students enroll for the latter half of their secondary education and 20 percent enroll for advanced education; Japan ranks second after the United States in rate of enrollment in schools of higher learning, and the tendency toward more and more years of education is gaining further momentum. In contrast, only 25 percent of students in West Germany go on to the latter half of the secondary education available to them, and only 6 percent take advantage of the opportunity for advanced education, yet we can hardly say that Japan is substantially ahead of Germany so far as democratization of education is concerned. This is a point we have to reconsider.

"The Central Council for Education has made public the fact that high school students in Japan who are capable of really profiting from advanced education account for only 30 percent of the total, while 50 percent barely manage to understand what they are supposed to learn and the remaining 20 percent do not understand any of it. When asked why such students were permitted to enroll in schools of higher education, a certain official answered by saying that they were permitted to enroll so as to maintain budget quotas for the public schools. How can we say that education in Japan is successful as long as such conditions prevail? Japan, since the war, has been forced to make the same mistake that the United States has.

"What Japan should do to correct this error is to discard the philosophy that regards school education as categorically imperative and important. Education at home should be emphasized, and the place of work should become a place of education as well. We should shed completely the idea that enabling everybody to go to high school and the university amounts to democratization.

"Neither in Germany nor in France can we find any such philosophy as the one we now see in Japan. Rather, individual potential must be considered, and there should be thoroughgoing guidance for individual students in the selection of courses —just as in France, where the nine years of compulsory education serve that purpose. Then the place of 'eternal' education (as the French put it) after graduating from school should be given consideration—which will urgently demand that we provide places and facilities for such study, formulate plans for work as it ought to be, and mold a tradition of social acceptance for such thinking. I heartily agree with Mr. Ibuka's insistence that what is important is not a diploma."

I agree completely with Mr. Hiratsuka's thinking as quoted here. At the same time, I cannot help but feel apprehensive as to the future of this country. What a waste, what a loss to our national economy, for us to permit the enrollment of those 70 percent of students who are not capable of understanding a high-school-level curriculum, who are not to be gainfully employed during the period when they are supposedly "studying," and who —it is proposed—are to squander money at the expense of the general public!

We at Sony want to contribute to the extent of our capabilities to the advancement of national education. The rationale for this, as Mr. Hiratsuka explained it, is that "the place of work should become the place of education as well"; thus the role played by the employer in the improvement of our educational system becomes extremely important.

Specifically, the first thing we must do is to eliminate diploma-oriented personnel management. (I will discuss this in greater detail in later chapters.) Second, we must provide opportunities and facilities that will enable our workers to continue studying as long as they have the will to do so; we must create jobs that take human beings into consideration; and we must endeavor to build an environment throughout every plant in which no job will be despised and all useful work will be respected. As indicated, I feel that Sony is somewhat more advanced than the average employer in this regard.

I now feel confident, moreover (and here I am speaking of the ordinary person), that we should be able to create just as fine a human being and just as useful a man or woman out of the middle-school graduate who enters our company as anyone who has gone through day high school and the university before taking his place in society. We already have engineers emerging from this group who can be ranked with any engineers in the world. What vexes us is the fact that this kind of thing seems to be so difficult to understand and accept, simply because it is so different from the situation we have today. I appeal to all employers to follow Sony's example—for their own sake if nothing else. I also plead for greater understanding on the part of families and schools throughout Japan.

The families and schools who send their children and pupils to our plant at least are beginning to understand our thinking, so it seems to me, in the light of our performance. Actually, in several agricultural areas from which we drain employees, the general inclination is to send a child to high school when he fails to get a job at Sony. We want to increase the number of such communities still more rapidly, and we want to help the children entrusted to us grow into fine, solid people. This will prove beneficial not only to Sony but to Japan as a whole.

We have too many half-serious teachers who are not equal to the sacred task of education, who act as though they were doing nothing more important than supplying workers for industry. Perhaps what we should do to cope with this problem is to reduce the number of schools and concentrate on the quality of those remaining. If we did this, then parents would not need to undergo excessive self-sacrifice in order to send their children to school—with all the resulting waste in tax money. We for our part are determined to provide those who have the basic potential and zeal with opportunities and assistance as they progress to undergraduate and even graduate study, and I sincerely wish that every company might subscribe to this idea.

This is what amounts to providing equality of educational opportunity. It is what real democratization of education ought to be.

True Education Within the Company

Obviously, the initial process of selection at the time of recruitment is highly crucial. Since we look, above all, for basic qualities in applicants and since a company's personnel requirements keep changing, what is of the utmost importance in creating an environment in which the right person can be assigned to the right job is capacity for education after employment. What, then, is this education to be? I am completely ignorant of any lofty educational principles, yet I believe that the fundamental task imposed upon the teacher—or, in the case of the industrial company, the manager—is to identify the individual merits and strengths of his pupils or subordinates. This can only be accomplished properly when the educator's judgment is candid, astute, and free from any self-interest. It is, needless to say, an extremely difficult thing to do. But, however difficult it may seem, the manager's duty is to view it as a primary responsibility.

Managers tend to place the job to be done ahead of people and to think of people as tools for doing that job. This makes them look chiefly for shortcomings in workers. In any case, be it strength or shortcoming, they are prone to judge people's characteristics incorrectly. Overcoming this tendency requires, therefore, that managers think of the workers first and the job to be done second—as a means by which the worker supports himself. Only as managers assume this kind of attitude will they begin to know their workers' strengths better.

This is an empirical fact. I don't know why it is so—probably because, when managers put jobs first, they try to fit into them workers who are entitled to independence as human beings. Naturally, some of these people may not be suited to the jobs in which they are placed; so the managers wonder what is wrong with them and start finding fault with them and misjudging them generally. When, on the other hand, managers assume an attitude that puts men first, they start looking at their workers in the same way that they look at themselves. In short, they begin to judge them as they are.

Once workers' strengths and merits have been identified, the next step in this process of education is to let them handle only jobs that are compatible with their strengths and with the degree of those strengths. I need not repeat here what I have already touched on in regard to letting workers handle their jobs on a basis of trust. The performance thus achieved will be far greater when proper personnel are placed in each job. What is more important, though, the workers tend to realize their true potential in the performance of their jobs and to grow rapidly as they experience in a very real way the great joy of working and as they then gain confidence in themselves. And, having attained this growth, we can hope for unrestricted and unlimited progress from people as we assign them to advanced work.

I hope my readers will bear with me when I say that the process by which I assumed the post of plant manager at Sony was the exact replica of the process I have explained in the preceding paragraphs. It was precisely the way my job was assigned to me that enabled me to achieve the greatest growth in my life while performing my duties. Indeed, I am deeply grateful to Sony's top management for this opportunity, and I mean what I say here.

Top management, however, was not the sole driving force which made my growth possible. The teamwork of all Sony, of which I am a part, and the teamwork in our plant, of which I am a leader, was obviously an even more pertinent factor. Clearly, teamwork has in it some mystical power to make people grow. Every one of us in the plant has experienced this power unmistakably.

The job itself—especially the one done by teamwork—is a true mentor. Nowadays there are many people who believe that education means only *school* education—a fact that may be the very root of the perils which currently beset our educational system. There are people, too, who believe that the royal road to education within industry lies in establishing in-company courses, seminars, and schools (as Sony has done). Yet these are all adjuncts, necessary but secondary. Schools in which knowledge is handed out wholesale are all but useless; pupils would be better advised to stay home by themselves and read books instead.

Companies which go to extremes in labor "stretching" while providing school-type in-house education for their employees are mistaking the means for an end. Indeed, their efforts are pointless.

4

The Essential Will to Live

TO go back a little—when you let other people handle a job on the basis of trust, it is important that you select the proper people to do that job. True, the effectiveness we gain in this way may vary depending on the attitude assumed and the effort expended by the manager. Still, overall effectiveness is greatly influenced by the basic qualities of the people selected.

The first opportunity for managers to participate in the selection of people comes at the time of recruitment. The multifarious jobs in a company require, above all, the selection of people with different qualities for different jobs. But, because there are some general guides and policies, I should like to describe those we have at Sony.

People with Determination Are Resourceful

I believe that every human being basically is determined to live—which equals "to work"—but that this determination may vary in intensity from one person to another. Therefore, it is our companywide policy in recruitment to select those people gifted with a strong will and determination to live.

I venture to use this simple phrase "to live" because there is no other way to express what I mean. People can be physically handicapped or mentally retarded, but, so long as they are determined to live and are full of spirit, they are potentially resourceful people who can be depended on if placed in work which is compatible with their aptitudes and abilities. Provided they are in earnest about life, they will voluntarily enrich their way of living—given the right kind of environment within a company.

There are many people in every walk of life who can meet this first requirement of good job performance. One should never be trapped by the fixed notion that certain people are inferior in this regard. A U.S. company named Abilities Inc., founded by a Mr. Henry J. Viscardi, Jr. (who is physically handicapped himself), is staffed only by physically handicapped and similarly "unemployable" people. This company produces fine electrical components and is becoming prosperous as a free enterprise without any assistance from government or any appeal to the sympathies of the general public. Nobody is qualified for work here except the physically handicapped, those with chronic ailments such as heart disease and epilepsy, and even mentally retarded individuals who could not otherwise be gainfully employed. Severity of handicap is not a valid reason for refusing job applicants, but people who do not have a strong will to be independent, to commute to their place of work without any help from others, are never accepted.†

We, for our part, deliberately prepared to receive this kind of people in our plant so that we could back up our convictions. Thus, in May 1966, we employed the first people from an institution for the mentally retarded, called the Sugina Society, which is located in Atsugi City. We are proceeding carefully with our plan to employ still more people from this institution; at present we have only four. They have a 100 percent attendance record and are working splendidly among their colleagues. The pride they have come to take in their ability to perform so dependably at the plant has contributed to an improvement in them beyond all expectations and has been a source of encouragement for others in the Sugina Society, enhancing their determination and will to live even further. We are sure that many people from the Sugina Society—all of them with high hopes—will come to work in our plant in the future.

Housewives Prove Their Worth

In Japan, working women are, for the most part, unmarried girls. Married women have not been generally accepted by companies, allegedly because their morale as workers is low. The recent shortage of juvenile workers is increasingly forcing some plants to hire housewives; however, the fixed notion that they are bound to be unreliable is still a relevant factor in the limited use made of them in industry, where they tend to be employed temporarily for unskilled jobs at low wages. Our plant formerly was no different from any other in this respect; so, under the circumstances, the morale of the housewives hired by Sony was indeed low. Their output was only about 60 percent of the average for our unmarried girls; and their attendance, as measured

† The moving story of these people who are doing their jobs like any normal human beings is contained in Mr. Viscardi's book entitled *Give Us the Tools*, published by Eriksson-Taplinger Company, N.Y., in 1959.

in hours worked, was only 70 percent of the unmarried girls' record.

The example of Western Europe and the United States, however, indicates the desirability of gainful employment for women regardless of marital status. The conditions existing in Japan were, I felt, not desirable when I lectured to that effect before members of a woman's club in Atsugi City one day toward the end of 1962. Intuitively, I sensed that I had surprisingly strong support from them, and this made me determined to shed established ideas about married women and introduce housewives into our plant as full-fledged industrial workers.

The main concern of the married woman, of course, still remains the household; therefore, we gave special attention to the requirements of her home situation, particularly since the social conditions prevailing in Japan are quite different from those found in Western European countries. But, even though special consideration was accorded these women, we made it a basic policy to treat them just as if they were regular full-time workers. Bonus and severance pay were to be offered them. And competent, determined housewives were to be promoted, as long as their family life would permit, to whatever higher positions they might be entitled to.

All the same, it proved a difficult task to introduce housewives into our plant without prejudice as dependable industrial workers. It could not be done by the plant manager alone; instead, it required changes of every possible sort within the plant. Special efforts were needed to wipe the stereotype of the housewife as an inferior worker from the minds of personnel in charge of recruitment, managers in charge of housewife workers at work stations, and colleagues who must work side by side with them. The relatively early eradication of anti-housewife prejudice among our plant people can only be ascribed to the fact that the plant was already being managed in accordance with the people-centered principles I have described and that a ready network of effective communication existed in our cell-type organization.

Yet the difficulty lay not only in the plant but in the housewives themselves. What I mean is that, understandably, these housewives were not sufficiently sure of themselves to accept

with confidence the fact that they could play a real part in industry. Fortunately, the plant environment during their five months
of provisional employment implanted the necessary sense of confidence in a natural way.

I have stated that we were required to give these women special consideration. This was essential, first of all, in the area of
wage administration. A wage system based on seniority or age is
inapplicable to housewives; therefore, we instituted a pay plan,
based on the skill grade of the individual worker, under which
housewives, as such, are not eligible for the periodic pay raises
received by regular employees. We reasoned that, because the
housewives' main business is basically their homes and families,
it would be necessary that the jobs assigned to them be decided
not by the women's abilities but, rather, from the standpoint of
convenience in relation to household needs. In addition, we
realized that the growth shown at work stations would be quite
irregular from one housewife to another.

The second area in which we gave married women special
consideration was that of working hours. In Japan it seems to be
reasonable for them to work about five hours a day. At our plant
they may choose either the regular seven-hour workday (plus
one hour of break) or a five-hour workday (plus 15 minutes of
break) on a two-shift basis.

Third, there was the problem of children. When I lectured to
the woman's club, I noted with surprise that the children brought
to the meeting outnumbered their mothers. That made me think
about establishing a home in the plant where we could care for
workers' children during the day. My idea was not simply that
we might set up a plant nursery. Rather, I had in mind a home
where, as in the Soviet Union, we might provide group training
and education for the children which would far surpass anything
that they might receive at home. This was the origin of the Sony
Atsugi Infant School, within the plant premises, which was to
accept youngsters over three years of age.

Fourth, we had to face the maternity problem. Giving birth
to a child carries with it the strong possibility of a big change in
any household; certainly, a great deal of inconvenience might
result if a housewife with a new baby attempted to keep on

working in the plant. This kind of situation could only add to people's distrust of housewives in the plant. Therefore, it is our practice at Sony for housewife workers to resign immediately at the time of childbirth. There is no explicit stipulation in our rules to this effect; it is simply a custom practiced in our plant. Mothers are free to rejoin the company, once they are fully re-covered from the birth of their child, whenever they wish to do so. So, as a rule, are girls who resign from the plant to marry and have children. In many such instances, the re-employed girl or woman often chooses to work a different shift or be assigned to a different job owing to the changes in her family situation. This system of resigning and rejoining, which eliminates unnecessary strains and inconvenience and contributes greatly to the friction-free introduction of housewives into the workforce, is, we be-lieve, an absolute must.

I was greatly surprised to note that, once housewives were enrolled under this new system, their rate of attendance climbed to 94 or 95 percent (as compared with 95 or 96 percent in the case of young girls). Virtually no difference could be observed in the work performance of the two groups. Many housewife workers participate in the "study-report meeting" to which I shall refer in later chapters, and I am always moved by their sincere, earnest attitude toward their studies. It also has become clear to us that, when young girls and housewife workers inter-mingle at the work stations, they exercise an extremely favorable influence upon each other.

Under these circumstances, the number of housewife workers in our plant has increased rapidly. At present, there are about 1,200 of them, and they account for about half of all the female workers at our work stations. Some of them are now being se-lected as leaders or subleaders. Many more housewives are, in fact, applying for work at our plant; so that, every time we hire housewives, we examine candidates in a ratio of four or five per vacancy.

Our housewife workers are all fine women, and lots of them commute to the plant in their own cars. At times they create the illusion that we are looking at a scene in the United States. (See Exhibit 3.)

EXHIBIT 3

MANAGERS' MEMOS: February 1966

[Excerpt]

*"The endless search for answers during my daily five hours at work,
when I forget about being a housewife. . ."*

The first day of the New Year unfolded, bright with sunshine. Normally, I look upon the first sunrise of the year with the hope that something good may happen in the coming months, but it was with somewhat different sentiments that I greeted this New Year. For, since the latter half of last year, I have held a job at Sony. Days I used to spend without any particular plans have come to be restricted for five hours, and this has made me streamline my household duties, which now have a special significance for me.

It was toward the end of last year that I was transferred from Section 244 to the Control Section. To tell the truth, I spent New Year's Day as if in a delirium, full of hopes for this new job and anxiety about unknown problems.

At any rate, I reported for work with my mind quite refreshed. On-the-job training started immediately in the Control Section. At present, after being given a quick course of instruction in the measurement job, I am being trained for administrative work. Here are my thoughts about what I saw and felt.

1. I observed with surprise that in this section transistors are handled with great nonchalance. (This may be justified by the fact that the job here requires accuracy on the one hand but speed in measurement on the other.) Precious transistors which were the focus of intense concentration on the part of workers in the assembly sections were lying around on the floor. I myself used to make transistors, and I could not help but be disturbed about this. It seemed to me that, since a single transistor goes through many hands, it should be measured honestly so as to send out into the world only a perfect and reliable product. This is the purpose and responsibility of those in charge of measurement in the Control Section, and, it is one of the important functions which eventually form the basis for statistical control.

2. I came to realize, also, that different climates exist in Units A and B. This interested me deeply in view of the fact that the people in both units, in the same plant, were pals—which may be attributable to the healthy rivalry between the two. But I felt, too, that the difference in climate could lead to insufficiency in horizontal relations, to discrepancy in standards of measurement with all the resulting waste. Though the number of employees in the big plant is large, I feel that we should strive for common goals. By being aware of such common

goals and getting to know ourselves, we can grow in the right direction.

3. One important thing, I believe, is that we should strive for perfection in the maintenance of measuring equipment, sockets, and accessory items. Poor contact and poor calibration should never have reason to occur. Even a strong, solid fort—so it is said—was once destroyed by holes made by ants. The basis for measurement must be accurately established; no reliability can be expected without it. Naturally, this calls for inspection of all measuring equipment before starting the day's work. One does not have to be a leader to make this inspection. It only requires a little extra attention and alertness to do this at the beginning of each workday, and I hope that everyone will come to approach the job in this frame of mind.

Lastly—although it is irrelevant to our work—I should like to touch upon the fact that housewives are now the sole occupants of the Control Section. This is a situation unparalleled in the company's history; and, since we do not have any great knowledge about transistors per se, we feel decidedly uneasy about it. Some say that a control section is just like an authoritarian control tower; but, to me, it is just like a home kitchen in which great care is taken. Both the authoritarian and the care-taking attitudes are important. Now that both are our duty, we have no choice but to devote our best efforts to them both.

The greatest problem inherent in this situation is that we could be restricted in our work by being housewives and that we do lack knowledge—either of which might prove to be an obstacle occasionally. Also, I feel that there are few housewives here who do not have any problems in their family lives. In spite of these problems, our five hours' work in the plant each day gives us the pleasure of working—and it may give us means of escaping from reality as well. Granted that this is indeed a place of escape for us, it is wonderful, though, if we can forget our problems as we concentrate on handling transistors one by one.

I want to hold a transistor in my hand and solve my questions about it in turn by asking myself why and how with the little I know about it. I want to feel in myself an urge to search endlessly for the answers to my questions within the time-frame of five hours a day, freed as I am from my consciousness of being a housewife. I would like to try this step by step, even with my premonition that it may be far beyond my capacity.

All the former leaders and operators are being transferred to other work stations to make room for us housewives, who have taken over the entire section. I know they will do fine at the new work stations they are assigned to, but I miss them because I like young people. What shocked us in the past was that we had nothing to give these young people. The active energy of youth drove them to work and play so hard. We, for our part, wanted so greedily to absorb their youthfulness, yet we had nothing to offer them in return. The discretion we have learned from experience means nothing and may even have withered away in the face of this youthfulness.

EXHIBIT 3 (*Continued*)

By repeated mistakes and youthful follies, I have grown—and so will these young operators. Perhaps our only duty toward them is to give them the benefit of our ideas so that their excesses will not be too great. A work station with no young people? How quiet and lonesome the place will be! I shall do my best, however, to put my heart and soul into my work within this precious time-frame of five hours a day.

Reiko Ishii (36 years old)
Subchief
Manufacturing Department 4, Control Section B

Results Are What Count

The primary qualification for employment in our plant—which I have already discussed in detail—is determination, will to live. I have also pointed out that generally accepted theories about this vital life force may be in error. A secondary consideration requires that we select people on the basis of personal abilities and characteristics. Any company must hire a certain ratio of personnel earmarked for certain types of jobs, and this means hiring people with different abilities and characteristics in accordance with corporate needs. Here, too, it is highly important that we not be influenced by any fixed ideas or mundane principles. Results are what counts.

For instance, young girls—graduates of junior high schools—once were considered best suited to our jobs. Then it became clear to us that housewives were equally well fitted. Again, women workers formerly were not thought to be leadership material. This also was a fallacy: In our plant, the majority of leaders with groups ranging in size from forty to fifty workers are now women—and many of them are housewives. Their performance is superior.

Another common idea calls for university graduates to fill jobs demanding a high degree of creativity. This, too, is completely wrong. Among seemingly well-qualified university graduates we find many people who are knowledgeable and have a capacity for understanding yet who are not gifted with creativity and who lack leadership ability. We can safely say that these characteristics have no connection whatsoever with formal academic training.

Sustained by Brinkmanship

These, then, are the processes by which our plant came to be what it is now. At any one time we still have among us perhaps two or three individuals out of three thousand who go wrong, who fail to measure up, and many of us naturally become skeptical and unsure of what we are doing on some occasions. However, we can no longer see any trace of the sorry kind of situation that prevailed during the days when I first assumed my post.

The plant has become a place where everybody can do his best on a voluntary basis, where everyone cooperates with each other in the belief that infinite progress is possible both in themselves and in their jobs.

Problems, of course, do occur continually. But, since immaturity is our *self-created image*, we should perpetually be burning the torch of energy, subjecting ourselves to the agony and joy of innovation while striving for growth and the achievement of ever higher goals. What we fear most is the gradual loss of this growth-consciousness, of our orientation toward higher and higher goals —that is, our *youth*. Should this loss be allowed to occur, it would result in the infiltration of formalism into our innovative organization at the expense of its vital spirit, in retrogression, and in self-destruction. We cannot deny, certainly, that these are the probabilities.

Fortunately, Sony keeps loading our plant with tasks that could easily overwhelm us. Viewed from a worldwide standpoint, we are pitifully small in terms of production volume. It is our responsibility, however, not to be swamped by the superior technology developed by the ever powerful semiconductor industry in the United States, to engage in healthy competition with companies there, and, if possible, to win in that competition. In short, all these problems of ours force us to indulge in the game of brinkmanship, and there is no possibility that our position and the resulting state of mind will change in the foreseeable future.

Up until a relatively short time ago, I could not help wondering with a persistent sort of anxiety whether such competition would really be possible for us. Not now. Number of engineers is not a factor here, nor is amount of capital. The real issue is whether we know what must be done and what must not be done; whether we have shrewdly established goals and whether our engineers as a group are zealous and dedicated, ready to bury themselves in their jobs for the sake of achieving those goals. It is in these areas that the real difference lies, with limitless variety in the degree of probable achievement. It is here that we find the key to victory, defeat, or something between the two.

This applies to other jobs as well. The question is whether technicians, operators, and clerks alike cooperate with their fellows and whether they can act with courage based on the will to succeed, zeal in pursuit of goals, and scientific attitude. Here, again, limitless variety exists in the degree of probable achievement, and any slight difference may be the key to either victory or defeat. I can truthfully say, however, that our plant has pioneered in developing a type of management—primitive though it may seem to be—which will enable us to realize this cooperative spirit. It is entirely different from management as it has traditionally been conceived, and we believe that it is the only road to ultimate victory. It is—to repeat—people-oriented management based on the principle of perpetual search for perfection and growth.

Bearing this thought in mind, I took advantage in the summer of 1965 of an opportunity to observe from an overall point of view how management functions in first-class corporations abroad, mainly in the United States. What I actually saw was a burning desire for management innovation, especially in the more progressive companies of the United States and Europe. I came to realize that the direction such innovation is taking was just about the same as with us.

I felt then that the Oriental way of thinking inherent in the Japanese mind might excel in creating a type of management centered about human beings; that the integration of this management with the scientific methodology we acquired from abroad might provide the basis for the management style of the future, not only in Japan but throughout the world. The Western tradition of analytical approach might, in itself, encounter difficulty in achieving people-centered management, or production based on the integration of men, machines, and processes. On the other hand, I believe that the concept of Mahayanist Buddhism which is manifest in the thinking and in the general makeup of the Japanese should be able to contribute greatly to the realization of this new management style.

Ours is an era of management innovation the world over. Rapid technological innovation demands it. Or—to put it differently—companies that will not accept management innovation will not be able to carry out the necessary technological innovation. It is in precisely this area of management innovation that we Japanese may be able to play a major role. Current Japanese employers, however, are solely occupied with importing management methodology from overseas; it's a pity indeed that their eagerness is directed so exclusively at implementing these imported methods and procedures.

What is important is for us to do our own thinking, grounded in a lucid analysis of reality; verify our conclusions by means of field tests; introduce innovation into management in an original way, however "immature" it may be accused of being. Whether or not such efforts will ever create any organized methodology is only of secondary importance. The basic problem is to be certain that our thinking is based on actual needs, that we are not trapped in established concepts and theories, and that we are courageous enough to experiment in the field with the results of our thinking.

Here, then, is the primary requisite—the decisive factor—in building management effectiveness.

Things I Live For

It is in work that human beings find their true worth and reason for living, yet on some occasions we all grow sick and tired of it. We may be lucky enough to be engaged in creative work; nevertheless, we sometimes get "fed up," suffering a mental slump even in the absence of external obstacles. It is in this context that I said earlier that managers should constantly move among their workers and encourage them in their work. However, a person receives less and less encouragement as he advances into the higher echelons of management—a situation in which artists and scholars also find themselves. So how are we to sustain this important—and entirely voluntary—zest or enthusiasm for the job? What factors contribute to it? Encouragement is not effective unless the person being encouraged is in some way responsive to it. My own thoughts on this subject, which I should like to present here, are based chiefly on my personal experience.

Dr. Hideki Yukawa, the Nobel Prize winner and physicist I have already quoted in these pages, tells us: "Creation is achieved through repeated failures. What, then, makes a person overcome this succession of failures? I feel it is his obsession. This sense of obsession is created in him by a certain kind of contradiction or conflict. It is important that he have a profound problem on his mind which he cannot get rid of. Should he come to resemble the sage who is untroubled by any such problem, his sense of obsession may vanish." This is, in fact, true—my own experience testifies to it.

However, Dr. Yukawa's explanation alone fails to answer my question. Everybody at times has a feeling of contradiction or conflict; therefore, the mere fact that a person has something on his mind is not in itself decisively important. What *is* decisive, though, is being aware of this contradiction or conflict, tormented by its presence, yet undefeated by the painful struggle it creates in the inner mind.

What gives a person this awareness? What makes him overcome the agony of this struggle? The real explanation of obsession lies in these questions. What is it? I really don't know; all I can say at present is that what keeps me in a perpetual torment of contradiction has something to do with what I might call my sense of mission. It has something to do with my wish to be of help to others and, on the other hand, the realization that I am surely an egoist. Should I ever lose my sense of mission and my desire to help people, then I would not feel the contradiction between these aspirations and my egoism; consequently, I would lose my obsession.

It was some time ago that I had occasion to chat with a group of young people working in various companies. I noted with surprise that these young people were quite egoistic in their thinking and, at the same time, apparently felt no conflict or contradiction as a result. Come to think of it, they can hardly be blamed for this! To all intents and purposes, life for them has been one long series of monumentally competitive examinations for entrance to schools at higher and higher levels and job applications to a variety of companies—simply for the sake of *personal success.* And, even when they are established in a company, the competition never seems to end; instead, it goes on and on. Such young people may well become hardened egoists whose real wish is that their colleagues may fail and drop out and who openly express their hopes to others.

However bright and clever they may be, employees of this sort can never contribute to the development of a company, simply because they lack creativity and the cooperative spirit. In school they may have gained a great many small pieces of knowledge; but they did not *learn*—and what a pity for them it is! I am relieved, in contrast, when I look at the young workers in our plant. Naturally, they also have a tendency to be egoistic, yet they are all troubled by it. That's the way it should be.

I, being plant manager, must encourage these boys and girls. And what encourages them is very clear: It is the effort I make, as their manager, to be of help to each one of them. It is the effort I devote to implementing this sense of mission that I have. Only in this way can I kindle a sense of mission in each of them and make them feel that they have something to live for in their work. Only in this way can I get them to display creativity and cooperativeness and insure that they contribute not only to their own well-being but to the development of this company. Yet this philosophy of mine, I want to emphasize, has nothing to do with so-called paternalism.

Part Two

Victory of the "Republic" System

1

Everyone Is a Manager

THE tendency of the current system of work to alienate people
—which, it is claimed, is one of the inevitable byproducts of
modern industry—means that human beings are destroyed by
working. How can we transform our present methods of production, under which human beings become slaves to machines,
organizations, and regulations for the sake of a temporary increase in productivity, into one in which human beings are the
masters of their work? How can we establish a system which
will make people work voluntarily and make them feel worthy of
living?

Let Us Make Men the Focus

Human beings, first of all, must become the central focus of
the workplace if we want to turn it into an environment which
can contribute to the growth and development of human beings.

75

I have mentioned in previous chapters some of the innovations that resulted in this kind of environment in our plant. For example, there was the abolition of the time clocks that gave birth to the cell-type organization. We can say that, for us, this was the starting point for the establishment of a production system centered about human beings. The introduction of cafeteria service counters without attendants, the establishment of the cells—these, too, were geared to the shift to people-centered management that placed its trust in human beings and in their will to improve. The activities of workers in the cells had to be consistently based on brotherly cooperation in an environment of complete mutual confidence.

Needless to say, industrial organizations are not fully autonomous bodies like villages and towns; they do not exist solely for the employees of whom they consist. The managers at the various echelons are selected by people other than the workers, and they report directly to managers at still higher levels. We must bear this fact clearly in mind. However, that authority which is inherent in responsibility must be exercised in a democratic manner. Despotic exercise of authority denies a worker an independent personality, turns him into a "cogwheel" or "pebble," makes him actively unhappy as a human being. It inhibits productivity, results in the misuse of authority, and leads naturally to the self-destruction of the company itself.

It is hardly likely that top management will always make the right decision. Therefore, one-sided, despotic exercise of its power and authority may create and perpetuate policies that are not right for the company. The development of any organization requires, if at all possible, the formulation and implementation of proper policies, and it is only when managers heed the objective voices about them and listen selflessly to what these voices tell them that they will know the right policy to follow in a given situation. This knowledge presupposes, as well, accurate, ample information and discussion based on that information. Managers and their subordinates alike should listen to the voices of objectivity humbly and obey them with confidence.

The famous words of Abraham Lincoln (". . . that this nation, under God, shall have a new birth of freedom; and that government of the people, by the people, for the people, shall not perish from the earth.") denote exactly the attitude I refer to here. Only when power and authority are exercised democratically—that is, scientifically—are managers able for the first time to fulfill their responsibilities to their superiors at higher levels.

What is primarily important, given this context, for our cell-type of organization is *not command and order but, rather, information*. For instance, let us visualize here just one small cell. Information flows into it from above, from below, or sideways. That which reaches it from above or sideways is supplied chiefly by the leader of the team, who is also a member of a cell one step higher. The information that comes from below or sideways originates with a member of the team who is also leader of a cell one step lower.

This information includes various goals and facts about the current status of activities in cells above, beside, or below the cell in question. It also includes all external information. Once everything is in, the cell holds a meeting which is attended by the entire team. In this meeting the team members establish or refine their goals and decide what methods they will use to achieve those goals. They discuss the role to be played by each member and the schedule to be followed, and then they start working.

The role played by a leader in this kind of meeting is, needless to say, one of organizing the available information and conducting the meeting in such a way that each member will be able to speak out freely and the team will arrive at the right conclusions, objectively, on the basis of prevailing conditions. It is entirely possible that such a meeting will occasionally fail to produce a unanimous decision; in this case, it is not appropriate to base the decision on the majority vote. Provided the leader of the team concurs, the opinion of those members who must actually implement the final decision should, as a rule, be adopted as the conclusion of the team.

In rare cases, it may happen that the leader does not agree with either the majority opinion or the opinion of those who must implement the final conclusion. This calls for great delicacy and discretion on the part of the leader. In such a situation, it is our rule to adopt the opinion of those who will be taking the required action but to make the leader assume ultimate responsibility for that action. In other words, we believe that the initiative and creativity of the individuals who are to implement the final decision should be honored and that their thinking should be given the most weight. We can then expect the maximum performance from these individuals, who will be strongly motivated to produce, find satisfaction in their jobs, display the utmost ability, and feel a strong sense of responsibility toward what they are doing.

Because the prevailing conditions will always be in a state of flux, decisions—regardless of who makes them—will not necessarily prove to be right. Therefore, they must be reviewed periodically during the process of implementation; in fact, action may be proceeding even as the decisions are undergoing delicate revision. This revision can be handled quickly and properly only by those engaged in the implementation process. If decisions are forced upon them which they must then implement, the advantages of maximum motivation and performance will not be fully realized.

I wish to emphasize again that the leader must account to his immediate superior for every aspect of cell performance. Therefore, our rule which calls for adopting the opinion of those who must implement the final conclusion while overruling the opinion of the leader may sometimes force unwarranted responsibility upon the leader if an important decision proves to have been wrong. In such a case, the leader may be completely frustrated. When faced with this possibility, there is no alternative for the leader but to explain the situation fully to his people and ask for their approval of *his* decision and plan. Past experience tells us that, so long as the right procedure is followed, those who carry out a leader-made decision will not feel that they are being imposed upon but will accept his decision as their own and display both initiative and responsibility in executing it.

I have said that a case like this calls for delicacy and discretion on the part of the leader. This is particularly true when the leader comes to judge the probable severity and extent of the aftereffects that might be felt if a decision were to fail. A leader who is too timid, too afraid of failure, cannot be trusted to be a real leader. We at Sony take the attitude that we can expect our workers to grow only if they know they will not be punished unduly for making mistakes. For this reason, we believe that a leader should have the courage to yield to the opinion of his people to the maximum possible degree without being excessively afraid of failure.

Enough about the process of decision making in our cells. All I need say in addition is that, while the decisions thus arrived at are being implemented, the leader is by no means required to keep watch over his people, standing by to interfere as traditional supervisors and foremen used to do. In my opinion, he should never have the sort of attitude toward his people that requires watching and interference. Our cell type of organization would be destroyed if he did.

What we must remember here is that we can trust human beings but not their behavior—and that human nature is frail. Thus, during the implementation of a decision, it always is necessary for the leader to maintain contact with the members of his team. The more frequent such contact is, the better it will be. Since work assignments are based on mutual trust, this contact can never be transformed into surveillance and interference. Rather, it becomes a source of encouragement and consolation for common frailties. We simply smile at people—or perhaps we say, "How are things going?" Or we offer specific, concrete assistance where it is needed. People who give of themselves voluntarily and feel a true sense of responsibility sometimes become overly anxious; they doubt the importance of what they are doing and their ability to do it, and their work slumps. On such occasions, the encouragement of contact with the leader may provide a stimulus which will enable them to keep up their spirits.

Once a project or job is completed—or, in the case of a continuous type of process, once a portion of the work is completed—the leader is required to review his people's performance and make pertinent comments about it. He should, of course, praise excellence of performance and mention any poor results—but warmly.

People will not shout at an echoless mountain. Thus managers should try to provide a good-natured, responsive echo to the behavior of their people. Any worker, hearing this kind of echo, will complete his job in the satisfaction he derives from being a whole man; it will fortify his determination to step forward and tackle yet another job. I believe that in this satisfaction lies the true happiness of every human being.

Basic Principles Through Experimentation

I have now described the basic principles involved in the administration of our cell-type organization and explained how we are putting those principles to work. They were not arrived at by any abstract process of thought. We simply experimented with ideas and attitudes formulated intuitively and in this way reached the obvious conclusions. Here are some more examples.

Monthly Meeting. Since the end of 1961, it has been our custom to hold a monthly meeting with the entire workforce of the plant at which I speak for about an hour. New members of the team who have enrolled during the month are introduced on each such occasion, and these introductions are followed by a general report on overall business for the previous month and by reports from various production units on performance and achievement against goals.

In the manufacture of transistors, acceptable quantity of output—that is, yield—clearly indicates overall performance in terms of personnel management, production control, and industrial engineering for any particular work station; so congratulations are extended to those units which have achieved new records. Comments are made in front of everybody as to why outstanding performance was possible here and why poor achievement resulted there. The plant manager hands out gifts to the managers of the successful units, who in turn distribute these to their team members. Everybody joins in this ceremony of congratulation by clapping his hands, but it is not by any means intended as a citation to the fortunate workers. The gifts are presented in a spirit of universal admiration and salutation for outstanding effort and performance on the part of respected colleagues.

The meeting concludes with talks on production plans for the coming month, on other plans which are to be implemented, and on the situation of the company or of the industry as a whole. We review the significance that this general situation may have for us and suggest how we might be preparing to meet it.

Nowadays we do not have any place large enough to hold 3,000 employees at one time; therefore, we schedule our monthly meeting in four sections. This puts a heavy burden on the plant manager, but we still continue to hold the meeting because it seems to be a source of pleasurable anticipation, satisfaction, and encouragement for the entire plant team. And—to sum up—it does serve the purpose of clarifying overall plant objectives, supplying pertinent information, and educating people in the methodology of achieving established goals and reviewing the final results.

Joint Leaders' Meeting. Over and above this monthly meeting, we hold a joint leaders' meeting 15 days later. This is attended by leaders of first-line crews, chiefs and subchiefs of groups, and all other managers and their staff; some 600 participate. During the meeting, which lasts about an hour, the monthly manufacturing cost for each product is shown, along with past records. In addition, other information which is too sophisticated to be passed on to participants in the monthly meeting is provided by the plant manager and other personnel in charge. This meeting, obviously, serves the same purpose as the monthly meeting.

Although the basic meetings held by each cell comprise the mainstream of communication in our plant, the monthly meetings and joint leaders' meetings supplement them well. It is a fact, however, that these two latter types of meetings came into being prior to the cell meetings. It was through them that I, as plant manager, explained the new principles of organization, and it was their structure which served as a model for the new organization that would later be established.

Thorough, Extensive Information—Without Embellishment

The most important feature of both these meetings is the fact that the information supplied by the plant manager and other top management personnel to every team member in the plant does indeed defy normal practice in its extensiveness, its thoroughness, its lack of any embellishment, and its candidness and honesty. At the same time, it still remains within the capacity of the participants to understand it. Among these people we have floor sweepers, gardeners, and equipment and machine porters; and, to each one alike, we give information relating not only to general conditions in the plant and the company but to the worldwide situation in our industry. Anything pertinent to our endeavor, satisfaction, and progress—both as a group and individually—is reported.

Thus each individual sees his own work and goals, and the significance of the information given him, in relation to the overall picture and comes to understand the relevance of that overall picture to him. Understanding gained in this manner is far deeper and far more effective than any based on one-sided lectures on the value of goals and what-not. Every floor sweeper, for example, comes to realize that his job is an integral part of the process of developing and producing transistors and that its importance makes it indispensable. Furthermore, honest information plentifully provided makes him feel that he is a trusted team member in the plant.

I would be remiss if I failed to mention the fact that meetings of this kind and the information they supply will never serve any purpose so long as they are used as mere means of coaxing people to achieve certain goals. Who can courageously report the true situation—just as it stands—while harboring false intentions? Who will listen to it as truth when it is presented with false intentions? Unless meetings grow out of a selfless yet urgent desire to transmit information to people whom we really care about, their potential can never be fulfilled.

Top Down and Bottom Up

But the core of management in our plant, as I have already said, consists of meetings held by the cells from the top down or from the bottom up. The top cell, composed of the plant manager and the departmental managers, meets every morning for about an hour. All kinds of problems relative to the plant as a whole are reported and discussed at this meeting, and the appropriate action follows naturally. No agenda are prepared beforehand. Everybody can speak up freely; the meeting adjourns quickly whenever nobody has anything else to talk about. Only when each departmental manager has problems that concern his function alone does he talk personally with the plant manager.

This meeting at the top triggers a series of meetings held that same day at various levels of cells. The procedure for these meetings is the same as for the meeting of the top cell, although the time required decreases as we go down through the different levels. All the pertinent facts and figures discussed at the top in the morning have been transmitted by the end of the day to the actual workers, and all the pertinent ideas or information offered by the workers will reach the top by the next day.

This series of meetings is held for the purpose of clearly indicating the goals that should be kept in mind at a particular moment by a particular group, modifying and revising those goals, receiving information, discussing methods to be used, establishing contacts, and reviewing the final results. In another meeting, held once every six months, we discuss long-range goals, methods of implementing them, and the evaluation of performance against such goals.

At the end of each six-month period, performance for that period is reviewed and goals and policies for the subsequent period are decided by means of discussions held from the bottom to the top of the organization in the manner described. Then, for several days, the plant manager, his staff, and the departmental managers meet at a hotel. The manager of each department reports on its performance for the period just ended and states the goals to be achieved and the policies to be followed in the coming period. Discussion centers chiefly about these reports and plans. The plant manager in turn presents a consolidated review of the work situation, as well as the goals and policies confirmed in this meeting, to the managing directors at company headquarters and receives their comments.

The effect of this meeting at six-month intervals is far-reaching, almost immeasurable. Each departmental manager becomes familiar with other functions and groups, learns from hearing their work reviewed, and participates in policy making. He learns the significance of his department's activities in relation to the whole company. Review and appraisal, goal setting, policy making, discussion—all are engaged in here by managers representing the entire plant workforce and embodying human behavior typical of its members' initiative and zeal in establishing goals for themselves and their sense of satisfaction with the results achieved.

This meeting—with its dual purpose of shaping long-range plans and reviewing actual performance against those goals—has been held continuously since 1963 and is increasing in liveliness year after year. The energy which is to be found in every corner of the plant and which seems to erupt on this occasion simply overwhelms me.

Establishment of Production Plans by Cells

The monthly production plan for each specific item is established at the planning meeting of top plant personnel for the coming six-month period on the basis of our optimum balancing of market demand and state of the art. What is important here is the fact that the detailed explosion of this master plan into plans for each individual production line is handled entirely by the sections concerned. Each section refines its own plan during successive meetings at crew, group, and section levels. In other words, production plans are indeed being established by the personnel who are in charge of producing the various items.

The heart of this process is the establishment of the yield (amount of work meeting quality standards) and work efficiency (speed of work). Workers never want to establish the same plans, month after month, once they are entrusted with a share of the planning activity. They always tend to make plans which will enable them to beat previous months' records. They won't find planning interesting enough if they can't make perpetual progress.

Production plans formulated in this way are implemented with enormous determination. Managers accustomed to the attitudes that workers used to display under the traditional system can hardly imagine the strength of people's will to achieve goals which they themselves have set. The production of transistors involves many uncertain factors beyond the control of human beings; even the most determined work group sometimes fails to achieve its goals. Therefore, the more challenging a goal is, the greater our joy when we achieve it. Such pleasure is unforgettable —no money in the world can buy it. The tasks assigned to the workers are indeed simple and repetitive; but, when each one participates in the process of overall planning and thus knows intuitively that every movement of his hands comprises an indispensable part of the resulting plan, his sense of responsibility is aroused. Every movement then becomes filled with significance, and he feels that both his work and his life are worthwhile.

Whenever I see a worker sincerely concerned about his group's performance for the day and overjoyed by its joint achievements, I am filled anew with a keen sense of trust in my fellow human beings and of the true happiness that life offers.

2

More About the Joy of Work

I should now like to illustrate this description of our production system based on human beings with another specific example. It has to do with work standards.

The establishment of work standards has two aspects. One is concerned with job steps and work processes; another with the efficiency and quantity of work. Thus the system originated by Frederick W. Taylor, which is the bedrock of modern industrial practice, calls for the establishment of the most efficient and detailed work processes, as well as standard times, by staff specialists using time and motion studies. These are designed to force people to work according to the prescribed processes at a certain rate of efficiency without any thinking on their part. The system, needless to say, is based on the concept which regards people as machines and negates their humanity.

The Defeat of the Staff

Our concept is completely different. To be sure, we used to have staff-prepared manuals describing work steps. Each worker was instructed by the staff to do exactly what he was told to do in the proper manual.

Actually, however, these manuals were abandoned in forgotten corners of the plant; they were little more than piles of paper. This was a constant source of trouble. Because the very nature of our plant made the work highly unstable, the methods used were always being changed—which was precisely why we needed genuine work standards. But, since the work standards we had at the time were not actively used, once a certain process got "out of tune" it used to take some time before operations became normal again.

A Manual for New Recruits

Today, such problems give us no trouble at all. Instead, the plant has been transformed into a place dedicated to work improvement.

The change began when, in 1963, the crew leaders took over on-the-job training for new recruits, following the example of the coach system introduced in the dormitories. Up to that time, such training had been the province of staff specialists; only then was it decided that leaders should train their own workers. At present, this system is being expanded still further in that the training is being handled directly by senior workers, rather than by leaders, on the basis of one worker to one recruit.

The basic principles involved in this improvement are the same as in the case of the dormitories. The opportunity to exercise initiative thus provided not only enhanced people's enthusiasm for the work but saves time and provides efficient, natural training. One might also predict that the senior workers, in training their juniors, would develop their own abilities as individuals and as workers and reinforce their confidence in themselves.

Training to be conducted by leaders for the benefit of newly recruited workers calls for planning and preparation for such training by the leaders. This was not easily accomplished. First of all, the leaders themselves received training in methods they could use to analyze their own work processes and communicate the results of their analysis to the workers. This training was provided by the staff specialists. On the basis of this training, the leaders drafted manuals of work standards for the various processes, consulting with their people about the contents.

These manuals were quite primitive. However, the leaders got together with their drafts, and each explained to the others his own work-standard manual for his own processes. Participating in this meeting were the leaders—who were the central figures—as well as section heads, their staff, chiefs and subchiefs of groups, and specialist engineers in the Technical Development Department. The explanations of each leader were commented on, questions were raised, and general discussion followed. Thus each draft manual was revised and improved. Section heads and higher staff members tried to refrain from speaking too much, so that the meeting would depend chiefly on discussion by the leaders.

Few remarks were made at the outset. Finally, though, our patient efforts paid off; and, as the leaders started to express themselves actively, the exchange grew lively. Each draft manual was written on a big sheet of white paper, on which corrections and additions were rapidly jotted in red ink. Full of these red-inked revisions, it was truly a source of heartfelt satisfaction to its author. And so, in the end, the leaders themselves succeeded in compiling work-standard manuals which they could use with confidence and pride. They then started to train the new recruits with the help of these manuals as guiding texts. (See Exhibit 4.)

EXHIBIT 4

RANDOM THOUGHTS BY LEADERS IN CHARGE OF TRAINING

"Well, a few more days to go before you finish training your new recruits," I was told—and I did indeed feel that time had flown.

Come to think of it, I was anxious and uneasy, wondering whether I could possibly handle such a big job as training new recruits. But, from April 1 on, I did my best for the newcomers, who, as my sisters, looked to me for help. Mr. Ojima [the chief] and others quite often expounded their high-sounding principles of training new recruits at meetings for leaders, and every time I listened to them I longed to make my method of training good enough. I studied it, trying to make it better and better, but I still had to train the girls in my own way—which may be far from the idealistic picture that was painted by Mr. Ojima.

I feel, though, that to me it was a kind of education—one which satisfied me. In the beginning, the new recruits were overly self-conscious, although they tried their best to do their jobs well. They made mistakes and had to do things over again. Some said they were so tired that they couldn't sleep at night and became sleepy during working hours. I think they were helped by a simple physical exercise done at the work stations during breaks and by the background music.

For the past three months of training I have talked with the new recruits at meetings on subjects ranging from technical problems to what constitutes ideal group living. I had only two new recruits to teach my process to, and still I learned a great deal from my experience.

> SADAKO ABE (21 years old)
> Leader
> Group A, Wafer-Alloy Crew

                *   *   *

Hard training it was, and the training schedules contained things which even I, as a leader, had not understood in the past. This forced me to study along with the recruits.

What seemed especially good to me was that toward the end of this training period some of the new recruits wanted to learn other processes as well. I told them we could not go into those then. Instead, we decided to go over again the explanation of each different process. The chiefs and leaders in charge of the various processes could have done this much quicker and better, but we decided that the newcomers themselves should do it. By having each one explain each process on his own, I succeeded in making them more confident about their work: They now know their processes much better and are able to teach others. I believe this kind of training session was very good.

> SHIZUKO TAKAHASHI (18 years old)
> Leader
> Group B, Wafer-Alloy Crew

                *   *   *

Section 245 is still a young organization, and its management capabilities are not adequate. I felt quite uncertain whether we could train 51 new recruits under such conditions. But, with this heavy burden placed on us, we got busy.

Workers were selected to be in charge of training, and we also established policies to be followed, plans for general orientation, and lists of

EXHIBIT 4 (*Continued*)

training equipment that would be needed. I feel we overextended ourselves a little in view of the large number of newcomers we were to have. I became a full-time trainer; and, as such, I immediately undertook to prepare a manual for instruction in the work. As I look back, that was the hardest moment, yet the process of writing that manual was the most worthwhile.

I want to say here for the benefit of others in the future that information about the impressions left by newcomers at the time when they were interviewed for employment examination may be good just for reference purposes but it cannot and should not be trusted at the time when you actually meet them. For the past three months, we have tried to achieve our training goals as well as we could, and all the plans we made have been implemented. I cannot say I am satisfied, yet we did our best. Being a trainer has made me recall the days when I joined the plant for the first time—and I envy those who are now coming in. But the important thing is how much of the knowledge we have all acquired so far will be applied to our work in the future so that it will prove of help to the development of Sony. We seniors, for our part, must study much more and should always be in a position to teach newcomers in the future.

> KAZUKO MIURA (21 years old)
> Leader
> Group B, Thermo-Compression Bond Crew

Victory of Human Beings

The effect brought about by the leaders' compilation of the manuals was incalculable. The rate of speed at which the new recruits learned quickened rapidly in comparison with the rates experienced in the past. What proved to be particularly outstanding was the growth shown by the leaders themselves and the subsequent improvement of teamwork.

These manuals thus compiled proved to be replacements for the staff-prepared work-standard manuals. On the basis of our experience in having these prepared by the leaders at work stations which had to absorb new recruits, we decided that the work standards should be established throughout the plant chiefly by the leaders—which meant that the workers would be behind them. This was done in exactly the same way that the training manuals were prepared, starting in June 1964, and the whole procedure made the leaders realize the significance of their particular processes with relation to the total process, as well as their responsibility toward other processes. It also stimulated the human instinct for self-improvement. Engineers who participated in the manual-writing meetings at which the work standards were put in final shape were impressed with what I may call the natural engineering wisdom possessed by the workers—they learned much from these girls. I value especially highly the fact that associations based on mutual respect have been created between workers and engineers by this means. The girls have come to grasp—to the extent of their capacity for understanding—the problems, both engineering and theoretical, which their processes entail. This has deepened their interest in their work and made them want to study more about the theory and practice of work in general.

Since this plan was initiated, mysterious phenomena have occurred. Month after month, between July 1963 and February 1964, the output of all types of transistors—of which there were more than ten—continued to show new records. I have mentioned before that the production of transistors involves markedly uncertain factors and tends to fluctuate. It was hardly imaginable, then, that the output of all types would steadily increase, nor can we cite any direct evidence for this fantastic achievement. I am convinced, however, that it was the result of our move to let the workers establish their standards by themselves.

The original work standards formulated in this manner were revised, one after another, for every six-month or one-year period —again by the workers. Thus they became a part of the workers' flesh and blood, so to speak, and are actually lived by at the work stations. And, during the establishment and revision procedure, the workers regained their humanity; they are not machines any more. (See Exhibit 5.)

EXHIBIT 5

ESTABLISHMENT OF LIVE WORK STANDARDS IN AN ENVIRONMENT
WHERE DEVELOPMENT AND PRODUCTION ARE ONE AND THE SAME

[Excerpt from *Factory Management* (July 1966)]

To Begin With

In most industrial companies, people seem to believe that fair amounts of labor and other costs must be expended in order to establish and maintain work standards.

EXHIBIT 5 (*Continued*)

Many managers, we suspect, deplore the fact that their work standards are not being observed by their workers. Why, then, are they not being observed? We can perhaps trace the reasons to these companies' thinking with regard to work standards and their general attitude toward their employees.

We can hardly say that our plant's condition is entirely satisfactory in this respect, but we would like to describe here some examples of our thinking with regard to work standards, which are now actively used in the production of our transistors.

Why Are Work Standards Not Used Effectively?

Quality cannot be assured unless each operator provides his own assurance and regards the next process in the manufacture of the item on which he is working as one of his customers. This he can do only when he is making an effort to be well informed about his work and when we have a type of organization which enables him and each of his fellow workers to know their jobs well. Work standards must be made a part of the work, they must be improved whenever necessary, and they must be completely understood by the operators as a means of guidance on the job.

A product is, after all, the work of human beings; therefore, it is influenced by the individual workers who make it. It is these workers who actually operate and maintain high-performance machines and automated processes and who make them serve the needs of production.

We can have fine work standards and working conditions to match. It is the workers, however, who alone are in a position to observe the work standards and to assure product quality. Unless we make an effort to implement them constantly, we cannot turn out high-quality products.

In this context, also, we are apprehensive about engineers and managers establishing work standards by themselves, *giving* such standards to the workers, and *forcing* the workers to implement them. We believe that the answer to the problems of establishing work standards that workers will live by and turning out products of high reliability and refinement lies in this very point.

A production engineering or manufacturing engineering department with its big staffs can devise impressive work standards. The effort cannot be justified, though, so long as the standards are not used. Actually, staff members from such a department should be helping the operators at the work stations. Granted, work standards produced by the workers themselves will probably seem inferior, in terms of the expressions used, to those prepared by engineers; however, self-made manuals have a much greater chance of being put into active use. . . .

An Example: Formulating and Revising Work Standards

How are we to handle work standards for jobs geared to the development of a new product (test production)?

The transistor industry, which faces rapid technological innovation, usually engages in developmental production, a method which can be regarded as one of the most effective production tools in a business like ours. It is for this reason that we say we cannot completely separate manufacturing, or manufacturing techniques, from techniques involving research and development. As in any other business, during the actual development phase the designs—by which we mean, not designs for machines, but, in the case of transistors, designs for functions incorporating designs for physical aspects of transistors—must above all be superior in order for us to produce transistors which are highly reliable, have excellent properties, are easy to manufacture, and can be produced in quantity with few rejects, thus enabling us to meet our cost goals. This phase is greatly influenced by the capability of individual engineers and the effectiveness with which the engineering teams are organized. During the next phase, in which products are made on an experimental basis, we follow this practice: Young men and women (in the case of women, subchiefs or operators of leadership caliber) who will have the principal responsibility for actual production at the time when we go into that phase learn their work under the guidance of development engineers. After a certain period of time, when the process requirements for test production have been established, provisional work standards are set.

In each case, a draft standard is generally prepared, with assistance from the engineers, by operators (those with leadership abilities) who are engaged in the work of test production. This draft is then discussed with everyone who participates in the processes of new product development and test production. By these means it is revised, supplemented, and made into a provisional work standard.

During this phase, processes, methods, and work requirements are likely to change freely and quickly; therefore, speed is called for in compiling such a provisional work standard. The man responsible for doing this, so that the standard may be used in the test production, is a chief development engineer. This procedure of establishing provisional work standards while going ahead with test production is quite helpful to the entire team in reconfirming the methods to be adopted and the requirements of the work to be done, but it is especially helpful to our engineers.

A provisional standard for use in development and test-production work must be such that it enables us to understand the purpose of the work involved and gives us an outline of it. Also, care must be taken to make sure that any problems which occur during these early phases are clearly reflected in the standard. All changes in work methods, processes, and requirements which take place after the compilation of the provisional work standard must be incorporated into it by going through the steps described under the heading "Revision of a Work Standard."

Work Standards for Manufacturing Stations. Once a new product is ready for full-scale production, some of the engineers who were in charge of development, along with those operators who participated in the work of

EXHIBIT 5 (*Continued*)

test production so as to become the core of the workforce at the time of full-scale production, get together to organize manufacturing stations. The women workers who participated in test production act as their assistants and are put in charge of training for workers newly assigned to the stations.

After production is firmly under way, a standard meeting these requirements is formulated on the basis of the provisional work standard:

1. Clear indication of purposes, methods, processes, and work requirements.
2. Outline of steps to be followed when defects occur.
3. Clear indication of methods, processes, and requirements involving quality inspection.
4. Manual for operation and maintenance of machines and equipment.

No hard and fast time standard is established. This is partly due to the very nature of our work. The basic philosophy is that each operator should establish his own goal in terms of volume of work to be processed and should function in such a manner as to incorporate his ideas for work improvement into the job. Accurate records are kept and displayed for his benefit in graphs, so that he can readily compare his rate of progress with those of others.

The actual task of formulation is accomplished in meetings of the groups concerned. All pertinent and necessary information is prepared by the leaders of the various processes, who then compile the original draft. Each process has two leaders; therefore, coordination of their thinking is essential. The draft compiled in this way is further checked for accuracy by chiefs, subchiefs, engineering staff specialists, and section heads. Meanwhile, each leader of each process has a copy of the draft, and they exchange ideas among themselves as to areas requiring revision.

As soon as the draft proposal for work standards covering the full range of processes required by the product in question has been completed, leaders, subchiefs, chiefs, engineering staff specialists, and section heads meet together to study it. At this meeting, each leader explains the proposed standard for his process, and all those present discuss the contents of the draft fully and arrive at the final, uniform wording. The responsibility for coordination lies in the hands of the section heads.

The final standards that result are compiled into a single volume for all processes, and a copy is distributed to each work station. Here operators, not to mention leaders, are free to look at this manual and use it often. If copies were merely placed on the bookshelves of section heads or department managers, it could not be fully utilized.

The fact that the people concerned with each process are provided with a work-standards manual which describes other processes as well is extremely helpful to them in learning the processes which precede or follow their own.

Managers should give due consideration to enabling everybody to utilize in this way the standards he has helped to establish.

Revision of a Work Standard. Once a work standard has been formalized, subsequent revisions are handled by issuing process-change instruction forms until such times as an official revised version is prepared.

The process-change instruction form is equivalent to a provisional work standard; it is applicable to work processes which are scheduled for change on the basis of process-improvement tests.

We pay special attention to the following points in proceeding with a process-improvement task:

1. Information relative to the purposes, methods, and schedules of process-improvement testing is to be supplied to the entire crew or group by means of organized meetings. (Such improvement testing is to be handled through the normal production processes.)
2. The leader assumes responsibility for the implementation of testing. He issues a test card, insures control (identifying test items as against production items), reports any discrepancies with current methods observed during the testing (instructing the operators what they should look for), and files the test cards upon completion of the testing.
3. The head of the testing function places special emphasis on planning on observation of differences in engineering requirements as compared with current processes and any abnormal phenomena during testing. He immediately prepares an engineering report, regardless of the final outcome of the testing, and provides materials to be discussed by the engineering committee.
   When a change in process is authorized, this man issues a process-change instruction form.
4. The secretary of the crew or group files test papers and process-change instruction forms according to category and serial number. The fact that such a secretary attends the appropriate meetings makes her work quite effective.

Upon final authorization of a process change, the leaders in charge of each process, who have already been directly involved in the implementation of the process-improvement testing and who have been advised in advance as to the final results of that testing, are of course familiar with its details and any important changes in the work that may be indicated. This facilitates the switch to the new work process.

The leaders of each process further check off, on the process-change instruction form, items to be revised in the work-standards manual which is permanently available at the work station, confirming in this way the necessary modifications. By means of this add-on method, they actually record in the proper work standard the portion of the work that is to be changed. The shift to the new work process is implemented chiefly by the

EXHIBIT 5 (*Continued*)

leaders with the assistance of the testing chief and other higher-level management personnel.

About six months after the formulation of the official version of a revised standard, it too is revised in exactly the same manner as was described under "Work Standards for Manufacturing Stations." Guided by the old version of the standard and the accumulated process-change instruction forms, operators and leaders prepare a draft proposal, giving further consideration to the expressions used and the contents of the manual. This virtually completes the revision of the work standard. It is, however, important that managers indicate their interest in revising a particular standard by specifying a timetable for such revision.

> KEIJI KURATA
> Manager
> Manufacturing Department 3

Doubts About the Suggestion System

At this point, I should like to digress a little and set down briefly my thinking on the so-called suggestion system.

Some people place the suggestion system on a pedestal. This may account for the fact that so many companies have one. But I personally have my doubts about such systems. I doubt, for example, whether they actually have any substantial effect on the companies that maintain them. I might even go so far as to say that in many cases the benefits claimed can be traced back to complacence on the part of staff specialists and their belief that a suggestion system *has* to have some effect. This is abundantly clear in the enormous amount of trouble that is taken to encourage suggestions, including suggestion contests, increased award money, and workers' names placed on machines they have helped to improve.

The original suggestion system must have been adopted because management believed it could alleviate the feeling of alienation so often experienced by human beings and enhance employee morale. It would then follow—or so management must have reasoned—that the employees, out of sheer delight at having such a system, would make suggestions voluntarily. If this reasoning is correct, it just doesn't make sense that all these various inducements are being offered *to improve people's desire to make suggestions*. Which proves that the suggestion system in itself does not deliver very much.

Why isn't it effective? Granted, we can point to many people of goodwill, subjectively speaking, among those who advocate or implement suggestion plans. But these are devised, after all, as a means of appeasing the workers or—in some cases—as a form of hocus-pocus that will delude them while still preserving the work system which alienates human beings. And, so long as this system remains essentially intact, the workers from the very beginning will have little desire to make suggestions and feel little pleasure in doing so. If you really want them to make suggestions in this kind of situation, you have to resort to many unwarranted measures. Even slight carelessness in handling the suggestions you do receive may lead to ostracism for those who made them or to distrust of the amounts paid. There could also be a furor if a "reward exempt" line were to be drawn across the management hierarchy on the ground that people above a certain level are paid a salary for making suggestions. All of which could create no insubstantial volume of work for an office in charge of suggestion handling.

There is no way out of such difficulties but to change the old work system which alienates human beings. When it is transformed into a work system based on respect for human beings, it naturally results in many suggestions, since the very act of making a suggestion—which amounts to a kind of creative action—is one of the basic impulses of every man and woman. Moreover, truly effective improvement in operations usually comes from ideas whose origin is hard to pinpoint; and everybody seems to subscribe to them spontaneously. This makes it clear that suggestions made by individuals under a traditional plan offer little in terms of potential effect but that suggestions made under a work system based on mutual trust and respect do indeed produce substantial effects.

The meetings held by our cells, especially those in which we enable workers to establish and revise their own work standards, can all be regarded as means whereby suggestions are made. Thus we can say that we work in an environment full of suggestions. Under this new kind of setup, reward money intended as bait or a perpetual promotion campaign for suggestions is not only unnecessary but harmful as well.

The act of making a suggestion is an expression of human pleasure. It is a reward in itself and, as such, does not require any promotion. It should develop endlessly of its own accord and prove effective on a voluntary basis.

Farewell to the "Carrot and Stick"

That other aspect of work standards—by which I mean standard times—has been made entirely unnecessary for us, as I hope I have shown by now. Standard times are required only when human beings who are being treated like animals are coerced into working in accordance with the "carrot and stick" principle. Human beings in their natural state want to do their best in jobs which will enable them to realize their own worth. Therefore, those workers whose sense of humanity has been revived see their jobs as the supreme reward. "Carrot and stick" measures and standard times thus become both useless and destructive.

It is in this context that I say the so-called semi-automatic machines which more or less operate themselves and require only that the workers synchronize the movements of their hands with those of the machines should be so designed that the workers can freely adjust the speed at which the machines are set. Otherwise, we may create a situation in which human beings are driven by machines. It is my belief that if all semi-automatic machines were modified in the way I have described, the result would be higher productivity and higher quality than are possible with machines lacking such flexibility.

Some time ago I had a discussion at our plant with an expert in work measurement, whose methods are one of the achievements of the Taylor system. Here is the conversation which took place between us:

HE: No business can exist without any quality standards. Likewise, no production work can be done without any time standards.

I: What you take so for granted is something we don't understand. For what purpose are these time standards required? You must believe they are necessary to make people work—as a kind of "carrot and stick," right?

HE: Yes.

I: But I believe that concept has now trapped itself in a corner. We don't require any such standards in our plant. As in the Olympics, we are constantly endeavoring to make a quality item still faster, still better. It wouldn't be fun if we did anything else. Maybe, if we established a standard for the 100-meter dash, nobody would participate in the Olympics. Nobody would care to *see* the Olympics. Can you, with your work-measurement methods, establish an objective standard for the 100-meter dash? How do you account for the fact that since the days of ancient Greece new records for the 100-meter dash have been made over and over?

Finally, the expert agreed with me, complimenting me on my ideas. But he also said: "There are very few managers who could implement such ideas. Your kind of management may be possible in small companies, but not in large ones."

Everybody with established concepts and notions invariably tells me the same thing. My answer is our cell-type organization —that is, organization based on teamwork. It means nothing, however, if we can't demonstrate how it actually works in the plant. Therefore, the expert and I were forced to terminate our conversation at this point.

3

Development of Multiple Systems

I have mentioned the chain reaction produced by the cell meetings which provide the main thrust in administering our new-type organization, the monthly meetings and joint leaders' meetings that reinforce this thrust, and the sessions in which the plant manager meets the entire workforce, the members of all the cells. These are not enough, however, and we have complementary systems that I must describe next.

Start of *Managers' Memos*

First, there is the system we have to supplement the monthly meetings and joint leaders' meetings, which, by their very nature, tend to provide only one-way communication from top management. Since 1963, all those individuals who are qualified to attend the joint leaders' meetings—about 600—have been encouraged to submit business reports to the plant manager at the beginning of every month through their immediate managers. They are not forced to do so, however.

Such a business report is nothing like the so-called production or engineering report; rather, it is a memo—a vehicle for random thoughts which are jotted down in the course of business during the month. The writer is encouraged to be straightforward and candid. The immediate manager writes his comments in the space left for this purpose and sends the memo up to the plant manager. It is later returned to the man who submitted it.

It takes an extraordinary effort on my part to read all these voluminous memos. But, since I feel nothing can be compared with them as a source of humor, satisfaction, and personal encouragement, I make it my practice to read them all in detail. Sections which seem to be outstanding and to merit reading by managers other than the immediate supervisors are then excerpted, printed in a pamphlet called *Managers' Memos*, and distributed to all parties concerned. (See Exhibit 6.) Occasionally, articles which have appeared in *Memos* are taken up and discussed further in the business reports of the following month. By cutting down through the various levels in the organization, this system enables us to supplement communications.

EXHIBIT 6

MANAGERS' MEMOS: June 1966

[Excerpts]

"Production goal achieved; everybody strives to make it . . ."

During the month of June, our crew's production goal, which is our single most important objective and responsibility, seemed difficult to achieve. This was because of the unexpected change we had after we established our production goal.

The Crew A girl who was most experienced in the process of inspection for Voltage Punch-Through had to be transferred to another process. Monumental efforts on the part of her replacement could not fill the resulting void. We simply could not and did not say that we couldn't meet our pro-

EXHIBIT 6 (*Continued*)

duction schedule on account of this change in personnel. We would do it in one way or another—that was our vow. Yet we felt our prospects were dark in the beginning. Since, however, determination without any specific plans serves no purpose, we started by calculating how much we would fall short of our scheduled amount with the help we had available at the moment and how we could possibly reach our goal by "stretching." Then we discussed these findings among ourselves.

Both our collected data and a common-sense view of the situation told us it would be impossible for us to attain our goal. However, we still didn't change our minds. Inasmuch as the present number of workers in our crew could not conceivably satisfy our manpower needs, we were afraid that the only hope left to us was for the company to give us some newcomers (an unknown factor). To rely solely on this possibility was, we thought, an indication of lack of resourcefulness on our part, yet we all—operators included—had little more to back up our determination to succeed. We felt uneasy.

We then decided to let each individual operator have her own production goal—although, in an emergency like this, it might have been more appropriate for us to say that we "allocated the work with a view to attaining the overall goal." Some of the workers, in fact, voiced their doubts by saying, "We can't do it." But: "We can do it so long as I can produce that many pieces," said others. Everybody decided to try. I truly respected these girls, who promptly started working toward their individual goals with all they had.

I felt, also, that it was because of these girls that I was able to get information quickly and make any necessary decisions spontaneously and accurately. For example, as far as Crew A was concerned, the schedule looked too ambitious because of the fact that the team had two newcomers and one temporary worker (a housewife). Deciding to give priority to the operation, we therefore took the step of having operators and leaders alternate their lunch hours (subleaders performing the jobs vacated by workers at lunch so as not to idle any machines). We overshot our intermediate target after about ten days, so the practice was then terminated. But it's easy to see from this illustration how determined and aggressive everyone was during the month of June.

Crew meetings every day were devoted to discussing our progress against target and yield. And how this did help in renewing our determination to realize that goal! Struggling with our innermost selves without any weapons in our hands—the month of June was that and nothing else.

But this struggle led us to victory. On the afternoon of June 30, we not only achieved our production goal but overshot it by 37,000 pieces—which was a record that nobody, in the beginning, had ever dreamed of making. And so we finished the month. The log for June 30 says, "We felt we had done everything we could to achieve our production goal; that was the only thing we had on our minds during the entire month." Which was indeed true. We did everything we could!

I was filled with the desire to say over and over to all these girls, "Thank you! You were wonderful!" We had exerted ourselves and made good on what we had determined to do—as was clearly indicated in the fact that the man-hours required per unit of production had been reduced and in the attitude shown by everyone during the month.

Needless to say, I am very happy that we could attain our original production goal under the adverse conditions we faced. At the same time, I rejoice in the fact that our minds fused so remarkably in the achievement of this goal. The effort has further fortified our ties with one another and has, I believe, made everyone feel a great pride and joy in our work.

I conclude this report by promising that we will do our best in July with the same zest we showed in June.

Masako Ishiguri (20 years old)
Leader
Section 213, Group A, Alloying Crew
Manufacturing Department 3

* * *

"Principles of education discussed in Section 244 . . ."

"Education" seems to me a big word, and I feel a little shy about using it. But I am not writing this to talk about the state of a nation. I just want to scribble down what we have said in our section in discussing what education is and what kind of principles are conducive to more realistic education and training.

It is beyond our capacity to come squarely to grips with what education is. It is simpler for us to approach it by way of abstractions, from which we can arrive at a concept of education with relative ease. Thus we compare it with plants:

Education is a flower . . . it enhances personality.
Education is a leaf . . . it absorbs higher energy.
Education is a root . . . it makes an effort in hidden places.
Education is a seed . . . it grows a next generation.

This sounds like a television contest for quick wits. However, we agree that the best of the lot is the comparison of education with a seed. It seems to us that education does not end with one generation; therefore, this allegory gives us a correct description of one aspect of education, and a bad seed should be weeded out.

We are a group of boys who share the feeling that "a human being like me should end in one generation and never be sent into the world again";

EXHIBIT 6 (*Continued*)

for that reason, we used to believe we might as well reject this thing called education. Thus the most responsible attitude we could possibly assume toward any kind of education would have been to decline any role we might play in the process of educating people. We may have become a little too frivolous in our approach to the subject of education, but this subject of teaching others bothers us seriously now.

If we reject our responsibility for educating others, we will not become involved in the process of education and thus will fail to play any part in training up succeeding generations, to help the world progress, and to grow ourselves. And that's something we can't accept. So let's get rid of this uneasiness of ours and try to teach whatever we feel we can, no matter how funny we may look in doing so.

There is a possibility that what we teach may be wrong; therefore, we prefer the word "assert" to the word "lecture." If we assert what we know, we can be sure that others will at least catch up to our level of knowledge. We can be sure, too, that they will grow further on the basis of what they learn from us.

Once we made up our mind about all this, we came up with many ideas. Thus our plan for education in Section 244 [1] was formulated as outlined here:

1. Education should be considered as a seed. And a seed must be planted.
2. We won't try to educate by lecturing. We will assert our opinions. But what we assert may not prove to be the truth; therefore, you should try to learn from us by detecting our falsehoods, not by memorizing our falsehoods without knowing they are false.
3. Once you have learned from us, try to plant your seeds upon other newcomers.
4. Once you have finished sowing what seeds you have gotten from us, let's look for others.

We wanted to believe we were right in asserting that better education would result from these four points. Almost six months passed, during which we held study meetings and prepared materials on the following topics: knowledge of electricity, basic principles and characteristics of transistors, basic principles and processes involved in the work of Section 244, control of man-hours, control of quantity, managerial accounting. About 69 hours were allocated for our "assertions" on each item. At the start of these study meetings, we were very timid indeed. Nowadays, we are quite high-handed

---

[1] In our plant, education and job training are chiefly the responsibility of each work station; therefore, each section or department has its own plan of education.

and caustic. To us, it is a happy moment when we can participate in one of these meetings.

YOSHIO KATO (28 years old)
Chief
Manufacturing Department 4, Section 244

Plant Manager's Comment: Very good indeed. I especially like your idea of education's being "assertion" rather than "lecturing." Let those professional educators listen to your ideas!

Short-Circuiting by Men in Charge Welcomed

Our second type of complementary system is one by which we encourage what we call the short-circuiting of management levels for business purposes. Thus we implement the group-management policy that makes our meetings a chief management device. Those problems which are irrelevant to other departments can be efficiently solved by consultation between a cell member and his leader. However, other problems may be impossible to solve in this manner and so call for consultation with leaders at higher levels or with members of different cells. It is our basic policy in cases like this to permit and even encourage those in charge to establish direct contacts with others who are knowledgeable about the subject. This short-circuiting may result in a situation in which one member of a cell bypasses his immediate supervisor and talks directly with managers at a higher level or with members of other cells to settle a certain matter. Or, conversely, leaders of upper-level cells may bypass leaders of lower-level cells to talk directly with the members.

Ordinarily, leaders who are bypassed in this way tend to take offense. We believe that this is an indication of petty power-consciousness and that such a reaction is wrong. The important thing is that the right decisions be made quickly. Certainly, our encouragement of short-circuiting has had only good results. The traditional method of requiring that the immediate manager be consulted and give his approval not only slows down the process of decision making but also may produce wrong decisions because of jurisdictional disputes and insistence on individual authority. We have encountered many such cases in the past.

Those who oppose this concept invariably protest that the immediate manager who has been bypassed cannot be held responsible for the decision made. But this cannot be a valid rebuttal. So long as a leader is successful in organizing a good team, any action taken by one of his members will naturally be reported back in the next meeting of the team or in individual discussion with the leader. Should a leader then learn of a decision which did not involve him and which he does not approve of, he can take appropriate action.

To judge by our experience, however, this does not occur under normal conditions. I as plant manager am encouraging all the workers to make any necessary contacts with the managers immediately above me at any time and—vice versa. The results thus far are extremely favorable, and everything is going smoothly.

We Discover the Importance of Lateral Relationships

Our third and most important supplementary system is that provided by our laterally interconnecting cells. The traditional industrial organization structure is chiefly based on vertical linking, as is the case with the participative, group-management type of organization achieved through our cells—to say nothing of the old-fashioned directive organization.

That this kind of vertical linking is totally insufficient is indicated by the increasing need for strengthening the horizontal relationships—that is, for cooperation among the various functional departments—and by the fact that vertical linking alone fails to eliminate departmental insistence on jurisdictional rights. Naturally, multifarious committees are resorted to, and they do not work either, for these committees are advisory bodies and authority for making decisions and implementing them remains solely in the hands of the vertically linked cells or other groups. Improvement in this area can be achieved only by giving substantial authority for decision making to the natural groupings which cut laterally across the various departments.

We became aware of this fact when we realized that quicker and far more appropriate decisions were made when the members of a cell who knew its problems most intimately made direct contacts with either leaders or members of other cells without going through the process of first holding an internal meeting and getting their immediate manager's approval of the conclusions reached. Why is this true? Because communication with other cells through leaders who have previously had discussions with their members may—in contrast to communication based on short-circuiting contacts—inhibit candid conversation and the exchange of objective data. Also, it may be further influenced by extraneous factors such as group egoism and leaders' consideration for "face."

For instance, we can readily visualize a conflict of ideas between the manufacturing and purchasing departments. Purchasing insists that, in order to reduce costs, changes be made in specifications for a part to be purchased from vendors. Manufacturing in turn insists that this part, if made according to the revised specifications, will not perform satisfactorily in the shop. (We all are familiar with cases like this.) Under the authoritarian type of organizational setup, the proposal to revise the specifications would be made by a man at a relatively low level in the purchasing department, submitted for discussion at various levels of management within the department, and finally approved by the department head. Then it would be discussed by the respective managers of the manufacturing and purchasing departments —whose views, growing out of lengthy consultation with their subordinates, are bound to be rigid and irrevocable. Conversation between two managers in this kind of situation therefore tends to proceed on the basis not of facts but, rather, of the need to save face. Furthermore, many more steps are required to reach a decision than I have described here; the process consumes endless time.

A great difference results when the men in both departments who are in charge of this part can communicate with each other directly from the start. These two men are in a better position than anyone else to know facts of the case, and they are more likely to arrive at a proposal for changed specifications that will satisfy the requirements of both departments: That is, it will reduce costs on the one hand and cause no inconvenience to manufacturing on the other. The reason is that neither man is likely to bother about extraneous matters. The procedure may not work well if the men in charge don't get along with each other or if they are inclined to be emotional, but this is the exceptional case. Once agreement is reached between the two, each man reports back to his department and the question is settled. No time has been wasted, nor have any unnecessary problems been created.

This "lateral contact" method is more quickly described than implemented, however, and in industrial companies it may not be easy to introduce. Some manager in the upper echelons, because he is inclined toward power-consciousness, may not like the results. In fact, the traditional, vertically linked, authoritarian organization may not be able to condone the results.

Further Means of Promoting Lateral Contacts

This method of operation was initiated and systematized with the establishment of safety and hygiene as a laterally linked function in our plant. The plant is categorized as being engaged in light industry; thus there is no danger of major industrial accidents. However, hydrogen gas and other volatile gases are extensively used, and toxic and volatile chemicals are often required at many work stations. Those who handle these chemicals are young girls, and critical accidents are always possible. Minor accidents, such as small burns, occur frequently.

Production jobs in our plant involve close work, and this constantly leads to eyestrain. In fact, poor health may influence work performance more noticeably than any other factor. We take every precaution in terms of providing the proper equipment and keeping it in good repair, yet there are still many elements in most jobs which call for care and attention on the part of the workers themselves. We can hardly make equipment perfectly free from danger unless the workers participate positively in our efforts. The safety and hygiene function, in short, requires interdepartmental cooperation of the highest order.

In view of the prevailing conditions, we—like other manufacturers—established a Safety and Hygiene Committee in compliance with national regulations. Under its guidance, the main problems having to do with safety and hygiene were handled by the vertically linked organization. This was not effective. We therefore decided to appoint someone to be in charge of safety and hygiene in each lower-level cell. Most of the personnel here are girls, so we called the appointees nurses. They are linked together horizontally throughout the plant under a central office in the General Affairs Department. Responsibility for safety and hygiene was then delegated to this laterally linked system.

Each nurse wears a white cross pin on her chest and receives training, first of all, in what she should know about safety and hygiene. Within her cell, she is a leader as far as the safety and hygiene function is concerned. She establishes and implements specific plans for the cell's safety and hygiene activities during a given month. Her ultimate goal—and ours—is to eradicate all accidents, however minor they may be, from the plant. The cell nurse, then, actively engages in safety and hygiene work at her station. Similarly, the lateral setup that links all the nurses in the plant also plays an active role; its status is not just advisory. It issues its own newsletter [2] on its own responsibility, conducts its own research, and provides opportunities for study. It also tries to improve plant equipment.

This lateral linking of the safety and hygiene function has achieved remarkable results. The number of accidents has been reduced drastically, and hygiene-oriented thinking has been further enhanced. But what is even more important than these direct benefits is the fact that intercell ties and lateral intercell cooperation have been fortified.

We learned a lesson from this success. It led to the subsequent establishment of many laterally linked systems. For instance, we now have the assets control system, which controls fixed assets and utensils; the reformer system, designed to improve administrative procedures; and the interviewer system, which carries out various types of research through interviewing.

The benefits realized by such systems are the same as those we have noted in the case of safety and hygiene. Why is it that they

[2] *Nurse News* is published weekly by the Safety and Hygiene Committee of Atsugi Plant. This periodical is aimed at enhancing awareness of safety and hygiene among the employees and contains such items as tips on nutrition and health.

can achieve these results? Similar functions in the past used to be performed by staff specialists, and their orders were forced on lower-level personnel through the mechanism of direct management control. Now this is all changed. The workers are the chief performers; the responsibilities of the staff specialists have been transformed into those of advisers or secretaries. Cutting across departments and sections, linking all the workers assigned to the same function, produces far stronger and closer ties among them than were ever observed under the old system.

Many people may wonder how a vertically linked line organization can be compatible with these laterally linked functions. Their curiosity is in fact justified, because true compatibility or coexistence would indeed be unthinkable in a vertically linked, rigidly directive or authoritarian organization. It is possible only in our cell type of organization where group management is the rule.

I have mentioned that the plant manager assumes full responsibility for our plant but that this responsibility is partly shared by the cell leaders at the various levels. Authority, however, is delegated to the maximum extent possible to the cell members, meeting together for purposes of joint planning or decision making and, in turn, acting as individuals. Yet authority can also be delegated to the laterally linked systems, and we incur no inconvenience at all by this sort of delegation. In the area of safety and hygiene, for instance, the plant manager as usual assumes full responsibility. Nevertheless, a portion of his responsibility is shared by the cell leaders on the one hand, and the nurses in their laterally linked function on the other are given authority in accordance with Sony's spirit of mutual trust to devise and implement their plans. (See Exhibit 7.)

EXHIBIT 7

MANAGERS' MEMOS: May 1966

[Excerpt]

"Safety and hygiene require persevering efforts . . ."

Every work station displays posters: "Nurse's Goal of the Month," "Safety Green Cross," and "Daily Safety Record." Such displays seem to indicate that the safety and hygiene function is firmly established, and they apparently serve as a barometer of interest on the part of operators and others concerned. We have, however, cause for not being able to rejoice. Aside from Manufacturing Departments 3 and 4, where the personnel in charge of safety and the nurses are cooperating closely with each other, the work stations seem to be sticking to the old method of operation. We feel we are responsible for this because the centrally established policies were not made clear enough to them.

In May we attempted to correct this situation. We invited ideas and opinions from the nurses at their meetings so that we would be prepared to establish overall policies on how they should operate. Obtaining their participation in this way, we felt, would enable us to suggest directions in which they could most usefully proceed. They themselves had paved the way for us in the past by performing the basic functions of nurses: measuring light, noise, and gas density; maintaining first-aid boxes; and administering first-aid procedures. But these functions are either, like preventive injections, geared to the prevention of contamination or aimed at post-accident care. They are negative or, at best, passive. The nurses should have more active, positive functions such as issuing a newsletter for themselves or making a slide presentation on "the health of our eyes." However, even these more active functions are becoming less essential now as a result of the gradually increasing level of hygiene at our Atsugi Plant. In other words, we are now in a position to go a step further in hygiene management and control.

The next phase of our activity should be for us to eradicate all kinds of diseases and to proceed with the difficult task of actual health improvement. This is the direction in which the nurses' functions should take them from now, but implementation of this policy will entail serious problems.

First of all, these new active functions require more sophistication and specialized knowledge on the part of the nurses. Job changes and the rapid rotation of nurses owing to work requirements, however, make it difficult for us to aim at a particular level of training. Second, implementation of our new policy calls for close, forceful cooperation from the medical office, which is taxed to the utmost at present by its therapeutic functions. The medical office should be able to devote more time to maintaining its position as a leader in this area. Third, the switch to the new activities creates problems within problems.

We used to have relatively quick feedback on the results of activities relating to our basic functions. The benefits they produced were specific. However, the types of activities we are proposing here will call for the more extended and more persevering efforts that the safety and hygiene functions inevitably demand. Each one of us must therefore become more conscious of health needs, understanding the importance of safety and hygiene, and cultivate that interest in these functions without which we will never succeed.

EXHIBIT 7 (*Continued*)

Furthermore, we need organizational changes. What we must do without delay is to establish lateral relationships between the heretofore virtually unrelated educational functions of the schools and dormitories in the hygiene area and the management of hygiene in the plant so that we can install an effective overall system of control without any duplication of effort. The urgency of setting up such a system cannot be overlooked; we will have tremendous waste in our nurses' activities without it. The fact that their functions have been limited to the plant so far may have saved them from encountering any difficulties. Now, however, that we are having to move out from in-plant control to hygiene in the life of each individual worker, a unified system becomes vitally important.

I have already said what I think about what the nurses have been doing so far. Other functions that they are proposing for themselves, as well as their activities to date, are all intended to prove that the concept which holds that work has a degrading influence upon the healthy development of people's minds and bodies is wrong. I sincerely hope we can develop means of controlling hygiene that will enable work to become the best possible method of developing healthy minds and bodies.

NAOMASA TSUNODA (22 years old)
Safety and Hygiene Group
General Affairs Department

Plant Manager's Comment: I clapped my hands mentally when I read the last portion of your memo.

Our Safety and Hygiene Committee of course insures conformance to national law; it is strictly a group of specialists, such as doctors and specialists licensed to handle hazardous materials. Their function is to provide advice and assistance for the nurses in the lateral system.

So far, I have limited my comments to those laterally linked functions that are directly related to our business and to the work. However, there are others in the area of employee benefits. For instance, we have the cafeteria system, the library system, and the recreation system, all of which control the appropriate activities.

To repeat—these lateral setups are not compatible with the authoritarian, vertically linked organization. Our experience tells us, however, that even under an authoritarian regime the forced establishment of lateral systems can lessen the power-consciousness and the petty jurisdictional conflicts that are inherent in the vertical organization. We can also say that, given the natural tendency of human beings, this kind of lateral system—empowered with the authority to make and to implement its plans—is quite effective in preventing power-consciousness, once eliminated, from reappearing in the unfathomable human mind.

Managerial Accounting for Everyone

At this point, I should like to describe the managerial accounting system we have in the plant. Established in 1963, this system has since shown such rapid development and expansion that it now comprises the backbone of our many management systems. Account items have been rearranged in such a way as to be directly related to the numerous controls possible in each department, and prices have been established for every interdepartmental transaction so that each department is able to control its income and expenditures as if on a self-sustaining basis. This method in itself is not new. We have added our own unique features to it, however, and it is through the way the system is administered that we are able to attain a high degree of effectiveness in its use.

This method of administration was not planned from the beginning. Like any other such group, Accounting—in consultation with each department—prepared budgets based on something close to managerial accounting principles. Then, throughout the year, Accounting prepared analyses comparing actual performance against budget and against the past performance of each department. During meetings with the plant manager, these data were presented, and we would simply make judgments by saying that performance was good or bad. In other words, our budgeting system failed to take into account the various actions taken by the departments. At this time, we were trapped into a procedure, not knowing why we were doing things in the way we were doing them.

It was only when this system was applied to our cell organization—including the very lowest level—and the members of each cell replaced the staff specialists and took over the cell's administration that the bad practices began to disappear. It was only when departmental staffs, instead of specialists in the Accounting Department, started to organize and administer our managerial accounting system in their own unique way that improvement was discernible. Nowadays, cell personnel at crew level participate in this accounting activity as if they were doing household bookkeeping; and the administration of the system, in general terms, is chiefly the responsibility of each section.

The Accounting Department simply offers overall training, makes comments or suggestions, and consolidates the work so that it can be reported to the plant manager. This is the way it should be. Under the old system, each department faced the threat of having the validity and solidness of its budgeting exposed by Accounting in front of the plant manager. Thus it was forced to try arbitrarily to improve its cost and profit picture—and the results could only be harmful. It is when each department tries to reduce costs for the sake of its own satisfaction in a job well done that we truly create a managerial accounting system which directly reflects individual department actions.

Improved yield and increased work efficiency are not the sole factors that influence costs. Improved processes, new ideas for jigs and fixtures, reduction in materials usage, ingenuity in the selection of materials, increased machine operating time, and a corresponding reduction in the man-hours spent on miscellaneous chores—all these have their impact. We have come to know that cooperation and ingenuity on the part of the workers at the various stations can achieve results which defy expectations.

Savings on such "fixed" budget items as gas, water, electricity, and chemicals are being realized voluntarily and spontaneously; each such cost has been reduced to the minimum level consistent with sustained operations. Of course, encouraging the participation of everyone in this system calls for many meetings and for much educational activity. The hours required are, however, made available—also spontaneously—by ingenious efforts to reduce the time needed for miscellaneous chores so that the maximum educational results can be achieved with the minimum number of man-hours.

The influence of our managerial accounting system upon cost reduction is—to sum up—immeasurably great. Here is an example which testifies to the fact that self-control offers maximum effectiveness in comparison with forced control by somebody high up in the management echelon. This, again, is a source of real satisfaction for me.

Birth of the Pair System

A fourth supplementary system is what we call, in our particular phraseology, the pair system. This was born out of necessity. The idea grew out of the fact that a chief, who is the coordinator and leader of a group (responsible for the single integrated line required to manufacture a product)—which is one step above the crew level—necessarily was a boy as a rule, but that all the members of the group (composed of several crews) were girls. Because these girls needed a coordinator among them to assist the leader, we decided to appoint one of them to be a subchief. With her chief she forms a pair, and together they manage their group.

These two are, as it were, a business husband and business wife. Just as in any other home, the daily chores are taken care of by the subchief and such functions as training, negotiation with other groups, and problem solving are handled by the chief. Thus the overall responsibility is shared. The ideal we envision is that the two should cooperate as one solid unit while still making use of each other's characteristics as boy and girl.

The success we obtained with this method led us to principles of organization based on the pair system and to its proliferation within the cells. For instance, a leader, who is the coordinator of a crew, has a subleader under her. The leader trains her subleader in the course of their work. This assures us that we are building a new generation of leaders on a sound, stable basis, and it also enables the leader herself to grow through the process of training others. In addition, we have pairs—that is, combinations of senior and junior workers—among the crew members.

Since we operate our plant on two shifts, different groups work at the same tasks in the morning and afternoon. This means that two girls will be using the same machine—a situation which lends itself well to a kind of intercell pairing. Machines have idiosyncrasies which demand the same frame of mind from the users; therefore, the pair system is effective in this area.

Why is the pair system effective? The smallest unit in a cell is a pair, and that is the unit which is most conducive to formulating and molding cooperative behavior among human beings. It may be, therefore, that it provides the most favorable conditions for the self-learning which occurs during teamwork. A married couple falls into precisely this category. Cooperation between the man and his wife means that the one makes up for the other in a slump, that they not only assist each other but take responsibility for each other. Similarly, a pair of workers offers the most primitive and most appropriate vehicle for training in that the two provide information for each other and teach each other. The cell, having pairs of this kind, accordingly delivers strong, well-developed teamwork. We believe that the supplementary capability inherent in the pair system throughout all the cells in our plant is inestimably powerful. (See Exhibits 8–10.)

EXHIBIT 8

MANAGERS' MEMOS: October 1965

[Excerpts]

"Increase in yield and the pair system . . ."

We had been more concerned so far with catching up on production volume and less concerned with yield. This could have led to over-etching and could have influenced yield, properties, and reliability. We felt we had to do something about it, and so we thought about the pair system that was being implemented in the Assembly Department.

The Assembly Department had set up this system on the basis of pairs from same class or age bracket. It seemed to be working well. We decided to implement the same system in our processes, in a slightly different manner, for Groups A and B. We were able to get good results after just one month of implementation—which made all of us happy. In fact, only two days after we set up our pair system we had our first results and couldn't resist smiling—we had a 100 percent yield! We now take our jobs more seriously and feel more responsible than we used to. In our A and B pairs, we make it our practice to turn out perfect lots and even do our own checking by microscope without any help from others.

This may account for the rapid improvement in our alertness and the fact that our yield now stands at 90.4 percent, far exceeding our goal of 75 percent. . . .

As soon as we introduced the pair system, communication between Group A and Group B improved; much misunderstanding was eliminated. Everything is turning out to our advantage. In the beginning, though, everybody was so nervous that we felt as if the room had been darkened, so to speak, but after about a week our surroundings regained their normal brightness and we started to make jokes. We are all right now.

At present, each of us inspects the lot assigned to us with the microscope to make sure that everything in it is O.K. When we find a Class A part, we smile. When we find a Class B part, we frown. When we find Class C or Class D parts, we're about ready to cry. We feel as if we were watching a face-making show.

I am moved to know that all the operators feel so earnest and responsible toward their work. I feel that I, as one of their leaders, am obligated to create an environment that will offer a pleasant place of work for them.

KATSUE KATO (20 years old)
Leader
Group 107, Group A, KPR Crew
Manufacturing Engineering Department 3

•　　•　　•

"Effect of the pair system . . ."

At the beginning of October, we started our pair system for the purpose of eliminating the over-etching of openings in the electrodes. KPR [Kodak Photo Resist] crews from both Group A and Group B got together for discussion and decided that we should establish three pairs, each composed of one member from Group A and one from Group B. Each pair would take care of a lot from the beginning of the process to the end.

The results of this plan are as follows:

1. Each of us came to have a greater sense of responsibility and to be more strongly motivated to work. One lot used to go through the hands of six people, and this may have diluted each operator's sense of responsibility.
2. Our production volume became somewhat stabilized.
3. The yield began to show improvement. The number of Class C and Class D defects decreased, while Class A and Class B parts increased in number. Parts of Class B workmanship also improved in terms of quality, . . .

EXHIBIT 8 (*Continued*)

Any need for very fine work, any abnormality observed during the process, and especially the results of inspection are noted down by each pair. One look at their notes tells us, though not completely, what happened with respect to the openings in the electrodes for a certain lot. We are now planning to have joint meetings of KPR crews from both Group A and Group B, either to review notes of this type together or to make some kind of presentation based on them. We haven't as yet had the opportunity, however.

> Yoshie Shoji (21 years old)
> Group 107, Group B, KPR Crew
> Manufacturing Engineering Department 3

＊　＊　＊

"Pair system introduced into 107 KPR crew . . ."

[First portion omitted.] The idea of having pairs with members from both Group A and Group B originated in discussions held among the members of KPR crews in the two groups who were troubled continuously by the over-etching problem and hoped to eliminate the resulting defects completely. It was uniformly pointed out during these discussions that (1) whenever a test item is placed on the line, the results are good all the time; and (2) such a test item is taken care of quickly by one girl, from start to finish, as her responsibility.

We therefore arrived at the conclusion that knowing the results obtained from one lot in detail and proceeding to the next lot on the basis of our knowledge should enable us to make the right decision on how best to handle it. All the members of the KPR crews, in both Group A and Group B, talked the matter over and decided that a girl from Group A and a girl from Group B should be paired and that a record of how a particular lot was handled should be kept by the first of the pair. Then, when the other girl took over, she would read this record and be guided by it.

Many girls had been involved in a single lot under the previous KPR setup. This meant that any record kept was quite unclear, which made it difficult for us to take appropriate action on the next lot. Hence the problem of defects. When we teamed up in pairs for the first time, all of us in KPR experienced difficulties; but, as both the responsibility for the work and the results of that work came to be clearly identified after the establishment of the pair system, we gained confidence in ourselves. At the present moment, the significance of the pair system is so well understood by everyone that we wouldn't be able to operate in KPR without it. Drawing one member of each pair from Group A and the other from Group B proved to us how important such interaction between the groups is and how magnificent results can be achieved by skillful administration of the pair system. This will help us in many ways in our future jobs. . . . Our success is due to the fact that we tackled our problems seriously in KPR.

HIROSHI TANAKA (33 years old)
Head
Group 107
Manufacturing Engineering Department 3

Plant Manager's Comment: The reason for your success was the fact that, not only did you "tackle" problems, but you also held discussions with all your team members and developed a unique pair system which linked Groups A and B on the basis of specific needs. If you had forced people to implement the pair system across the board, the result would probably have been failure.

EXHIBIT 9

MANAGERS' MEMOS: JANUARY 1966

[Excerpt]

"Pair system enables us to help one another . . ."

The pair system for Section 245 was initiated in July of last year. I was a TCB [Thermo Compression Bond] crew leader then, and I would like to comment on how I felt at the time and how we can improve our system in the future.

Our principal objective in implementing the pair system was to develop, first, ourselves and, second, our abilities. During the initial phase of implementation, all I can say is that we paired up and that it is doubtful how effective this was. Gradually, though, we started to introduce specific procedures such as the preparation of the daily report by each pair. Although we had been somewhat apprehensive about the effectiveness of this daily reporting prior to its implementation, we feel that it actually proved to be doing us good.

I was quite impressed by the fact that the system helped us to tabulate our results easily and that the paired operators were helping each other to do their jobs. We are making our living in a group, and self-centered thinking creates people who lack thoughtfulness and are egoistic.

Because I wanted to know how much the two members of a pair understood one another, I became deeply involved with the operators at the various work stations. I made it my practice to communicate with each pair at least once a day. This convinced me that they had at least established common goals and that they were coming to the rescue in case one or the other member suffered a slump.

They are unable, however, to analyze the reasons for defects or to establish appropriate measures for improving yield. They still need guidance

EXHIBIT 9 (*Continued*)

from us leaders. Thus we should perhaps motivate ourselves more strongly to do our jobs well. Before we talk about enhancing others' satisfaction and improving others' work, we must give further study to our own job attitudes and performance.

We leaders, in other words, should identify ourselves with the operators more closely even as we establish our own work goals. There are lots of things, however minor they may seem, which can lead to unexpectedly big results.

> KIKUE KAWAKAMI (21 years old)
> Leader
> QC Crew, Section 245
> Manufacturing Department 4

EXHIBIT 10

MANAGERS' MEMOS: FEBRUARY 1966

"Let's introduce the pair system in to our department . . ."

[First portion omitted.] Why don't we introduce the pair system as a means of finding out how quickly newcomers are developing? A newcomer and an old-timer form a pair, establish a single goal, and then try to attain this goal. When one of the two is in poor shape, the other makes up for her so that they will reach their goal without fail.

The process of attaching a lead is a one-man job, and this new system may enable us to make progress here. It should not necessarily be limited to newcomers only; pairing old-timers as well will definitely make for better results. I am given to understand that Department 4 is getting good results since implementing this system, and we should imitate whatever may be good for us. It is a really wonderful way of getting to understand each other, and it may also result in the spontaneous creation of a true spirit of cooperation.

The notes we keep on our process are headed "Sincerity." As the word indicates, everyone scribbles down what she thinks quite frankly. Most of these comments are directed at the work; and, as leader, I am delighted to know that people are devoting such sound thinking to their jobs. I only regret that I cannot necessarily give them answers to all their problems.

> TOSHIKO KIKUCHI (18 years old)
> Leader
> Lead Attachment Crew, Section 212
> Manufacturing Department 3

Comment by Mr. Kurata, department head: I hope you will try to realize your plan for achieving a truly cooperative relationship between newcomers and old-timers. It is important above all to have meetings so that everyone will understand your plan.

Democracy, I suspect, may not be possible of achievement except as it is applied to small groups. The sort which respects human beings and literally places its trust in them cannot really be established in large organizations—or, at least, it will find conditions there extremely difficult. Certainly, true industrial democracy will never grow out of any system of consultation between labor and management. It will come into being only where a plant is organized into numerous small groups interconnecting with one another vertically and horizontally. We have great numbers of leaders at the points where such small groups (cells) connect with each other. These countless individuals, comprising a large stratum in themselves, develop into democratic leaders on the one hand and develop their members into leadership-minded human beings on the other. In our plant we use the slogan "Everybody is a manager." This may sound a little odd, yet everybody in the plant accepts it without any sense of contradiction. As a matter of fact, I can't help feeling that at least these 400 leaders in the plant may have a much purer consciousness of being managers themselves than I have. This may, in fact, be the true form of industrial democracy.

Mr. Jiro Kawakita, professor at the Tokyo Institute of Technology, has said, "A good leader is also a good member of a group." I agree with this picture of the ideal human being.

Part Three

Creative Organization

1

Organization Based on
Anti-Organization Principles

THE actions described so far were intended as a slow but steady struggle against established principles of organization. I should now like to elaborate on our experiences and draw certain lessons from them in order that we may explore this new type of management still further.

When I became manager at Atsugi Plant, I can truthfully say that Sony was facing a critical moment. Starting virtually from scratch, it had grown into a young company of 5,000 employees within the short span of 15 years. Such a company, full of vitality, invariably reaches a turning point after its rapid early development. It also is likely to face a real crisis at this turning point.

The intrinsic worth of a company, like that of a human being, lies in its vitality. Unfortunately, this very quality—which enabled the company to grow—has a tendency to be weakened by the large numbers of personnel employed, one after another, during the process of development. The people who joined during the start-up period were fighters who staked their future with a company that might turn out to be a failure or a success. Those who came in after the company had grown to a respectable size are inclined to "ride" with it, counting on the stability it has achieved.

The spirit of Sony at the time of its establishment can be summed up as conducive to the creation of opportunities for work in which people could make use of their vitality without coercion while keeping their personalities intact. Stability, however, weakens this original spirit in people's minds.

Moreover, as a firm grows in size, it increasingly demands an organization structure. On the other hand, Sony is a company which is opposed to a rigid organization structure, for a stage on which people—uncoerced—can display their talent for creativity and independent activity implies characteristics contrary to those of the old-fashioned industrial organization. And this freedom, this lack of coercion, assured Sony, as we have seen, of its dynamism and flexibility. As it grew, though, it could no longer maintain control without any form of organization, and this led to the establishment in turn of departments, sections, subsections, and what-not, all leading to smaller and smaller subdivisions. In this way the management hierarchy of department managers, section chiefs, subsection chiefs, and so on was created, with detailed rules and regulations for all jobs. Such phenomena were inevitable in spite of the underlying Sony tendency toward anti-organization.

Since, however, Sony did aspire to this philosophy of anti-organization, the need for organizing was accepted with reluctance by its managers—people who could not possibly give the necessary time and attention to the task involved. And this in itself created a problem. The managers' reluctance made them listen too willingly to the opinions of staff specialists who moved into Sony after it became established and who made immature, half-baked suggestions based on ready-made principles of organization.

A company structure based on ready-made principles of organization was bound to conflict with the spirit that characterized Sony in its pioneering days. It was void of any human personality.

Nowadays, some people in our plant worry. "What will happen," they ask, "if Kobayashi leaves?" Yet it would be quite natural, if I did leave, for the way in which the plant was operated under the new management to be different. This would not create any inconvenience whatsoever. It seems to be the general belief, however, that changes in management style due to changes in personnel are not desirable. Why do people think like this? Simply because they regard organization as something that overrides human beings. I even venture to say that people regard organization as something which operates of its own accord by fitting people without any personality into a mold—something which should not be colored by human beings and is just like an automatic machine. This kind of thinking leads them to stipulate job authority, for instance, in detail. They are so accustomed to the idea that rules and regulations take precedence over the individual that they view these as absolute, as requiring people to do whatever "the book says"—unquestioningly—for the benefit of the company.

The same thinking prevails, not only in the management area, but at the work stations as well. The inhuman factors inherent in the Taylor system are the expression of such thinking. It is the duty of human beings to do whatever they are allowed to do, as stipulated, with efficiency. There are jobs to be done, ways in which those jobs are to be done, and people who are to be used by being fitted into those jobs as may be convenient. When these people turn out to be misfits, or when they are completely used up, they are replaced by others. The system also trains people to mold other people who will fit easily into the available jobs. What is sought, under such conditions, is a mere fraction of human capacity; that is, a fraction which will respond mechanically to orders to do whatever needs to be done. This, then, is what many of us call our labor resources.

The ideals expressed in the letters of intent leading to the establishment of Sony presuppose a company in which uncoerced people see their own well-being in the well-being of the company and in which everyone can work freely to achieve personal satisfaction and develop himself to his fullest potential. Thus it follows that a big contradiction naturally arose when principles of organization were adopted which took away people's "planning" and "controlling" functions and forced them into a "doing" role—this in spite of the company's aspirations to the contrary.

The motivation of workers deteriorates rapidly when management is dehumanized. This deterioration is clearly visible, especially in middle management and on down to the worker level. The result? A strong inclination toward labor unrest.

This, in brief, is the pattern that Sony experienced. The injuries sustained by the company were not fatal, however, thanks to the fact that top management resisted (and was alone in resisting) these established concepts of organization. In figurative terms, the patient was still in the initial phase of his sickness despite his high temperature.

Allopathy Offers No Cure

Labor unrest, according to generally accepted ideas, is contained by taking various measures against the company's workers. Such measures, however, are meaningless. It may, on some occasions, be necessary to reduce the patient's temperature by the use of ice packs, but this, in itself, will not eliminate the cause of the sickness. And what was needed more than anything else by Sony—which can be likened to a patient with great vigor and vitality in the early stages of a disease—was the elimination of the constitutional reasons for its running a temperature. In short, the establishment of management principles designed to effect a revival of humanity was one of the basic measures needed to cope with the situation.

Sony's aspirations to "do away with organization" notwithstanding, there can, of course, be no large-scale company without some form of organization. Human dynamism and vitality alone could not support such a firm. It therefore becomes necessary for us to organize in such a way as to permit the transformation of this human dynamism and vitality into company dynamism. Were we, on the other hand, to define organization as a method of structuring the company which leads to the negation of human dynamism, no management would be capable of solving the inherent contradiction.

At the time Sony faced its crisis, I thought there must be some type of organization, and some style of management, which would motivate people, but I didn't know what they might be. Presumptuous though it may sound, I made up my mind then that I had to find one way or another of bringing to life the philosophy of vitality to which Sony aspired and that we could and would continue to grow while rejuvenating and maintaining this philosophy. That was when I talked with the entire workforce in these terms: "Let's make this plant the best in the world. It may be difficult for us, but I believe that such qualitative advantages as our technological and innovative capabilities, our vitality, and our capacity for human growth can literally make us the best plant in the world. Anyhow, there's no other way out for Sony—so let's try it!" Such was our ambitious vision at the time.

A type of organization that would be conducive to this approach demanded that we base our effort on creative teamwork and that we destroy the static and dehumanizing aspects of traditional organization patterns. Establishment of a divisional profit-center system is one method which is being applied in decentralizing gigantic corporations, but it fails to solve any fundamental problems so long as it is viewed as a means of decentralization in the context of traditional organization.

What should an organization be like in a new era? It should be an organization capable of changing freely from moment to moment, one which will not fetter human behavior. It should be an organization which was created by people and which they can change of their own volition. It should be an organization in which the effectiveness of teamwork is never lost under any circumstances and in which every team member is able to take action based on his own free will and initiative in his own unique way. In other words, what is required is an organization which can motivate people and insure voluntary action on their part without being disintegrated and which will enable everyone to strive for the accomplishment of group goals. This kind of organization may be possible for a ball team, but applying it to a large company is an extremely difficult task.

Achieving an organization that will meet our specifications calls, in fact, for constant creative action aimed at formulating a pattern for ourselves on the basis of trial and error. What we must avoid under any circumstances is the stabilization of an organization structure through organization charts and rules based on the concept which views organization as a vehicle for directive management, authority, and status. Teamwork is possible only in small groups. Therefore, we had to redesign our large organization as a collection of interlinking small groups.

Breaking Down the Power Structure

I should now like to describe, first of all, how we set about breaking down the concept of organization as a means of insuring authority and power. By way of illustration, I shall draw chiefly on examples from the plant.

It is, of course, in this concept that sees the organization chart as providing lines through which directions and orders may flow, or as clarifying the power structure, that we find the reasons why the typical organization is dehumanized and static. What pleased me most at the time, prior to my employment, when I had my earliest contacts with Sony was the fact that top management didn't have a speck of power-consciousness. That was particularly gratifying because, since my childhood days, I had not been able to stand being ordered around by other people. When I started my work at Atsugi Plant, however, I realized that the people of Sony—contrary to the philosophy of its top management—did subscribe to the generally accepted notion that superiors do their jobs by using their subordinates.

This phrase "using people" is quite common; we even find the same thing in legal terminology. I can't endure it, however. The analogy with the idea of "using *things*" reminds me of people's attitude, in the old days, toward slaves. There was an occasion when I severely reprimanded a senior manager—the one, in fact, who was closest to the plant manager—for using this kind of language. As I recall it now, I feel that this could have been the very first step I took toward destroying authoritarian organization in our plant.

Underlying the general idea of superiors doing their jobs by using people is the notion—easily detected—that those who really love and care about their companies and their jobs are, first, presidents—followed by directors, then by managers. Mere workers are seldom given credit for caring about their companies or their jobs in the slightest degree, much less loving them. Hence the justification for managers' using their subordinates as tools—as slaves who must perform in exactly the way they are told to perform. This rationalization is virtually accepted as an axiom of organization and is reflected in invincible power-consciousness.

To me, this sort of thinking is no more than superstition. Presidents and workers alike care about their companies and their jobs. This is self-evident—just like the proposition that the earth rotates around the sun. Naturally, people are different from one another; so, just as there are some workers who don't care about their companies or their jobs, there are some presidents who couldn't care less. Therefore, the mere fact that a person is a manager cannot be accepted as justification for his regarding workers as tools.

Mary Parker Follett, the Boston-born social worker who became an outstanding management scholar during the 1929s, lectured at the University of London just before her death in 1933. Her classic *Freedom & Co-ordination* * has been translated into Japanese. In the lectures contained in this book, it is clear that she foresaw our modern times even during her *belle époque* days; her pages are filled with clarity of vision, intelligence, and wisdom. As the introduction to *Freedom & Co-ordination* says, "To her 'power over'" anyone was an obsolete idea, a contradiction in terms. Thus, to develop real power, we must abandon the idea that anyone is "over" anyone else; we must try to develop power "with" people. Here are some actual excerpts from the book:

> I said to one girl at a big factory, "What do you think would be the best improvement that could be made in a factory?" She replied instantly, "To get rid of foremen". . . .

> The arbitrary command ignores one of the most fundamental facts of human nature, namely, the wish to govern one's own life. "I don't like being bossed," a man in a factory told me.

* Mary Parker Follett, *Freedom & Co-ordination,* Lectures in Business Organization, 1949 (London and New York: Pitman), pp. xii, 19–20, 21.

Another workman said to me, "I am willing to obey but I won't be commanded." I think that a very interesting remark. Probably more industrial trouble has been caused by the manner in which orders have been given than in any other way.

It is often the command that is resented, not the thing commanded.

I have read that it is characteristic of the British workman to feel, "I know my job and won't be told how."

Again and again we disregard the fact that workers are usually as eager to attain a certain standard, as wishful that their performance shall be maintained at a high level, as their employers. We often tend to think that the executive wishes to maintain standards, wishes to reach a certain quality of production, and that the worker has to be goaded in some way to this. Again and again we forget that the worker is often, usually I think, equally interested, that his greatest pleasure in his work comes from the satisfaction of worthwhile accomplishment, of having done the best of which he was capable.

Right of Decision Making in the Hands of Facts

It is normally accepted that in an organization the top man is vested with the supreme power and authority and that he in turn delegates appropriate authority to the vice-presidents, the managers, the chiefs, and so on down to the first-line supervisors. Is this really so? It may be, physically and legally, as seen from a static viewpoint. However, such a concept cannot make an organization function in real life. Or perhaps I should say, rather, that it is rapidly becoming very hard to operate an organization in accordance with this concept.

Miss Follett says in this connection, "So much goes to contribute to executive decisions before the part which the executive head takes in them, which is indeed sometimes merely the official promulgation of a decision, that the conception of final authority is losing its force in the present organization of business." † I, however, go a step further than Miss Follett.

† Op. cit., Ch. 1, "The Illusion of Final Authority," p. 1.

Let me illustrate my point with a simple example. It would be impossible for me to make decisions as I please about discharging workers on the grounds that the right to do so is vested in the hands of the plant manager. In reality, I am just a watchman for reasonableness. Judgment as to the reasonableness of discharging a worker might be compared to a similar judgment of a doctor's final diagnosis. The *de facto* right of the doctor in this case is not vested in him because of his high position; it is his professional abilities that give him this *de facto* right. Should I (or the doctor) make a decision with the notion in my mind that I am entitled to make it by virtue of my position alone, it can only result in disaster.

There is no assurance whatsoever that the top man will always make the correct judgment. Thus I say that the concept which vests power in the top man just because he *is* the top man can do us great harm in any real-life administrative situation. To say arbitrarily that power is located at the top of the organization is equivalent to saying that the top man can make decisions as he pleases. What assures reasonableness of judgment is not the sort of thinking which automatically places all power at the top but, rather, that which holds that power and authority really are adjuncts to knowledge and experience having a bearing on the decisions to be made. Our ultimate purpose here should be to achieve reasonableness of judgment; therefore, to consider power as a concomitant of knowledge is indeed logical.

This may sound a little reckless, but once I said to my people: "Gentlemen, please don't obey me simply because I am your plant manager. The ultimate right to make decisions lies in the hands of facts and situations surrounding us. Facts are numerous, and authority and power are vested in those that will give us insight and understanding. Let's listen to what they tell us with our minds open, discuss them among ourselves, and obey their voices."

Naturally, I didn't make such controversial remarks to everyone; I resorted to this kind of peroration depending on whom I was talking to. However, I always tried to listen to the facts myself and behave accordingly whenever I spoke with people in our monthly meetings, in our sessions with the departmental managers, and in any other such gatherings. Sometimes I may have left the impression with my audience that I was contradicting myself. In fact, I erred constantly in this way—and admonished myself for doing so. It is the truth, nevertheless, that I always made a sincere effort to hear what the facts told me.

Harmful Status-Consciousness

Management based on power-consciousness became less obvious as time went by. But a certain obstacle in the way of improvement also was clear: hierarchical position as found in the traditional delineation of jobs.

To review briefly—our plant organization consists of the crew (at the lowest level), which has about six members; the group, which includes several crews; the section (though some sections would be called "groups" in English), which includes several groups; and the department, which includes several sections. (See Part One, Chapter 2.) The first obstacle arose in connection with the titles given to the individuals in charge of these various units. Department superior (*ka-choh* in Japanese), section superior (*kakari-choh*), group supervisor (*kumi-choh*), and crew supervisor (*han-choh*) all reminded both managers and workers of the old superior-subordinate relationship. We therefore decided to discontinue the use of the suffix *choh*.[1] The department superior and section superior were to be called simply "manager" (*shunin*). We also decided to use English words for titles—for instance, "leader" (in the case of the crew) and "chief" (in the case of the group).

We also encouraged people, as I have said, to address a man with a managerial position not as "Mr. Department Manager," for example, but simply by his last name.

A second obstacle that soon emerged was the fact that titles like "department superior" or "section superior" represented social status as well as company position. For instance, anyone who was promoted to department manager could never be transferred back

---

[1] *Choh*—meaning "superior," "head," or "chief" in Japanese—usually is affixed to the word indicating the organizational unit. For example: *ka-choh* (department supervisor) or *kakari-choh* (section superior).

to his old job as section manager unless for serious personal mis-conduct. The entire staff was so thoroughly imbued with status-consciousness that to move a person under any circumstances from the position of department superior to a section superior's job would have been considered an outright demotion. And this status-consciousness was irrevocably linked with power-consciousness.

We therefore decided to change our job-assignment policies when we changed our titles. People who are not yet considered eligible for such elevated status are sometimes made department managers, and people who *are* eligible are sometimes made section managers. In short, our practice became flexible. A man could be appointed department manager and, immediately thereafter, could be reappointed section manager, and vice versa. This new practice, once established, virtually eradicated status-consciousness due to hierarchical position.

The organization climate in which people must be accorded status because they are "somebody" and are expected to exercise the authority of their position to use people was gradually eliminated.

Managerial Responsibility and Participative Decision Making

How, then, are managers to do their jobs if they are not to use people to get the work out? I believe they should *assist* people to carry out the necessary tasks voluntarily.

When managers use people to do their jobs, orders are needed. When managers assume a role in which they assist people, they need only to explain the general situation and the relevant policies. Then all they need to do is teach people how to *act*.

Overdoing this sort of explanation and teaching is not recommended; it would be detrimental to people's initiative and willingness to act. Since we are not ordering them to do anything, it is now their duty to oppose, question, discuss any explanation or instruction they may receive from their managers. True, the use of the word "duty" may sound a little odd here, but it is only through discussion that we can find out what the facts have to tell us. Neglect of this duty is therefore tantamount to betrayal of the organization. Workers who are not fulfilling it deserve a severe reprimand from their managers. On the other hand, managers should never allow themselves to close their minds to conflicting ideas or opinions from their workers. If they ever allow themselves to be actually disturbed by remarks from their team, that means they are still harboring power-consciousness—they feel their prerogatives are being attacked.

What is right is right regardless of who says it. Everybody should express himself with an open mind and listen with an open mind. Managers and their workers alike must search jointly for the truth behind the facts.

All this, however, will not always result in a consensus of ideas or opinions. That's because time is limited. It is the generally accepted theory that when any difference arises subordinates should obey their superiors, be guided by what they say. Such an attitude, however, brings us back to authoritarianism. Employees' ideas and opinions should, as a rule, be adopted—if only because it is the workers, not their managers, who actually implement the decisions made. No policy or procedure will prove perfect in most cases. Success or failure often depends on whether the policy or procedure is being revised at the right time in the right way, during the process of implementation, and whether it is being approached by the workers with the right zeal and earnestness.

Some will of course argue that managers under such circumstances cannot be held responsible for anything. This is, I feel, the crux of the matter—and I have made this point before. Managers *must* assume responsibility for results, and it is because they must that they ought to obey their workers and thereby insure greater success. Those who insist that they will not assume responsibility for any action unless that action is consistent with their own ideas are not seeking success in any wholehearted way. What they are really looking for may be self-satisfaction in exchange for the sacrifice they feel they may have to make in assuming full responsibility.

The reader will recall that, just before I took over as manager of Sony Atsugi Plant, Mr. Ibuka said, "I shall not mind if this plant has to be shut down. You are free to do what you like." I still can't forget the shock this remark gave me. Mr. Ibuka may not have given any deep thought to his words, but I interpreted him as saying, "You are free to do what you like, and I will take the responsibility for the consequences." This attitude should, in fact, be the attitude assumed by any man willing to delegate authority. Employees who are given the authority, by such a manager, to do a certain job as they see fit come to feel that the last thing they want to do is to let him down. Thus a true sense of responsibility on the part of a manager is transformed into a true sense of responsibility in his men. We should all take account of the profoundly important principle of human relations illustrated by this example.

Those managers who are not willing to take any responsibility for an employee's ideas, once adopted and implemented, are not truly and seriously taking any responsibility for much else, either. The worst type of manager is the one who blames his people in case of a fiasco yet who wants to exercise his power and authority by taking credit for their successes. A manager who will not allow himself to dodge any responsibility has no other course but to trust his people. This boldness of spirit, when shown by a manager, kindles a similar spirit in those people and assures their voluntary cooperation. Here we have the real basis of leadership.

After the prevailing situation has been explained, the relevant policies are clear, and the necessary decisions on education and training have been made, action shoud be entirely in the hands of the employees. There should never be any form of surveillance or interference. What managers can do during this phase of any project is to establish as many contacts as possible with the employees and encourage them periodically. Upon request, managers might provide tips on revision of established goals or methods.

Then, once the job is completed, managers and employees together should review the results. This is what recognition amounts to. There are, however, innumerable forms which the review process may take. It ranges from a casual, personal survey and evaluation to a systematic procedure. What is basically the most important point to be made in this connection is that managers should evaluate performance seriously and wholeheartedly and that any appraisal should be carried out only in such a way as to further the development and growth of the employees concerned. Participation in the process by colleagues of those who are being appraised also is desirable.

2

Self-Imposed Rules and Regulations

LIKEWISE to be dreaded, apart from the concept which justifies managers' using their men, is that which places manuals and rules above everything else. These two notions play a major role in making organizations static and killing human beings.

The "Rule Is Everything" Attitude

There exists in Japanese companies a type of thinking which defines the act of organizing as drawing up detailed charts, precise job descriptions, and statements of job authority to avoid any misunderstanding. These generally are formulated by staff specialists working out of the executive offices or perhaps an organization planning department. This brand of thinking further insists that the company takes the initiative in implementing all rules and regulations, which everybody employed in the company then must abide by. Those who cannot obey such rules and regulations are to be regarded as organization dropouts.

Nothing could be sillier. Rules and regulations are stipulated so as to permit efficient administration of an organization under a certain set of prevailing conditions. There are no perfect rules and regulations. Even if we could indeed achieve such perfection, some of our stipulations would immediately be made impractical by the inexorable change of circumstances. To say, therefore, that organization men must abide by every last regulation is equivalent to saying that they must behave impractically if the rules so stipulate. And, if we define "organization man" as a person who would do something impractical because the rule required him to, we would be contradicting ourselves in our use of terminology. Such a "cogwheel" man simply is not a human being; he has disqualified himself.

The following episode occurred in our plant some time ago. For the summer only, we had some students working on a part-time basis at clean-up jobs in the warehouse. The place was full of dust, and very frequently the students' overalls quickly became soiled. They explained the situation and requested that the overalls be laundered every day, but the man in charge flatly refused, saying that it was against the rules. Overalls, it was stipulated, were to be laundered twice a month at no cost to the workers. This is the sort of thing that happens far too often; when I heard the story, I reprimanded the man severely. Yet I felt miserable about doing so because the man was very earnest and took his job seriously.

It is the dogmatic approach of putting rules and regulations above all else that makes a bad employee out of an earnest, serious individual. Instead, rules should be reduced to the minimum. They should not have an air of rigid formality, standardized uniformity, and authority. Anything coming under the heading of unwritten law should be left as is. True organization men should try, first of all, to understand the intent and purpose back of rules and regulations and place less emphasis on the formality implied. Second, they should temper conscientious administration with flexibility and take the initiative in proposing revisions where necessary. If possible, organization men themselves should endeavor to formulate suitable rules and regulations. With conditions around us becoming more and more fluid, initiative in this area is needed increasingly.

Rules Exist to Be Revised

The proposition I am about to set forth may cause understandable concern over the possibility that it would tend to disrupt order and the end result would be confusion and inefficiency. I declare categorically, however, that no such possibility exists. I believe rules exist, not to be adhered to, but to be revised. And I have never known any harmful disorder to result from this point of view.

People who are forced at all times to abide strictly by rules and regulations tend to lose their perspective on the organization as a whole. They have no understanding of the situation that led management to establish a particular rule. Also, it is a well-known fact that rules which are forced upon people have little chance of being adhered to. Those in the seat of power fail to see the reason for this and brand workers as good-for-nothings. And they are entirely wrong. People need not be deliberately trying to disturb peace and order when they ignore a rule. Disturbances, confusion, chaos—all are caused by the forcible imposition of rules and regulations.

It is only when an individual realizes that a rule exists to be revised that he becomes the master of that rule and arrives at an understanding of the circumstances leading to it. This realization makes him try to live with it and thus maintain order. It is in this realization that we find true freedom and discipline.

It is a gross mistake to assume that order will suffer where rules and regulations are not enforced. For instance, we have no company-made rules and regulations in our dormitories, yet strict order prevails. An Italian gentleman who was shown these dormitories commented, "They look like a convent." This may be an exaggeration, but to some extent the observation is correct, although a Japanese might have been reminded of "student dormitories maintained by high schools requiring in-house residence of all students." People who are spellbound by normative dogmatism can hardly be blamed for believing, upon looking into our dorms, that they are managed like prisons without bars and that the workers who live in them must be suffering from deprivation of freedom. Such is the degree of order we enjoy without rules or regulations.

Quite some time ago, an outside organization whose self-imposed mission is to create disturbances in labor relations dispatched agitators to the plant. These agitators passed out leaflets at the gate to the dorms, offering them to the girl workers who were setting out toward the plant. The leaflets urged the girls to rebel against the company's oppressive practices, but the occasion proved to be a sorry one for this interfering organization. The girls failed to understand the meaning of the provocative leaflets. Because the order in the dorms was something they themselves had created and vowed to maintain (though, admittedly, this may be a rather exceptional case), everybody observed it strictly. Yet bright smiles were universal; these girls' cheerful faces presented a startling contrast to the dark, ominous-looking men lined up in front of the gate to thrust soiled leaflets into innocent young hands. Not only did the girls wonder what the leaflets were all about, but they also—understandably—came to feel a sort of physical revulsion against them.

Defining Our Own Job Duties

Texas Instruments Incorporated maintains a highly commendable position on rules and regulations. It says that in a tradition-bound company departmental managers are given job specifications which bear the approval of top management. These

traditional job specifications have been prepared by staff specialists employed by the company; therefore, they do not necessarily
meet with understanding and support on the part of every manager. However, those managers who are committed to long-standing
policies on procedures feel that such job specifications suffice.

A good example can be found in the typical government office.
If someone wants to establish a nursery school, for instance, the
duties assigned to the man in charge will be directed not so much
toward the school itself as toward the way the necessary papers
should be prepared, the correct method of stamping the prescribed seals, and the channels through which the papers must
be processed. The matter of efficiency is completely ignored. Nor
is this an isolated case: We are surrounded wtih this kind of "rule
is everything" or "organizational jurisdiction is everything" principle patterned after government "red tape."

At Texas Instruments, managers define their own duties in
such a way as will best serve the company's interests under the
generally prevailing conditions. They do this on an annual basis.
Their statements of job duties, however, are not static but are
reviewed, revised, and adjusted as the need arises, depending on
the requirements of the company during a particular fiscal year.
By sheer coincidence, we follow exactly the same practice.

I wonder what kind of duties could ever be performed effectively by those "cogwheel" types who put detailed rules and
regulations on a pedestal. None, I imagine. We as human beings
should not wait for someone else to stipulate the duties we are to
perform. At Sony Atsugi Plant, we do not subscribe to this kind
of passivity at all.

For instance, imagine that I am appointing a man to be manager of the General Affairs Department. I ask him to write down
what he thinks the problems of the department are and how he
anticipates solving them. This man and I then discuss what he has
written. I don't force my ideas upon him; I simply let him do
whatever he seriously considers must be done. If, after a while,
he wishes to revise his plan, he and I again hold further discussions.

Those who fear that self-made job descriptions could lead to
the total disintegration of a company tend to regard men as totally

incapable of thinking through what they should do in the context of the total organization. They belittle the capabilities of human beings. Yet no organization can be effectively managed as a whole in terms of the old concept that job duties should be stipulated and everyone must conform as prescribed. Nor are organizations, in reality, being operated by this logic. They simply fail to recognize this fact and persist in fettering men and their minds with rules and regulations. But they are fighting a losing battle, and eventually they will end up in confusion.

Suppose we have a situation here in which everybody is doing work that he spontaneously decided to do. During the course of this work, however, a certain mishap occurs. Faced with such a situation, an authority-oriented leader and his staff would tend to conclude that their men were mishap-prone; that accidents could be prevented only by stipulating rules and enforcing them rigidly. But the imposition of rules doesn't work that way. It may at least prevent the same mishaps from recurring, but it cannot prevent other mishaps thereafter. Thus the power-conscious leader may keep thinking his men can't be trusted and try to ramify his rules still further, but he will only succeed in bogging himself down completely without getting anywhere.

It is therefore necessary that we not concern ourselves too much with small mishaps so long as our people attack their work with vigor and determination. Should vertical or horizontal coordination with other operations or processes be required in the course of defining job duties, workers can discuss matters not only with their immediate managers but also with people in other functions to arrive at a proper statement of their responsibilities. It is they themselves who should assume this task on the basis of their relations with the organization as a whole.

It is highly unlikely, therefore, that the manager of general affairs will define his duties as being similar to those of the purchasing department manager. Moreover, when the present manager of the General Affairs Department is replaced by another incumbent, the definition of the job will change as well. Even the same man may define the same job in a different way, once he has gained new experience or he finds his situation altered. Not only is he perfectly free to do so, but he is obligated to do so.

3

Teamwork and
Multiple Organizations

WE have already seen that an organization which can motivate
people and insure voluntary action on their part without being
disintegrated, one which will enable every member to strive for
the achievement of common goals, can be realized only in small
groups.

During the initial phase of management innovation in our
plant, we became aware of this fact. That's why we began by
organizing lower-level production functions on the basis of the
small group which we call a crew. (See Part One, Chapter 2.)
This, it will be remembered, is composed of two to a maximum of
twenty people. Those people who work in the same process in the
manufacture of transistors are grouped together, and we may have
one or two or even three crews, depending on the number of work-

ers in a process. Crew-type organization thus is very common throughout the plant. What is important about it is that each crew comprises a small team and that this unit provides the basis for the organization of the entire plant.

The Secret of Small-Group Success

But what is the difference between such a team and the equivalent unit in the traditional organization? First of all, the leader of a team, in contrast to the crew chief (*han-choh*) in the traditional organization, is not a supervisor who gets the work out by using his men. Most of the leaders in our plant are girls 18 to 19 years old; and, in the ranks of the operators, we have many well-established housewives. Moreover, since our leaders are free from status-consciousness, they assume and resign leadership quite freely. We aspire to an organization in which everybody can become a leader; in fact, appointments are now made spontaneously by the operators themselves.

Second, it should be kept in mind that a team is a group of human beings and is managed chiefly through meetings of its members. Herein lies the basic difference between the team and the work group in the traditional, directive type of organization in which superiors give instructions to their subordinates individually without holding any meetings. It satisfies the human need to belong.

Professor Rensis Likert, of the University of Michigan, writes in his *New Patterns of Management* as follows:

> The most important source of satisfaction for this desire is the response we get from the people we are close to, in whom we are interested, and whose approval and support we are eager to have. The face-to-face groups with whom we spend the bulk of time are, consequently, the most important to us. Our work group is one in which we spend much of our time and one in which we are particularly eager to achieve and maintain a sense of personal worth. As a consequence, most persons are highly motivated to behave in ways consistent with the goals and values of their work group in order to obtain recognition, sup-

port, security, and favorable reactions from this group. It can
be concluded, therefore, *that management will make full use
of the potential capacities of its human resources only when
each person in an organization is a member of one or more
effectively functioning work groups that have a high degree of
group loyalty, effective skills of interaction, and high performance goals.* ‡

I agree with him completely. All our experience testifies to the
truth of what he says. The large, traditional organization fails to
take advantage of the mystical power possessed by small groups.
It is this power, of course, that is the secret of small groups everywhere, enabling them to deliver superb performance. Sometimes
this performance exceeds the wildest limits of the imagination; the
aggregate abilities of people comprising a little team can produce
results that defy expectations. To quote Professor Toshihiko Toki-
zane, of the Medical School of the University of Tokyo, "A discovery in the area of cerebrum physiology tells us that the desire of
human beings to belong to a group is the strongest desire of them
all, and yet it is the least realized in terms of its existence."

We don't call the meeting which comprises the core of team
administration a "conference." To us, this term implies a type of
meeting which is commonly held in many groups but which we
try to avoid. I have already described how we provide access to
information, how we establish action plans, and how managers and
workers discuss them through our meetings in general. Here a
meeting is performing the same function in a more organized way.
What is above all needed to make this kind of meeting successful
is a climate that will promote flexibility and freedom. A "conference" [2] is too ceremonious; its customary procedures require well-
prepared agenda, submission of proposals, question-and-discussion
sessions, and final action by asking participants to "say yes if you
agree." Such formal procedures would stifle us.

Before I was employed by Sony but after I had begun to have
some contact with it, I had occasion to attend one of its managers'

‡ Rensis Likert, *New Patterns of Management* (New York: McGraw-Hill Book
Company, 1961), p. 104.
[2] The Japanese word is *kaigi*—denoting, in the case of Sony, a type of meeting
conducted in accordance with a prepared agenda.

meetings. I was amused by what I heard. The managers started their meeting without any agenda in their hands. They talked spontaneously and freely, and they seemed in no hurry to arrive at any conclusions. When they adjourned, I wasn't at all sure whether they had reached any conclusions or not. In short, the manner in which the meeting was held was quite informal, and I liked this informality more than anything else.

People may feel some apprehension because of the fact that a meeting like this one sometimes appears to produce no tangible results. Yet implementation follows with vigor and determination. This means that everyone reached his own conclusions mentally during the discussion in his own way; in fact, it was because everyone had his conclusions well in mind that the meeting came to an end. Ideally, the perfect meeting by the perfect team should yield such results all the time. We always try hard at Atsugi Plant to achieve meetings of this quality, although we have not quite reached that degree of perfection yet.

Growth Through Teamwork

Another difference between organization into teams and traditional organization lies in the fact that a team doesn't function on orders from above; rather, it functions on its own initiative. The same thing can be said about the individuals who make up a team. Team goals and plans are set by the team, and the implementation and revision of those goals also are handled by the team. In other words, they work as a unit.

Professor Jiro Kawakita, of the Tokyo Institute of Technology, has published a book, entitled *Teamwork,* in which he describes some cases in which he himself has been involved. He says in connection with one such case:

> We found out that the following three points were important in conjunction with teamwork: development of people, harmony among people, and formation of a culture (that is, formation of something close to a rule), all of which are closely interdependent. It may be because of this close interdependence that our effort to develop each factor in parallel does not seem

to work out well in practice. For instance, suppose we have a teacher here. The theme of his lecture for the first week is "On the Development of People." During his lecture, he stresses impressively how important it is for teamwork to further the growth and development of each individual team member. He concludes his lecture by saying, "After all, it's up to the individual." In the same manner, he lectures on formation of culture by teamwork. He might achieve a degree of effectiveness from lectures given in this manner if he were one of the most charming and venerable men of his time. However, we have only a handful of such teachers in the world.

There exists in this world something which is a far greater teacher than any human being. That is work.

Suppose again that a team is organized here. At the time when this team is newly formed, each member is no great human being. Each is definitely insignificant, but each is in the process of development. The extent to which they will attain harmony cannot be predicted. They have no common assets in terms of knowledge of how a team should be managed. But a team once formed is a team, however insignificant it may be, and as such it has goals to achieve as a team. All the members have to do, then, is to tackle the task of achieving their goals, and this they may be able to do if their teamwork is correctly managed. It is through experiencing this joint achievement of goals that development of people, harmony among people, and formation of a culture are to some degree realized.

Now this team is ready to select a slightly more difficult goal than the first one it achieved through teamwork. And once more, having achieved this new goal, the members make positive progress in teamwork. Indeed, when this pattern of challenge and response to challenge is skillfully repeated over a sufficient period of time in assigning the jobs to be performed, the team is likely to grow at an astounding pace. An important condition must be met, however, before work can really become a "teacher." That is, the teamwork applied to each job must be good teamwork. And what constitutes good teamwork? In a nutshell, it is *creative* teamwork. To put it more plainly, it means the achievement of pressing goals that are worthy of achievement by way of innovative ideas.

I sincerely agree with every word in Professor Kawakita's statement. I myself mentioned in Part One of this book that individual growth is realized through work. Now I must add that a team grows through teamwork. The astounding capacity of people for growth in a team situation must be experienced to be understood. Anyone who thinks education is a mere matter of lectures is to be pitied.

Vertical and Lateral Linking of Teams

It is our plant goal to reach the point where the full range of our activity is based on teamwork. This means that each team must necessarily be small in size. The plant, on the other hand, is large. How did we solve this conflict? We solved it with the establishment of our cell-type organization. In other words, we linked small teams with each other, as in a living organism, to make up a single large body.

This did not call for any changes in the way the plant was currently organized. The various groupings could remain as they were, and so could the managers at the various levels. The only things that had to be changed were management style and management attitudes. In order that my readers may understand this more clearly, I should like here to talk a little more about this process of change.

First of all, the monthly meeting—in which it is intended that everybody participate—demonstrated the management style and attitudes of a new plant manager who denied power-consciousness. Gradually, then, the new climate came to be understood and permeated down through the entire plant with the help of talks, the way in which those talks were handled, and a succession of new policies that were implemented one after another. Everybody came to savor the good feeling that grew out of working in an atmosphere of mutual trust as exemplified by the abolition of time clocks and the introduction of the cafeteria without attendants. About this time, too, the crew system was implemented. Up until then, the first-line supervisors—called group chiefs—had managed every process in the plant. Under the new setup, however, crews were created within the old groupings, and each was assigned to one work process. Operators who composed each crew selected a leader from among themselves. Both steps—creating the crews and permitting the operators to select their leaders from their own ranks—proved highly conducive to the growth of the crews as teams. From the very beginning, the members lacked any of the status-consciousness which would have been inevitable with the usual superior-subordinate relationships.

The initial task of the crews, as I have explained in detail, was to record and control attendance after the abolition of the time clocks. This used to involve the exercise of authority and power; but, when such an important control function was delegated to the crews, the result was the spontaneous birth of teamwork. The girls did a beautiful job. Their checking, in clear contrast to that previously done by the Personnel Department, had a truly humane touch; it was intended not for surveillance but for encouragement. Now control of attendance is not simply the tabulation of figures; it is a drama itself, abounding in the warmth, tears, and blood of human life. This was the inspired start of our spiritual awakening. When, to autonomous checking, we added autonomous control over attendance, that in turn led naturally to autonomy in production control at crew level. Teamwork made the team members grow, and this enabled them to realize a still higher degree of teamwork.

To this day I remember the intense pleasure and inspiration I felt at this early success. I was so moved by these girls' performance that I wanted to embrace each one of them—and this is no overstatement. From then on I placed my trust in human beings.

Then there was our practice of holding a meeting for the department managers every morning. "M.M." (Morning Meeting), we call it now. Any matters pertaining to the plant as a whole were to be reported and discussed in this meeting and the resulting decisions then implemented. The participants in this meeting formed a team in themselves, one composed of the plant manager and the entire department-manager group. I, as the newly appointed plant manager, knew nothing about transistors—or about the plant. From the very beginning, therefore, it was impossible for me to direct and lead the others, even on an individual basis. I could take no action on any matter which a department manager came to consult me about unless I asked for comments and ideas from the other department managers.

Thus the top team was by accident formed simultaneously with the teams at lower levels. And these teams at the top and bottom led to the formation of intermediary teams in a chain-reaction effect.

Don't Stifle Team-Formation Effort

I have gone into considerable detail about these matters of team administration just because the teams were so important to us in formulating our cell type of organization. However, a certain amount of clarification may be in order.

To begin with, a team is a small group of people and team-orientation is strongest in people who have close contacts through their jobs. In our case, team-orientation is strongest in the crews, at the lowest level. They are the foundation of the cell-type organization in our plant. All teams above the crew level, viewed from the standpoint of maintaining and improving this organization, exist for the purpose of cultivating the team-orientation of the crews; they provide a sort of servicing. A smoothly functioning cell is possible only when it encourages and cultivates the team-orientation that is inherent in people as a particular work station instead of destroying it. Upper-level cells, in order to supply the needed encouragement and cultivation, must make a conscious effort to let the crew members organize their own teams.

I often receive questions from other companies as to how they too can organize cells. I always answer by saying that the best way is to scrap a certain management style which tends to stifle team-formation effort and which fails to promote management understanding of the fact that such effort is the expression of a natural human need.

Second, it should be mentioned that another key to success in organizing cells lies in the managers who act as interconnecting points for teams at upper and lower levels. It is only through these people that nourishment from the upper cells can be transmitted to the basic teams down below—that is, the crews. Differences in both managerial level and managerial quality lead to differences in the way teams are formulated. The extent of the influence which a lower-level manager can wield is limited, increasing as we go higher in the management ranks. Moreover, we can't escape the fact that there will always be differences in the relative quality of people in spite of improvements in their overall quality. And such differences, depending on their severity, may disrupt harmony and balance. In order to minimize these differences, it is necessary that we place as few layers as possible between upper and lower cells and that we not depend on any one manager for connecting the various levels—a point that is the very antithesis of the old authoritarian management style.

With the number of plant employees exceeding 3,000, the number of departments standing at 20-odd, and our lines of business diversified, we seemed to have reached a stage where we could no longer manage and control our affairs unless we established divisions. I hesitated to increase the layers of management, however. That was when we solved our problem by dividing the morning meeting into four sessions: general meeting, meeting for general affairs, meeting for semiconductors, meeting for calculators, each of them to be held once a week as a rule. (For details, see Chapter 4, "Systems to Support Communication"—particularly the section entitled "Meetings as Creative Organisms.")

The plant manager attends all these meetings of top management, and the acting plant managers, who assist him directly, attend in accordance with their particular fields and specialties. In the absence of the plant manager, the acting plant managers attend in his behalf. The regular participants in the divisional meetings are, of course, the managers of various departments, but no clear line is drawn as to which meeting any one manager is to attend. It is entirely possible, depending on the nature of his business, for one man to attend two or three such meetings.

A divisional meeting is similar in its functions to a meeting held within a single department. However, this meeting is more flexible than its intra-departmental counterpart, and the plant manager participates in it personally. The general meeting also differs from a departmental meeting in that it is attended not only by department managers but by section chiefs. This enables the plant manager to establish direct contact with both.

The general meeting, because of its very nature, draws many attendees and therefore inhibits any detailed discussion. In a divisional meeting, the discussion is likely to explore in detail information supplied by the lower organization levels. In the general meeting, top management makes overall plant information available to the attendees, and discussion follows on that basis. The intra-departmental meeting, in turn, is being modified, and its procedures are being improved along these same lines.

As a result of all this, both plant manager and everyone else are involved in only three layers of meetings. Indeed, one of the biggest disadvantages of the new procedure is the reduction in the number of meetings at the top. Previously we used to hold top-level meetings every day. Now, for those management personnel who attend only one divisional meeting, the number of meetings attended has been reduced to two, including the once-a-week general meeting. The density in communication has thereby been reduced proportionately, but this is something we couldn't help. The results, however, do show that the merits of the new arrangement far outweigh its drawbacks.

For a moment, though, let's return to the subject of organization by team formation. The third difference between this type of organization and the traditional type—which I have not yet reiterated—lies in the fact that meetings alone don't provide enough opportunity for team members to participate in the control process at their level. And it can't be said too often that team members *should* play some role in this process. We ourselves have taken several steps in this direction: Multiple systems as described in Part Two, Chapter 3, under the headings "Further Means of Promoting Lateral Contacts" and "Managerial Accounting for Everyone," are good examples. All are being reconsidered and revised as time goes on.

Teamwork and the Pair System

A similarly important role in team development is played by what we call our pair system, already discussed in some detail.

A pair, remember, is a combination of two workers whose relations on the job are just like those of a man and his wife in the home.

The fundamental difference between team formation (including the pair system) and the authoritarian, directive type of organization—so far as human relationships are concerned—lies in the fact that, whereas the latter results in human relations based on the ruler-and-ruled dichotomy, the former bases its human relations on partnership. Where partnership prevails, one member, it is true, is the leader and the other is a follower. We can compare this relationship with that in a social dance: The man leads his partner, and she dances by following his steps. They could not dance together if each were to make moves at will. But this relation is not the relationship between the ruler and the ruled.

To repeat: The pair is the smallest, most primitive sort of team and the easiest to form. But the performance it delivers is more than the sum of one plus one. Because the man and the woman cooperate with each other, sharing the jobs to be done, they do these jobs better. Significantly, they cover for each other, make up for their respective shortcomings, and reinforce one another in areas of strength. It was our growing awareness of the merits of such a pair that triggered the start of the pair system in the plant.

In this regard, I want to quote a story I once heard from Mr. Minoru Genda, ex-general of the Japanese Self-Defense Forces. The formation of the old prop fighter planes was based on a unit of three: Two such units formed a unit of six planes; two such six-plane units formed a unit of twelve planes. Modern jet fighter planes in action, however, have such speed and mobility that they are organized in units of two planes.

Also along these lines, Dr. Hideo Itokawa, formerly professor at the Space Institute of the University of Tokyo, once told me about a difficulty he had faced in organizing a team for the development of space rockets. He finally paired two scientists with different academic disciplines and eliminated his problems by building such pairs into an organization.

The characteristics inherent in pairs of this kind are comparable to those of the man and woman who automatically make up for a temporary slump in either partner during times of stress, encouraging and complementing one another. They are the building blocks with which teamwork is constructed. Learning teamwork on the job is best accomplished through the pair system. Three in a unit makes it rather an arduous task.

Of course, for the pair system to be effective, a pair must necessarily be composed of two individuals with different characteristics. Man and woman, teacher and pupil, senior worker and junior worker, worker on the morning shift and worker on the afternoon shift, manager and secretary, scientist and technician, two professionals with different academic disciplines and skills, two men with different personalities—all lend themselves to pair formation. The requirements are that the two individuals be heterogeneous, that they be performing the same job to achieve an identical goal, and that they assume joint responsibility for their work.

We and our staff specialists did not introduce the pair system in our plant so as to impose our ways on workers at lower levels. The concept is not new in Japan. Professor Jiro Kamijima, of St. Paul University in Tokyo, has mentioned in commenting on old Japanese social organizations and the underlying mentality that a sort of pair system carried a certain significance even during ancient times. Basing my remarks on these comments of his, I suggested at one of our morning meetings that we should perhaps introduce the pair system as a micro-unit within the crew on the strength of the chief and subchief system with which we had already experimented successfully. Upon hearing what I had to say, the workers at some stations expressed interest in the idea and started to develop a pair system of their own volition.

We always try to approach organizational matters in this manner. Neither I nor any member of my staff dictates to people how they should proceed with a particular organizing job. Rather, a certain idea seems to emerge spontaneously from nowhere, and workers at the various stations who are interested in it begin implementing it in their own way. As a result, our pair system differs from one work station to another with regard to both method of operation and timing of application. To this day we have work stations that are using systems which have yet to be set up on an organized basis like those I have cited so far.

The prime requisite in developing basic organizational patterns and systems is never to force any particular method upon people across the board. It is only when a pattern or system is created by the individuals who will be required to function within it that we arrive at a means of motivating and stimulating people instead of stifling people. The pair system in particular, because of its intrinsic nature, could never be developed if people had to be coerced into forming pairs. Voluntary forms of human organization are impossible unless they are grounded in the willingness and initiative of the people concerned.

4

Systems to Support Communication

WHAT is most important to organization by team is information. That's because in a team type of organization people are not individually directed or commanded to perform tasks expected of them. They perform these tasks of their own free will.

Teams Base Action on Information

Each team member does his own sizing up of a given situation, makes his decision, and takes action in accordance with the facts. Unless each member correctly understands the information which comes to him from above, below, and around him, the sum total of the action will not be properly coordinated and may lead to the destruction of the team system.

Communication which supports the team type of organization cannot be improved by merely providing access to information. All those who have occasion to make information available must necessarily do so in an atmosphere of mutual respect. Moreover, the recipients of that information must place importance on it. No communication will be taken seriously by the receiver if it comes from a person whom he holds in contempt, or vice versa. Nor will information serve to establish information unless both parties are free from prejudice and favoritism. Research in the United States tells us that, upon listening to the same speech by President Kennedy, Republicans and Democrats interpreted its meaning quite differently. All of which makes us realize that team relationships play an important role in effective communication and that communication is essential to forming a team.

Communication tends to stagnate in a power-conscious organization—a fact that endangers the authority-oriented structure itself. Typically, in an authoritarian organization, superiors give detailed instructions and directions to their subordinates, using those subordinates as freely as if they were the superiors' hands and feet.

Under such circumstances, superiors do not feel obligated to make information accessible to their subordinates. They may not even want to do so, in order to protect their cherished decision-making prerogative. The subordinates, on the other hand, will seldom reveal their true selves under this hierarchical form of human relations; instead, they are likely to embellish the information contained in their reports to their superiors in all sorts of ways. And, in their horizontal relationships—that is, with their peers in other departments—they will try to conceal information, keep their mouths closed during meetings, and get credit from their superiors for themselves alone by skillfully coaxing the bosses into approving their plans or ideas.

Superiors in the authoritarian organization can hardly be expected to know their subordinates well, although contrary claims are always being made. Such superiors make decisions based on their own insufficient understanding of the information at hand and give their subordinates the orders they think are needed to make the subordinate perform. This surely dooms the organization to malfunctioning.

Information for the Sake of Creation

Communication cannot be accomplished simply by recording, reproducing, and transmitting messages to company levels above or below the speaker—or sidewise, to other departments—as with a tape recorder. Communication has to be established among live human beings, and it must be the source of creative action on the part of those human beings. True communication makes possible the creation of new ideas based on useful detailed data which are derived from a combination of our own and others' information and judgment. Communication by any other definition is not only meaningless but harmful as well.

Let me cite, as an example, a disgraceful experience we had in our plant. It is our practice to permit department managers to send men to the morning meeting in their place when they cannot attend in person owing to absence from the plant. Such deputies dutifully note down all the information they receive in this meeting and report it back in their respective departmental meetings with positively clerical meticulousness—and the sincere belief that communication is indeed the backbone of our plant. Despite their honest aspirations, however, misunderstanding and suspicion as to the true meaning of remarks made by others but reported by the deputies began to emerge at lower levels; and, to aggravate the situation still further, some participants in the morning meeting started to insist that they might as well refrain from disclosing full information at that meeting and, indeed, should insure secrecy for their work by providing less information.

The emergence of this misunderstanding and suspicion can be attributed to the fact that the deputies were functioning as recorders only—and bad ones at that. Our management always must act as if in a goldfish bowl; even matters pertaining to plant personnel are no exception to this rule. The deputies were quite free to transmit what was discussed during the morning meeting to lower levels; the problem lay in the managers who sent their deputies to the meeting. They should have tried to listen to the resulting reports on their "recording machines"; to understand the reported information fully; and to transmit it personally, as they saw it, to the members of their teams at their own risk. Had they done so, they wouldn't have had any problems later. They erred in that they regarded communication as the act of passing information *as it is* on to others.

This is a case of failure on our part in this communication area. It demonstrates that we must at all times guard against being trapped into this kind of formalism, the emergence of which is always possible even in a relatively mature cell-type organization.

A Climate Supporting the Flow of Communication

Each of us may well have to be the master of his own job in order to establish communication as we believe it should be. For it is the climate of an organization—that is, the existence or non-existence of teamwork—which entitles us to think that prevailing conditions rather than authority will determine whether we achieve the initiative and voluntary action that are the prerequisites of effective communication.

We need not be troubled any more about misunderstanding of a message when communication takes place in the right kind of organization climate. This is a very important point. Verbal transmission of information is bound to be misunderstood if you consider just a mechanical process. When information is transmitted mechanically through multiple layers of people, you probably won't be able to find out, in the end, what the original message was.

There would be no transmission of information at all, however, if we were unduly afraid of this possibility. As I have stated, changes in the context of information during the transmission process create no harm so long as the intermediaries in the process try to transmit the facts in a creative way—that is, so long as the climate favors their being able to think subjectively about the information in question, grasp its true meaning, and convey this meaning on their own responsibility as if the information were their own. It is this creative deviation from information as it is that is indispensable to truly effective communication.

We are talking here, not about inaccuracy of transmitted information and the ensuing misunderstanding per se, but, rather, about the undesirable effect which is created by such inaccuracy and misunderstanding. What assures us of a consistently desirable effect is not the mental attitude which is apprehensive of misunderstanding; instead, it is the favorable climate existing in an organization.

When managers address their subordinates in an authoritarian manner, as if commanding them to accept what the boss says or to think the way the boss thinks, communication cannot help but be degraded. The message received is bound to be full of misunderstanding which creates nothing but undesirable effects. When managers address their subordinates, instead, in a spirit of mutual inquiry, asking what the subordinates think about this or that, effective communication invariably results. In short, it is in the managers' own thinking and mental posture that we find the causes of ineffective communication.

The establishment of a climate conducive to *creative* communication may bring astounding changes. For instance, operators' casual remarks about a certain phenomenon observed on the job— remarks which the operators themselves are not sure have any importance—are transmitted to staff specialists. A great engineering discovery results, and profits are handsome. (I shall touch on this again in Part Four.) It is not too much to say that this kind of information is becoming an important basis for technological innovation in our semiconductor industry.

Communication of the kind I am urging may look as though it could be established with ease. Yet it can never be established in an authoritarian organization. Why? The problem lies in the other end of the communication pipeline. What workers see at this other end is a glum-looking superior or engineer, for example. Workers feel as if any information they might pass along relative to a certain phenomenon or minute change in their jobs would be sneered at and brushed aside. Workers feel that the man at the other end of the communication pipeline is looking down on them as though they were a bunch of ignorant good-for-nothings without any knowledge or formal training. It takes casual, earnest, heart-to-heart relationships among people to pry open the door to the treasure chest of technological innovation.

Crisscrossing Information Channels

We have a rule that relates to the screening process involved in sending up plans for final approval by higher-level management. In reality, we simply report what we have decided to the higher level. This does not create any inconvenience, because the plan in question will already have been discussed at directors' meetings or at plant-management meetings before the decision was reached.

As I mentioned in Chapter 2 of Part Three, rules and regulations play an important role in maintaining coherence and consistency in our established systems. Should we be forced to live strictly by formal rules, however, people's creativity and sense of responsibility would be lost and management action would turn into a lifeless thing. At Sony, systems and teams aren't really functioning in accordance with such management action as approval, decision making, and order giving. Instead, *people* are functioning—each in accordance with the full authority delegated to him in his job and making use of the information passed along to him.

Final responsibility always remains with management—in the case of our plant it rests with the plant manager. Everyone in the plant understands this. But, in a climate like ours, everyone makes his decisions and takes the indicated action without embarrassing anyone else or causing any problems. His sense of responsibility toward his job and toward the man who irrevocably places full trust in him without any regard for self far outweighs any tendency in him toward self-centeredness.

Once more, what is needed even in this climate is information—information without any embellishment from those people who provide access to it. Information transmitted irresponsibly, like information which is twisted for purposes of self-protection, is of no use.

Here I should like to review briefly several kinds of information which flow through our plant. I exclude accounting or production-control paperwork.

Information Derived from Meetings. As the reader will be fully aware by now, we hold many meetings at Sony Atsugi Plant: directors' meetings, department managers' meetings, department and section managers' meetings (these three on a companywide basis), monthly meetings, joint leaders' meetings, long-range planning meetings (these four on a plantwide basis), and team meetings. All the information presented at these meetings is discussed by the participants, and the end results are passed on to others. (I will have more details in later chapters.)

Weekly Report. All plant personnel above the level of chief, including department managers and staffs, are required to submit reports once a week. In these reports the writers describe problems that have come up on the job and explain how they are being solved. Reports are submitted in a predetermined format (one sheet only) to the immediate manager and, finally, to the plant manager, in whose office they are compiled. Some of these weekly reports may, if necessary, be circulated among the departments concerned; all are returned to the originators with written comments from the plant manager.

Business Report. All plant personnel above the level of leader, including managers and their staffs, are encouraged once a month to submit comments or opinions regarding their jobs to their immediate managers and, finally, to the plant manager. These reports are returned with pertinent comments from the people who read them. And, as I have said, some that are deemed worthy of wide attention are excerpted, published in the periodical called *Managers' Memos,* and circulated to everyone who is qualified to submit such reports. No one is obligated to submit this kind of report, however.

House Magazines. Companywide magazines are *Sony News,*

published monthly, and *Weekly Reports,* published once a week. At our Atsugi Plant we have *Atsugi Topics,* published every other day, and the monthly *Home News.* This last, as its name indicates, is directed at employees' families. We also have many publications issued by dormitory residents and by members of work stations.

Informal Information. Channels for this type of information are not hard and fast. Informal information is transmitted in the so-called "little conversations," which we feel are highly important.

Informal information is the most readily communicated. All sorts of people can and do originate and transmit such information—from the president down to the individual worker. The way such information is channeled is extremely fluid and flexible; transcending management level, it will flow into any corner in the company where there is some form of human relations.

Once Mr. Morita, executive vice-president, told us, "We will try to transmit information from the top as much as possible, but it is wrong to assume that each manager here can't make a move unless he receives such official information. Don't count on it. You should actively seek informal information on your own." Someone commented on this statement by remarking, "Such informal information is bound to vary. We can have information on the same subject from two different sources and be at a loss as to which to rely on." Whereupon Mr. Morita replied with a faint expression of pity, "Isn't it the manager's job to exercise judgment on information received? Top management always evaluates such information and takes action accordingly. If we can't do that much, then we're not managers." This is a very important point. I suspect that Mr. Morita may have been disappointed at the time by certain Sony managers who were beginning to show their tendency toward formalism.

The reader will probably gather that we attach much importance to the unrestricted flow of informal information, that we always try to have as much information as possible and judge it correctly and unerringly on our own responsibility. Texas Instruments Incorporated feels much the same way: It points out that the active flow of informal communication prevailing in the company is one of its main characteristics; in fact, it has produced such an excellent slogan as "Get ahead with your communication."

In contrast, the management which gets *behind* with communication is bound to make an enemy out of informal information, to become defensive and end up by creating a gloomy and destructive climate that operates against it.

"Dial 2000." This Sony information system may be unique. We inaugurated it with a slogan of our own: "Let's actively seek information and give information." Any Sony employee can dial this number directly without going through the company switchboard and get or give information through the personnel who respond to his call. All are encouraged to "dial 2000" under the following situations:

1. To confirm the validity of rumors being circulated or of unconfirmed "tips" from other employees.
2. To get information on whom to approach about problems concerning our jobs, to find out more on topics we want to be better informed on, or to get helpful ideas about certain matters.
3. To get information as to which groups or people within Sony are trying to do or are already doing things we are planning to do in our jobs.
4. To get information as to who should receive information, proposals, or opinions which we consider will be of some help to Sony.

Workers at the Bottom Make Big Decisions

We operate our plant with the help of the types of information I have described so far. No orders are given anywhere in the plant. It follows, then, that we never take any action based on orders.

The difference between obeying orders and taking action based on information lies in whether we exercise our judgment and decide on our own responsibility to act or not. No decision on the action to be taken is required when we are simply following orders from others, nor are we required to assume any responsibility for our action. This may be an easy way out, but it is not exciting and will not result in *creative* action. Neither can we expect to further our own growth and development in this way.

The majority of the people in our plant are expected to do their work in the same circumstances in which I do mine. I cannot, of course, vouch for the across-the-board implementation of this method of plant operation, because each person's mental habits come into play here. It is much easier for us all to act in accordance with orders given us; and everybody, to some extent, likes to do things the easy way. This, however, does not result in the inner satisfaction we need. Only as we begin gradually to feel the pleasure of engaging in creative activity do we human beings free ourselves from the vicious cycle of giving and taking orders. This is the goal to which our efforts at Sony are being directed, and I believe that—in relative terms—we have made considerable progress toward its attainment.

We must, at the same time, continue and rejuvenate our efforts in this direction for the benefit of those newcomers who keep coming into our plant and who already have grown used to being "cogwheels" in the world in which they previously lived. We must make them experience a genuine feeling of fulfillment in their life with us. This naturally requires managers to repress their desire to give orders to their people and—what is the most difficult task of all for managers—to repress that resentment of decisions made without their approval which originates in their power- or authority-consciousness. Finally, managers must repress their fear of possible failure by their people.

Workers at the lowest level in our plant make major decisions. In the same way, my secretary makes some decisions for me. People outside Sony are surprised at this. What the situation demands, obviously, is that workers and their managers have a meeting of minds, which can be realized through effective communication (information and discussion) and that workers report back on their actions. It is true that mishaps may occur; however, the circumstances may have been such that the managers themselves would have made the same mistakes. Any loss or damage resulting from those mistakes probably will be greatly outweighed by the profits accruing from our contribution to the growth of people who are full of creative vitality.

Information-Oriented Organizations Welcome Short-Circuiting

Traditional principles of organization regard short-circuiting—
that is, the circumvention of established channels of authority—as
inadvisable. When it is resorted to—when, for example, direct
contact is established between the managing director and a department manager, bypassing the plant manager—the plant manager is offended. And perhaps the managing director and the
department manager may feel guilty at having circumvented the
plant manager, who insists that he cannot be held responsible for
the outcome of their decision. This is the real-life situation in
many companies, and the traditionalists in organization approve
of it.

This situation prevails because their power-oriented organization structure necessarily centers around order and approval. But
such a fallacy never prevails in the information-oriented organization. It should be remembered that we value informal as well as
formal information, that we include in our definition of informal
information those talks that take place between managers and
their people, and that the information exchanged is—in principle—held in the same regard as any other informal information.
This means that comments or opinions expressed by managers
are not meant as orders or approval, simply to be observed and
obeyed. As a matter of fact, Mr. Ibuka himself freely changes his
position on certain specific matters—excluding, of course, those
pertaining to the basic principles on which he stands. We just
cannot afford to obey his every word, because it would involve
too much risk. Blind implementation of his ideas on our part
would probably meet with criticism from him later. In an information-oriented organization like ours, each person has no alternative but to exercise his judgment, decide what action to take,
and implement that decision on his own.

Any discussion of the advantages and disadvantages of circumvention becomes meaningless in this kind of information-oriented
situation. In simple terms, each person has access to a place where
he can easily obtain the information he needs and discuss it with
someone. When circumvention seems appropriate, he can short-
circuit his immediate manager, but he has to exercise his judgment
and plan a course of action on his own responsibility. Even if he

were to act on the advice of his immediate manager, he could not and should not be permitted to "pass the buck" to that manager in the event of failure. I often believe that what makes talks with managers convincing to employees is the judgment of those employees that what they hear is indeed persuasive and convincing.

An information-oriented organization makes information out of every member's actions. That is, each person acts on the basis of his evaluation of the data transmitted to him "through channels," by short-circuiting, or via other media. This information immediately becomes input data for his immediate manager or his team members, who in turn review his actions. Thus it also provides the basis on which other people act.

It becomes quite clear, then, that organizations supported by free-flowing information and by responsible judgment and actions on the part of every one of their members are lively organizations, without any confusion or chaos to disturb their order. They represent genuinely creative organizations firmly based on effective communication.

Traditional authoritarian organizations, in contrast to their creative counterparts, are pitifully troubled with arteriosclerosis: they are in danger of becoming immobile in the effort to maintain order. For, in such organizations, order disintegrates when people try to move in directions which are not provided for by their rule books. People weary of reporting to immediate supervisors who show their displeasure openly when employees short-circuit them and talk directly to higher-level managers. Then, naturally, communication soon ceases to exist. The immediate superiors may want to fence their men in and leave open only such channels of information as will lead directly to them. This doesn't work, however. *All* communication ceases to exist, and they are left with either the complete disorder that results from lack of information or inaction for the sake of safety.

The Interviewer: Listening to the Silent Voice

Communication unquestionably improves, in comparison with that found in the authoritarian organization, once teams are formed. But this still doesn't satisfy us—our aspirations know no limits. There are, we realize, many elements of imperfection in our communication methods, and this led us to establish the interviewer system in our plant. Like any of the other systems we have, it is not forced upon the departments; each decides voluntarily whether to implement it. Let me further clarify the nature of this system by going back to its start.

The theme of the New Year poem ceremony held at the Imperial Palace in 1966 was "voice." His Majesty's poem read as follows:

> Daily in my effort to make my way aright
> I search for voices of people out of my sight.

I was moved by this beautiful poem. The use of hypermeter in it vividly and impressively stresses His Majesty's honest thought. It imparts the urgency of his desire to listen to the voices of silent people.

It is in the very posture assumed in this poem that we find a quality that is highly desirable in a team leader. The trouble is that, for worldly laymen like us, it requires courage to listen to candid, straightforward comment on our thinking and actions. We may hear biting criticism, harsh voices suggesting self-reflection. My managers and I can't help feeling that we don't want to listen to these scathing voices; yet the mental posture which is most important in a team leader is just this willingness to listen, however unpleasant the voices may be. No team organization will tolerate in its team leaders the assumption that no one should dare to criticize them or that they are entitled to punish those who speak up forthrightly. It is hard for us to recognize by ourselves what is wrong with us. This makes it necessary that we look to others for their comments.

I finally told my managers that I wanted a system which would enable us to listen to the silent voices. I was then informed that one department had already implemented such a system. This department was most successfully run at that time; its manager was an indefatigable fighter—the kind of manager who can easily frighten people. He knew this, had searched his soul in an effort to mend his ways, and still couldn't help himself. Concluding that he ought to improve both his skills and his management style, he appointed a man to find out what his people were thinking, to tap them for ideas and comments and advise him on this basis. The plan worked so well that it gave us the idea for our interviewer system. The first interviewer, the man appointed by the manager I have just referred to, played a leading role in organizing the system throughout the plant.

Giving Advice to Managers

We still have a couple of managers who are quite sure they don't need the interviewer system. They don't, in fact, have any interviewers in their departments. It is our thinking, remember, that no system can work well if we attempt to implement it in places where people feel it is unnecessary. It's obvious—the success or failure of this system depends on the manager.

The way in which interviewers are selected differs from one department to another. Some choose women, some choose men from among the section heads. Some choose staff specialists. Some interviewers are old, and some are young. Each place of work has its own criteria. We deliberately left it like this in the belief that no interviewer would be regarded as trustworthy by people unless they themselves selected him on their own initiative and of their own free will.

During the system's early phases, some of the interviewers told us, people were concerned lest it prove to be a needlessly roundabout way of tackling the communication problem. In some cases, the interviewers themselves shared this concern. The human instinct for self-defense is deep-rooted and is further fortified by seas of suspicion. It is because of this human instinct that we must search out and listen to the silent voices even when everything seems to be going well.

The role of these independently selected interviewers in each department is to gather advice from people on subjects which they themselves (or their managers) choose or to meet with people who are seeking advice and listen to the opinions or comments offered. The information derived from the interviews is passed along to the managers, occasionally with the interviewers' own thinking. Approximately once a month, all the interviewers meet together to exchange notes and study particular problems. Outside lecturers are occasionally invited to these meetings for counseling purposes.

A report on each meeting is submitted to the plant manager. It is generally quite helpful, and on some occasions it gives the plant manager very important leads. The managers also seem to benefit. For instance, workers may say, "Managers should visit our work stations more often." Or, "What I can't stand is my chief standing behind me during work hours and saying nothing to me. He might as well say *something* to me. Oh, how I hate my chief!" Such comments provide helpful clues and provoke much managerial soul searching.

There is nothing fancy about the work of an interviewer. I am given to understand, however, that, once a person becomes serious about it, he begins to find real significance in his job. It seems, also, that interviewing is proving to be an effective aid to individual growth. Some companies engage outside counselors to tap the voices of the employees, but I believe that the number of such counselors who are really qualified is too small to fill the existing need. Moreover, being outsiders, they are not in a position to be well informed about the companies that engage their services, and they are not getting very substantial results. This makes me inclined to recommend the internal-interviewer system.

This system demands, of course, that managers share the mental attitude exemplified in the Emperor's poem and take energetic steps to establish the interviewer system. It also demands that their people trust them and their intention. The system will not succeed unless it is supported by this kind of prevailing climate.

Meetings as Creative Organisms

The chief function of meetings in our plant is to serve as a medium of communication in administering the team as an organizational unit. Meetings abound, owing to the proliferation of the omnipresent team throughout the workforce. Part Two describes many aspects of meeting administration. All are undergoing some changes as time goes by. Here, however, is a brief summary:

- Meeting by plant manager, his staff, and department managers (held every morning). Commonly referred to as M.M. Divided into division meeting for general affairs, division meeting for semiconductors, division meeting for calculators, and general meeting because of limit on maximum number of people attending. Four meetings alternate so that all participants are not necessarily required to gather every morning at the same time.
- Meeting of department managers, their staffs, and section heads (held every day).
- Meeting of section heads and their staffs plus chiefs and subchiefs of each group (held every day).
- Meeting of chiefs and subchiefs of groups plus leaders and subleaders of crews (held every day).
- Meeting of leaders, subleaders, and entire membership of crews (held every day).
- Meeting of entire plant workforce (held every month). Plant manager discusses general state of business; and sectional performance against goals also is reviewed.
- Joint meeting of plant manager, all managers, and their staffs, including leaders of crews (held every month, 15 days after the monthly meeting).
- Meeting of plant manager, his staff, and department managers (held toward the end of each six-month period). Takes place in a hotel, lasting several days. Performance for previous period reviewed; goals and policies for coming period discussed.
- Planning meeting of top plant personnel (held monthly). Establishes monthly production plan for each product line; sets up meetings of crews, groups, sections, and departments for exploding master plan into detailed plans for each line.

Over and above these meetings, many others are held for the specific purpose of improving lateral relationships. Their purpose, and the basic principles involved, are the same as for the meetings described. They have been fully explained in other chapters; thus I need only recapitulate briefly.

In a word, then, meetings are intended as occasions for creative communication. Those who conduct them are not actually leaders;

rather, they should be called *organizers*. Meetings that are mere aids to stereotyped decision making and approval of action taken or means of exchanging information mechanically will not serve our purpose. Pertinent, candidly offered, *necessary* information must be presented at our meetings. All are held in such a way as to enable every participant to decide on his own, through discussion, what action to take. It doesn't necessarily follow that all he has to do is simply take action in strict compliance with the consensus at a particular meeting. In our plant, meetings are not based on the principle of irresponsible group decision making, which spreads the accountability over everyone involved. Each one of us, instead, must assume responsibility for his actions. And, if meetings as such are not viewed as decision-making tools, neither are they designed for simple consultation. They are, as it were, organisms for doing, for creation.

This kind of ideal meeting isn't easily achieved. It must be developed on the basis of day-to-day experience and practice. We sometimes go right back to where we started. Trained personnel also are a must; we have many newcomers, and even old-timers sometimes falter. Trying to arrive at the ideal meeting is just like walking on an endless road—it's the infinity that inspires us to accept the challenge. We can't give up, since there is no other road. We do know, however, that our efforts to review and improve our performance will definitely be rewarded. Sometimes, we can't help but feel it's our persistence, rather than the degree of perfection achieved in our meetings, that is so valuable and significant to us.

Ten Minutes Every Day

Although the condct of all our meetings is based on common principles, the manner with which individual meetings are handled, as I have said, differs a great deal. So does the degree of sophistication found in meetings at the lowest level. This is partly due to the fact that the participants are girls and that rapid changes frequently occur in the membership, including leaders. We must not, however, try to tell these girls how they should conduct their meetings. It is necessary for them to create meetings which will best serve their purposes.

Even I don't know much about the way in which many of these low-level meetings are actually administered. The time required is more or less standardized at something between 10 and 15 minutes a day. The girls meet at their work stations, standing. They receive information from upper-level cells or from the plant manager himself. They discuss current yields, possible reasons for any problems in yield, or actual production figures for the previous day. They may take up matters scribbled in somebody's notes— for example, the leaders are talking all the time, while the other team members aren't expressing themselves often enough.

Here is one example of such a meeting: The members are considering the problem of low yield. They discuss the matter and conclude that too much dropping of the pellets that make up the transistor core may be contributing to this low yield. (The pellet is an extremely small object, only 0.4 millimeter in length.) The girls decide that they will take a look at the floor before going home. When they do, they find pellets lying all around, just as they suspected. The next day they pick them up, use them in their work, and get different yields. They then conclude that dropping too many pellets is definitely the cause of their trouble; therefore, they should see to it that fewer pellets are dropped and an improved finish should be devised for the floor so that any pellets that fall can easily be identified.

Topics differ, let me repeat, from one meeting to another, but this is the kind of thing discussed. In most cases it is a specific problem relating to the work. Discussions designed to keep team members up to date on the status of the work are most important.

Holding sessions every day, of course, reduces the time required. The idea is that we should not save problems for discussions at some future date (when they may have become acute) but that we should solve them as they occur. In any case, it is quite helpful for people to see each other once a day; it refreshes them mentally. I have often been asked whether meeting participants mightn't run out of topics with the meeting held every day, but the truth is that we don't run out of topics, nor do we have too many. Once a team gets used to this kind of meeting, business is transacted quickly; then, if there is nothing else to talk about, the session is immediately adjourned. No time limits are imposed, but it seems to me that the teams have their own time standards for their meetings.

When they have particularly big topics to discuss, teams may hold special sessions in addition to the regular daily meetings. They freely schedule such special sessions at night, when they are not on duty, and often at some place other than the work station.

Some readers may point out that the man-hours we lose on account of multiple meetings probably amount to a considerable total. I can't agree that we ought to be using all those lost man-hours for production purposes, although I do agree that we should shorten the time required to the minimum and make the meetings still more effective. Work efficiency varies enormously, depending on whether people are motivated to work or not. In fact, the difference between the lowest and the highest efficiency may involve a ratio of as much as three to one. And this difference becomes even more pronounced when we take into account the factor of quality.

It is because people regard labor as a tool, just like a machine, that they talk about the loss involved in meetings in terms of cost. Granted, when workers are using semi-automatic equipment, this can be a problem. Since the speed of the machines is set, any reduction in man-hours means a corresponding reduction in output. The workers alone, no matter how motivated, will not be able to make up the loss incurred. Thus production definitely goes down in inverse proportion to the time spent in meetings. It is in cases like this, I believe, that we might perhaps have machines whose speed could be freely changed by the workers. With such variable-speed machines, we might in reality attain much higher speeds. Also, at stations where workers perform their jobs along conveyor belts, the conveyors should be so made that the workers are able to adjust their work pace. In any event, work which produces less on account of man-hours lost in meetings is not work as it should be.

My own experience tells me that under no circumstances will meetings which are efficiently held disrupt or reduce production. Meetings enable workers to think their problems through, plan for action, implement their plans, and control their actions. In other words, meetings—as one means of enriching jobs vertically —have far-reaching effects upon the quantity and quality of production and upon the health of the organization.

5

Leaders Without Power or Authority

IN the traditional authoritarian organization, no rigid requirements are imposed upon leaders from the standpoint of human qualities. That's because they can manipulate their employees through the use of their power and authority. Nowadays, however, power and authority are increasingly losing ground; they can no longer guarantee smooth functioning. Efforts are being made by managers to regain the old power and authority or, alternatively, to appease employees, and some of us are still trying to depend on the power and authority inherent in position rather than on the human qualities of leaders. Hence we become preoccupied with hierarchical status as indicated in organization charts and in such ludicrous symbols as size of desks.

Team Leaders Must Have Charisma

In the team type of organization, on the other hand, it is the charisma of a leader, and his worth and quality as a human being, that come to play the central role. One must excel, not only in skill, but in these two characteristics of charisma and individual worth, to qualify for leadership. Leaders who do not possess these gifts may destroy the team spirit, debase their men and themselves. Thus the appointment of leaders in the team-type organization must be based strictly on capacity and talent. Appointment on the basis of formal education and seniority must be avoided by all means.

What, precisely, are the components of what we have termed a man's worth and quality as a human being? I have been giving some thought to this matter, and I have come to the conclusion that the top management personnel of world enterprises which show consistent growth on a long-term basis are, without any exception, people who possess true charisma. I have met some of them in person, and I have read books written by others, and I feel that they all have real personal appeal. The same thing can be said, moreover, about our leaders at the lowest plant level. Where does this appeal, this so-called charisma come from? I have the feeling that it may be innate in the courageous yet gentle personality exemplified by the heroes of certain old fairy tales.

Let's analyze this thought further. Courage implies an exceptionally strong will and sense of responsibility. It also implies vitality. By "sense of responsibility," I don't mean responsibility in a passive sense. I mean a positive, stubborn feeling of obligation, a willingness to assume responsibility, and the determination to complete the necessary tasks, however difficult these may be. Real courage and strength derive from this sense of responsibility.

We often hear that top management personnel should share in the ownership of firms. Our human mental habits being what they are, managers may then be expected to have a strong sense of commitment and responsibility. I don't necessarily agree with this viewpoint. Men who are both owners and managers of a company tend to be power-oriented, but the great determination and sense of responsibility that they require must be based upon intrinsic human values on a much higher plane. Lofty humanity must accompany courage in the leader, and here we have the first requisite of charisma.

The second requisite, I suggest, is gentleness. This means that one must have a capacity for understanding human beings. A proverb says, "Warriors would die for those who understand them." It is this kind of understanding that is important—we might say it amounts to "trusting" people. Mr. Thomas J. Watson, Jr., board chairman of the IBM Corporation, once said, "I trust every one of the 150,000 IBM employees," and this is exactly the kind of trust I am referring to.

Trust cannot be built upon fear that one's trust may be betrayed. Trust can flourish only when one is willing to abandon oneself in the act of trusting. When a man who is truly willing to assume responsibility sincerely trusts his people, a corresponding sense of responsibility will be aroused in them. Courage and gentleness, therefore, are like the two sides of a shield.

I have made the point several times that trust does not imply trust in human behavior. We must recognize here that human beings are indeed imperfect. It is in this context that we place our trust in people who have the desire to be perfect, instead of pitying or upbraiding them for their imperfection, and admire and encourage their efforts to fulfill the desire to be perfect. This is the true meaning of gentleness.

It seems to me that we come to feel almost a sort of charm in those people who are gifted with the qualities I have described. At a monthly meeting, I once stated, "What I think is most important is that one be charming." Our many girl workers appeared to understand what I meant by this instantly. Since then, this expression of mine has become very popular in our plant; such exhortations as "Let's give our work stations charm!" are typical. "Charm" is a good word, because it is not sensually misleading. Charm of individual personality, not in the sense of being a beautiful woman or a handsome man—that is what I say is essential to true leadership.

You Aren't a Leader Because You're Somebody

I believe everybody has the qualities of a leader in some degree. Leadership therefore can be developed; it doesn't require any special kind of trait that a person must be born with. Nor do I regard the position of a leader as a special one. Ordinary team members are leaders in the sense that they are their own bosses in the work entrusted to them. It is only in the degree to which individuals possess leadership qualities and work skills that differences exist.

A person, in order to be entrusted with a certain job, is required to have both a fair amount of leadership ability and adequate specialized skills. When we appoint him, we must make sure he is capable of performing the job successfully so long as he exerts his best efforts. Such a man should not be *too* capable, nor should he be prone to fail. Thus the critical judgment required in this area becomes an important factor in placing people effectively. Placement without this kind of critical judgment means less motivation and hampers individual growth. This results in unhappy workers, and it doesn't benefit the company, either. Hence the importance of staffing based solely on ability.

Notwithstanding this importance, staffing based on ability is in reality extremely hard to achieve. One reason is that each job carries with it a certain hierarchical status, which fact makes it extremely difficult to make ability the criterion in hiring or promotion because of human factors involved. For instance, suppose we are looking for a competent person to fill the job of department manager. We find a qualified man who is a section manager; however, we cannot appoint him because the move would be viewed as a demotion. Or, conversely, we are seeking a suitable candidate for section manager, and the appropriate man cannot be appointed because he is now a department head—again because he and his associates would think he was being demoted.

We really must abandon this ridiculous practice of ours. And the only way to do so is to destroy completely the concept that attaches hierarchical status values to jobs. Although it is true that we no longer downgrade as outcasts slaughterers, beggars, and entertainers (the way we did in the old days), we still look down on sweepers and road workers and reserve our respect for people in managerial positions. As we have seen, the authority which has traditionally accompanied managerial status may be necessary in the authtoritarian, power-oriented organization, but it is quite harmful in the team type of organization.

Every Job Is a Respectable Job

In short, we have done everything possible to rid ourselves of the need to value jobs in terms of hierarchical status. I, as plant manager, was free of such notions from the beginning, and I can say now that we have practically eliminated this kind of thinking once and for all.

Several years ago, certain people from the development group at company headquarters were being transferred to the plant. With the help of some workers, they were carrying machines and equipment into their new quarters. A man happened to see the section manager trying to move a quantity of baggage; and, perhaps intending to flatter the manager, he said, "You should let the workers do that kind of thing." Upon hearing this remark, the workers left angrily and went home for the day. I didn't blame them for what they had done when I heard the story. On the contrary, I felt they had been justified in acting the way they had, and I reprimanded the little intellectual quite severely. I am not saying, of course, that engineers should always carry their own baggage. I am simply talking about their habits and their mental outlook.

In the beginning, also, our many part-time housewife workers seemed to be paying too much attention to the senior workers, who in turn seemed to be looking down on them slightly. We human beings are indeed to be pitied in that we always—or it would appear—have to look down on others in order to take pride in ourselves. Relations among junior high school graduates, high school graduates, and university graduates are based on this pitiful sense of superiority/inferiority, and so the relations among clerical staff, engineers, and workers. In our plant, however, all such distinctions are gone now—a prevailing condition which seems to be quite a rare thing in our present society. Regardless of the particular jobs we hold, all of us here are truly proud of our equality of status.

There is no status-consciousness among personnel in managerial positions, either. In our kind of team organization, those who have come to be leaders will again go back and be plain team members, if necessary. Among our chiefs we find one who finished high school only two years ago and is still just 19 years of age and another who is five years out of the university and 27 years old. Since the abilities required by a chief vary from one job to the next, we simply fill all such jobs according to the rule which calls for placing the right man in the right job at the right time. Should the need arise, any chief may revert to leader (*boy* leader in this case) or even just team member. Since he has no status-consciousness, neither he nor anyone else views a change in assignment as a demotion.

People outside our company are intrigued by all this; but, if I may say so, *I* am intrigued because *they* are intrigued.

True Ability-Oriented Staffing

Once managerial personnel have shed themselves of their status-consciousness, it now becomes possible to fill positions freely on the basic concept I have just referred to: the right man in the right job at the right time. We can perhaps call this *ability-oriented staffing*. The phrase, however, is generally accepted in the public mind as meaning the sort of staffing that is practiced by the traditional hierarchical organization; hence it carries with it a certain aura of status-awareness. Therefore, I shall avoid using this phrase here. As far as I am concerned, what I mean by true ability-oriented staffing—the kind which can eliminate the evil practices of diploma-oriented staffing—is staffing based on the "right man" rule.

As I have stated, the basis of diploma-oriented staffing is the power-oriented organization. We really can't change over to ability-oriented staffing if we are to keep this authority-oriented organization intact. If we force the new system onto the tradition-bound organization, we will be creating another bad practice. Why? Because ability-oriented staffing in the hierarchical, power-oriented organization means that status in the hierarchy would have to be decided not by formal training and academic background, as used to be the case, but rather by ability. And how can we truly evaluate people's ability in the tradition-bound organization? It would be an impossible task.

Ability cannot be evaluated effectively on the basis of hierarchical relationships. It can be evaluated only by weighing the respective merits of countless ability patterns. We could not possibly arrive at any scores for the various characteristics or skills in terms of one unit of measurement. If we were to enforce the practice of scoring according to a single unit of measurement in the traditional job hierarchy, we would end up by placing people and staffing positions on the basis of a completely haphazard evaluation of the available candidates. This would result in the stifling of human motivation and in wrong staffing—evil effects that would equal, if not exceed, those created by the seniority- and diploma-oriented system.

For these reasons I am convinced that staffing based on people's capacity can never be effectively realized unless we adhere to the principle of the right man in the right job at the right time. It is under this kind of system that people are assigned challenging and responsible tasks, feel that their jobs are worth doing, and develop endlessly through the achievement of job goals.

I commend to the reader's attention in particular the phrase "at the right time." For instance, an ambitious, impatient, energetic man may be a suitable person to head a certain section at a certain time. There are many such people among the younger generation who still have no special reputation. And there are perhaps fewer such people among those older personnel who already hold positions as department managers. However, we can't let the young, aggressive, ambitious, impatient types monopolize the section-head jobs indefinitely. As a particular section grows larger, it may at one time or another require a manager who is mature, patient, and well seasoned. We will probably find him in the older generation, and we will not hesitate to appoint him to head this mature organization.

This kind of flexibility can never be expected under the system in which position and status go hand in hand. But, especially in companies based on technological innovation and new product development, it is all too often required.

And take the team analogy I have used previously. It is not necessary for the manager of a company ball team, for example, to come from the ranks of the department managers. If he *had* to be selected from those ranks, what would happen were he to resign as team manager? We would immediately be confronted with a problem: What status should be assigned him after his resignation? And suppose, again, that a certain department manager is duly appointed to head the team. If he is the patient, mature, wait-and-see type, he may prove a burden rather than an asset to the team.

What we must realize here is that traditional organizations are forever committing the folly of mismatching people and jobs. In our plant, we managers always strive to be just like team managers without any status, whether we be department head, section head, or group chief. Once more, we cannot say we have achieved perfection, but we are endeavoring faithfully to achieve this ideal of flexibility in staffing. We are convinced, in fact, that this subject of staffing is far more important than wages and salaries or anything else.

Pay Plan Based on Job Description

A real bottleneck in implementing flexible staffing based on ability and the principle of the right man in the right job at the right time is the fact that pay scales are geared to the job hierarchy. This seems reasonable when we consider that wages are paid in return for work performed; however, this very concept is wrong (as will be further explained in Chapter 3 of Part Four). And, as long as this deep-rooted idea persists in people's minds, it will be difficult for us to change our staffing criteria. Because the wage system itself is hierarchy-oriented, just as are position and status, it becomes emotionally difficult for people to accept such a practice as appointing a department manager and giving him a salary commensurate with that of a section head or appointing a section head and allotting him the salary of a department manager.

It is next to impossible for a company to reduce anyone's salary, and all too often it is not possible to increase salaries. In other words, the salary system tends to be inflexible. And, when this rigid system is tied in directly with particular jobs, changes in those jobs also become impossible. It is in this context that I oppose the familiar pay plan based on job description as it exists in our country. I believe we should handle wages and salaries as flexibly and realistically as we can, depending on the situation we are in. Generally speaking, I feel that basing a pay plan on job description, like the incentive-pay system, is old-fashioned.

In our plant, wages and salaries are not directly related to specific jobs. In the case of personnel holding managerial positions, we do, however, pay a small allowance for their being managers.

Part Four

The New World of Management

1

Emerging from Destructive Management

THE difference between the past and the future, as I see it, lies in the rapidity with which technological innovation is taking place today. Needless to say, the years to come will see change occurring at an even greater rate—at unparalleled speeds, in fact, that mankind has never before experienced. Naturally, this will affect the management of industrial companies.

Up until modern times, the curve shown by technological innovation was rather flat. This prolonged the life cycles of given products or production processes. It follows, then, that those companies which succeeded in grinding out products or utilizing production processes in a better, more efficient way won out over companies which tried to move ahead in technology.

The "Machine Is Everything" Principle

To comment briefly on management methods during this period—these can be described, in a nutshell, as emphasizing efficiency more than anything else and as placing machines ahead of
people. The ideal envisaged in those days was a completely automated plant without any people in it. Human beings, as I have
said over and over in this book, were considered part of the machines. "Modern Times," the superb motion picture by Charlie
Chaplin, presented this phenomenon beautifully. I shall call this
type of management *machinelike management;* it is, of course,
synonymous with *dehumanizing management,* which still is the
basis of present management practice.

Fortunately, from now on, this kind of management will not
be able to adapt itself to changing conditions. What with the un-
precedented speed of technological innovation and the shortened
life cycles of products and processes, companies which can develop
new products and new processes ahead of their competitors will
outpace those companies which are merely efficient producers of
goods. That this is true is clearly exemplified by today's successful
"growth" companies.

Efficiency is indeed important. However, when we begin to
place innovation ahead of efficiency, we necessarily negate the
principle which puts machines ahead of human beings. The outstanding characteristic of machines or machinelike organizations
is their fixed stability, which is the antithesis of the basic fluidity
of innovation. To cite a hypothetical example—suppose we are
able to achieve high efficiency by mechanizing the manufacture of
a certain line of goods. We then have no alternative but to produce
the same line of goods for a prolonged period of time, simply to
depreciate the enormous capital investment required. So what
happens if newer products or superior manufacturing processes
become available in the middle of the depreciation period? We
have two choices: to replace the old machines with new ones,
writing off an enormous loss, or to manufacture the new line of
goods with the old machines at a higher cost.

It is only human beings who can provide fluidity. It is only
human beings who can provide innovation. Therefore, it is time

now for us to focus on human beings, to motivate them on the job instead of denying them their humanity. In other words, it is high time that we switched from machine-oriented to people-oriented management. The urgent need for truly people-oriented management becomes unmistakably clear when we look at the practices and policies that are making some companies more successful than othes at present.

There is an erroneous idea in the minds of the general public that technological innovation leads to denial of humanity. Technological innovation, as people see it, is synonymous with past change in industry—that is, the shift to machine-oriented production geared strictly to high efficiency—which did deny them their humanity. Since so many people can see only the surface of things, I say it's no wonder that technological innovation is regarded as a sort of scapegoat. On the contrary, rapidly advancing technology and the resulting innovation will necessarily negate production engineering and techniques which fail to treat people like human beings.

Free from Slavery to Machines

In the past, we have always had a limit imposed on the degree of mechanization we could achieve. It was either an engineering or a technological limit on the machine or process itself or, alternatively, a financial limit. Now we have another sort of limit— that created and complicated by the fixed, dehumanizing characteristics of today's machines. Therefore, we can no longer consider mechanization solely in terms of the attainment of efficiency. We must think about it in the framework of a broader, overall view of efficiency.

The philosophy behind mechanization was formerly one of saving labor and, at the same time, controlling human activity (the speed at which hands and feet moved). But it is one thing to save labor and quite another to turn human beings into extensions of machines. No man or woman can stand this kind of treatment, which resulted in the destruction of human beings in modern industry. In fact, it had a boomerang effect on industry that is clearly manifest in acute labor shortages and in lack of creativity among workers.

I am by no means a man who denies the necessity of mechanization. However, I believe that it should be directed at freeing human beings from the drudgery of mechanical work rather than at controlling them. We should not be too preoccupied with machine performance and efficiency per se. We must move toward increased mechanization with a view to overall efficiency while giving due thought to human needs and fluidity of process. I always like to express this idea of mine by saying that we must think of machines as integrating men and processes.

The management innovations we have been implementing at Sony work stations are intended to relieve human beings of the drudgery of mechanical work so that they can be assigned tasks involving perpetual creation and innovation.

An End to Traditional Principles

The inflexibility and inhumanity inherent in the traditional process of mechanization also exist in the traditional organizational structure, it will be remembered. The traditional principles of organization are synonymous with the machine-first principles. They put organization ahead of human beings, who are forced into a hard-and-fast structure and are expected to work just like cogwheels.

The Taylor system is one classic example of the result of such thinking. It seeks methods of simplifying work and producing goods with machinelike orderliness. Staff specialists even tell workers how they should move their hands. These same specialists propose work procedures, which companies force upon workers by hierarchical pressure. Do exactly what the book says, people are told, and those who can perform accordingly are called exemplary workers. All that is needed or wanted here is hands, not brains—not to mention hearts and souls. Workers, however, are human beings. They have brains and minds. They naturally feel and think. And this complicates matters.

Nor are we talking about production work only. The same thing can be said about administrative and clerical work in the traditional organization setup. Experts draw charts for departments and sections, delineating clearly the functions to be performed by such units, and they bind each and every individual with detailed work manuals and statements of job authority. People who perform routine work dutifully are praised.

We can only say that this kind of management kills people psychologically. It naturally makes people regard labor as an evil. Traditionally, managers claimed that this evil was something they couldn't help. They offered, by way of compensation, to shorten working hours and pay more money to people who would work like machines or animals. This is how the so-called higher-wages-for-greater-efficiency principle operates.

Inhuman management is never capable of coping with the technological innovation of modern times. Technological innovation is the result of human action, and that can be provided only by human beings.

Workers who are forced to become machines prefer to do their jobs the easy way. They reason that their jobs are not worth doing anyway. Also, they resist promotion or transfer; they prefer to remain in the same jobs. They oppose changes in processes or products and even changes in staffiing. Yet this standpat attitude serves no useful purpose in an era of rapid technological advance which develops new products and changes production methods one after the other. White-collar people—including managers and engineers—who become slaves to organization or to orders can hardly be expected to innovate anything. They have lost all the conscience, passion, courage, and determination which are the foundation of the creative, innovative capacities possessed only by human beings. They have become cogwheels with no inner drive.

Nowadays, modern industrial complexes are growing larger and larger. Therefore, some form of organization is an absolute must; we cannot deny the need for it. But, granted that we do need organization, then what we must create is a type of management which is capable of putting people ahead of organization structure, of enabling the individuals who compose the organization to revitalize it for themselves. We will never be able to eliminate the factor of inflexibility inherent in the traditional organization unless we strive for such a goal.

The type of organization I envision is not, naturally, an author-

ity-oriented organization. It is an organization with its own personality. When I had the opportunity to meet with Professor
Harold D. Koontz, of the University of California at Los Angeles,
he said to me, "This is an era of management innovations rather
than technological innovations." I agree with him completely. In
order for companies to be technologically innovative, they must
first of all be innovative in management. And moderation applied
as a stopgap measure to the traditional management axiom which
equates men with machines, horses, and cattle can never achieve
management innovation. The whole basis of the traditional management concept must be changed so that we can have organizations which will motivate people as human beings.

Management That Creates Labor Unrest

We can perhaps better understand the devastating effects
that machine- or organization-orientation has had on humanity by
examining the phenomenon of labor unrest, which is one of its
byproducts. For, if we were to take labor unrest as a simple manifestation of economic pressures or wage drives by the unions, we
would be very careless in our recognition of the facts. No human
beings are willing to take the risk of waging a strike just for money.
The desperation with which they resort to the strike weapon involves emotional factors.

We will be interpreting the history of the labor movement correctly if we see it as a rebellion against denial of humanity.

Sony experienced a strike on its 15th anniversary—an incident
which I recalled in the prologue of this book. It caused some com-
motion among the general public. What I felt keenly at the time
was that the girls involved—middle-school graduates who were
making transistors—were bored by having to commute to the company day in and day out. They were, as it were, shoveled into
trains, taken from where they lived to a strange place, told to move
their hands and feet exactly as they were shown. And all the time
they were living with their small-pebble complex.

We managers may be well advised to ponder this situation
more deeply. We ourselves would certainly be disgusted if we had

to work under the conditions those girls faced. Why is it that we ask people to do things that we would find repugnant? Why do we keep them in intolerable jobs on the one hand and praise all who work hard at those jobs on the other? Naturally, they begin to hate us managers and to revolt against us.

Labor unrest should therefore be regarded as a manifestation of people's frustrated vitality, of their need for ego-actualization; and, as such, it has some constructive meaning for us. Moreover, the same thing may be said about juvenile delinquency. Neither the workers nor the juveniles themselves are aware of the true reasons for their hatred and their unbearable sense of dissatisfaction. In the case of the workers, they become so self-destructive as to take violent action directed at increasing their wages even at the cost of the company's well-being rather than at recovering their humanity on the job.

The only way for us to turn labor unrest into constructive rather than destructive channels is to revive humanity on the job. No coercion or appeasement will work. Nor will our problems be solved by the establishment of workers' governments through revolutions triggered by energy born of labor unrest. The history of modern times attests to this.

The Downfall of Work Segmentation

Work segmentation was one of the pillars which supported the traditional type of management. The manufacturing process was broken down into many minute jobs. One worker handled this process, and another that. The final product was assembled after undergoing many small processes assigned to as many workers. (The same procedure, obviously, can be applied to services as well as to manufacturing.)

The processes that are involved nowadays in making a product from materials or components are indeed complex, and the technologies required to plan and maintain all those processes also are numerous and diverse. There is no one worker who is capable of handling the procedure all by himself. Even if we had such a person, it would be highly inefficient for us to have him work on each process, one after the other, till the product was complete. Thus segmentation of work is necessary. We should not forget, however, that it has both advantages on the one hand and some basic disadvantages on the other. Moreover, its disadvantages are gradually becoming more pronounced these days, and are being viewed more and more seriously.

Needless to say, one of these disadvantages is, again, the fact of inhumanity. Workers who are forced into segmented work are destroyed. Despite explanations and protestations to the contrary, they fail to see any significance in their work as it relates to the whole product or service in question. They feel intuitively that they are being asked only to repeat simple tasks over and over and that they can never expect to advance to higher-level jobs. Human beings work like machines under this system. The more segmented the jobs, the greater the evil. And, when such inventions as the conveyor belt are added to control the speed of work, conditions become almost unbearable.

Traditional managers were fully aware of the disadvantages of work segmentation. As long as the resulting risks were limited to occasional unrest among the workers, employers took downright oppressive measures—or they would appear to relax their posture by offering higher wages on the one hand while, on the other, they persisted in their search for greater efficiency through work segmentation. The phrase "higher wages for greater efficiency" aptly describes the employer mentality of those days.

But the time when, however agonizing the workers' suffering might be, the search for greater efficiency was justified so long as higher wages were being paid them is fast vanishing. The speed with which change in this area is taking place is astounding. For instance, labor turnover in plants where conveyor belts are used in mass production of automobiles is extremely high; managements find it difficult to recruit replacement workers even at higher wages in spite of constant advertisements in the newspapers. And human beings who are willing to serve as inhuman, machinelike laborers for a price are becoming fewer and fewer. Certainly the tendency is far more prominent in Japan, which consists of one homogeneous race of people, than it is in Western countries with their greater or lesser admixture of races. However, anyone is completely wrong who thinks that he still can rely on the old concept of segmented work, in the belief that Japan is still a relatively less developed country in terms of management innovation and, therefore, he will not be caught up in waves of recurring modernization.

The days are gone when the big advantage of work segmentation was considered to be the opportunity it gave employers to hire unskilled workers at low wages. We now have an emerging situation in which unskilled laborers command higher wages than many others.

What is significant here is that we are now at the threshold of an era of quality. The sophistication and complexity of products and their functions are increasingly emphasizing this importance of quality. So what are the factors that can insure ultimate product quality? Machines sometimes malfunction, or they break down. Can inspection alone eliminate defects in machines—or in products? Inspection is, as it were, like a school entrance examination in that it is not capable of evaluating the true quality of today's complex products. Moreover, how can we insure the accuracy of the inspection process itself when it is carried out by people? In the final analysis, of course, it is people who really insure quality in any product. But the people I am referring to are not those people who have come to resemble machines. This quality factor makes me doubly convinced that work segmentation is an enemy of quality.

People, like machines, sometimes malfunction. What makes the difference between true human beings and machines is that human beings hate to make mistakes, they try not to make mistakes, and they immediately correct their mistakes of their own accord as soon as they realize they have made them. Yes, it is only people, who can assure quality, and work segmentation is destroying such people.

The Start of the Zero Defects Program

A good example of the classic relation between the machine-centered system of work segmentation and human beings is the zero defects program which is now being popularized in Japan. This was initiated by Mr. James F. Halpin in his capacity as director of quality at the Orlando Division of Martin Marietta, in the United States. I have met him in person, and I should like to introduce here some of his concepts as these are demonstrated in the program he introduced.

The Orlando Division manufactures missiles. It has a high level of engineering capability, and it inspects its products rigidly to the highest degree possible. For a time, however, the company still failed to achieve zero defects. It was groping for measures which would enable management to achieve this goal when someone made a certain suggestion. This made people realize that the only thing which they could count on, but which had heretofore been overlooked, was the attitude of the company's workers. When they cast about for ways to motivate these workers in an organized way, they came up with the idea for the zero defects program.

The substance of this idea was deceptively simple. Each worker was to be so motivated that he would think of his workmanship as though he were a parent thinking of his children at home. We realize the true significance of this idea only when we compare it with the concept of statistical quality control. According to established statistical control standards, four or five defective items out of 50,000 or 60,000 missile parts are quite acceptable; performance at this level is worthy of citation. No parent, on the other hand, would ever accept the idea that it was quite all right for his son to be killed in a traffic accident in view of published statistics on traffic accidents. He would never accept anything less than 100 percent safety for his son. Mr. Halpin termed this kind of thinking the "proper attitude of people"; that is, the correct mental posture for human beings.

This proper attitude of human beings was lost within most companies. The zero defects program, created by much painstaking effort, was designed to revive it. The result was an astounding improvement in quality. But the program's impact did not stop there; its far-reaching effects at Orlando improved, not only efficiency, but the health of the organization itself.

The benefits attributable to the zero defects program are, in short, no mere immediate, temporary improvements. For example, it realized a tremendous reduction in overall costs. Savings were huge—far beyond those due simply to the reduction of direct manufacturing expense through increased yield and efficiency. The U.S. Department of Defense noted all this and took the trouble of introducing the zero defects concept to defense contractors, bringing an immediate response from the numerous companies that adopted it.

Many company people have heretofore failed to take the proper attitude of workers into account. The reason for this failure is that they have thought of cost only in terms of manufacturing cost. Yet the loss incurred because of the need for post-sales servicing and damage to the company's reputation also is an intangible cost. We are beginning now to realize what tremendous amounts of money we spend on reliability! And we are realizing, too, that work segmentation for the sake of improved efficiency results in more than the alienation of human beings. It also results in increased overall costs for manufacturers and customers, thus offsetting the increased efficiency.

One-Man Production

Just as we can't negate the values of mechanization and organization, we can't deny that work segmentation per se has its importance. We can say, however, that excessive work segmentation is gradually being eliminated. To put it a little dramatically, the work segmentation that remains is a necessary evil. A basic error in the concept has to do with the fact that, while segmentation is necessary, the process itself was tied up with the segmentation of human beings.

It is now possible for us to separate human beings from work segmentation and to let one worker handle several segmented jobs as a single integrated process. In the United States, the need for so-called job enlargement is much discussed, and I feel that this is due to the fact that management realizes the need to integrate segmented jobs.

I am sure that we have many means of meeting the requirements imposed by this need. Traditional management was insensitive toward it; therefore, this is still an untapped area. Many measures must be devised and developed to fit practical situations. In fact, I believe that we have two such measures at the present time. One I shall discuss here; the other, in the chapter which follows.

The first measure is to reduce horizontal work segmentation. Typical is the so-called one-man production method, designed to enable one man to assemble a whole television unit, for instance. A table which looks like the lazy Susan in a Chinese restaurant is placed in front of a worker. Around this table is placed one lot of 20 chassis, and on both sides of the worker there is an arrray of parts. For his first process, he takes up one part and attaches it to each of the 20 chassis, turning the table as he does so. Next, for the second process, he picks up another part and adds it to all the chassis. Then he proceeds to the third process—and so on. In this way he does a complete job on the product.

This method, in a nutshell, tries to make use of the efficiency inherent in work segmentation by adapting it to one-man production. Many sorts of equipment similar to the lazy Susan table are being developed for various kinds of products. The method is not necessarily applicable to all jobs; however, the basic principles involved in the one-man production method can be freely applied to all jobs, including clerical work. The extent of application that is possible will vary, depending on the extent to which we are willing to eliminate simple and repetitive work so long as we do not lose money as a result. There are in fact lots of ways, other than work segmentation, that we can devise for handling jobs.

One-man production admittedly does require time for training, but the higher intelligence level of workingmen nowadays makes it easy for us to implement the method. Also, workers are better motivated to work. One-man production creates a strong sense of responsibility in a man because of the identification of his workmanship with a final product such as a television set. However, nothing like this sense of responsibility would ever exist under the conveyor-belt system. Hard work on the part of Worker A, for instance, would not be reflected in the final product if the man next in line did a poor job, and this could well lead to detachment and irresponsibility on the part of both. Under the conveyor-belt system, the quality of the products turned out is not assured by human beings; rather, it is determined by imperfect machines called human beings.

An item made under the one-man production system clearly identifies its maker—Worker A, for instance. Nobody else produced it. Therefore, the pass rate of Worker A's products at inspection becomes a source of encouragement to him—or generally, in our case at Sony, her. Again, the reliability of her products after they are sold to customers is a matter of concern to her. This easily induces her to maintain the "proper attitude" specified by Mr. Halpin.

We applied this one-man production method to jobs that used to be meaninglessly segmented, and we achieved excellent performance in these work areas. In fact, phenomenal improvements in quality and efficiency resulted. What is more, we found the response of the workers assigned to the jobs quite interesting.

Naturally, a person has to have a certain amount of experience to be ready for this type of work. Newcomers, therefore, are not assigned to it; they have to learn each process on a segmented basis. Once they have acquired all the necessary skills, they are ready for one-man production. This represents a kind of promotion to them, and they are highly motivated by it. The minute a certain worker is told that her products do not need item-by-item inspection any more, that she will from now on be producing goods on a sampling-inspection basis, she is filled with satisfaction and pride in her workmanship beyond any verbal description. The company is then able to reduce its inspection costs, and all is very well indeed from the managers' point of view. The workers, for their part, have a series of opportunities for self-improvement and the pleasure of being able to see the results of their work from the very early days of their employment with the company.

Where the work-segmentation system uses a conveyor belt, workers are instructed in one process which they must then perform forever, year in and year out. For this reason they tend to hold a rather pessimistic outlook on the future. For their sake we must discard our old concepts and start all over again in this area of our responsibility as managers.

2

From Meaningless Labor to Meaningful Work

THE second method of separating human beings from work segmentation is relief from work monotony through the vertical integration of jobs. In the traditional organization, hierarchical work segmentation is utilized quite thoroughly. Not only does the Taylor system force workers to move their hands and feet exactly as they are told, but it also inhibits them from thinking. People higher in the hierarchy think out what hand and foot movements should be used. The poisonous effect this system has on humanity is far more devastating than that of horizontal work segmentatioin.

No More "Slavelike" Labor

Our exploration of new management principles and techniques led us to the elimination of hierarchical work segmentation in our plant. In brief, we let workers handle their own jobs. We let them plan, perform, and control their work.

The American Telephone and Telegraph Company is another firm that is directing a great deal of effort toward job enrichment based on the principle of vertical integration. One official of the company has told me that the results are exciting and fantastic. These words "exciting" and "fantastic" certainly express vividly the sentiments of those who are implementing the job-enrichment plan, and we at our plant share the same feelings. Human beings are capable of achievements that exceed the limits of the imagination.

I myself had never entertained any thought that people could be so capable. My surprise, like that of my fellow managers, truly testifies to the fact that industrial companies have been utilizing only the "cogwheel" portion of their human resources and that they have failed to make use of those qualities in human beings which determine their true nature. If each and every employee were to behave like a president, we would be able to mobilize a tremendous amount of energy from them. What could be more exciting and fantastic?

Should we be able to establish an ideal work system in our plant, people here would feel a tremendous joy in their work of producing transistors. And we can honestly say we are now coming closer to this ideal. Technological innovations are replacing obsolete types of transistors, one after the other, with new ones; and our boys and girls actually shed tears over the fact that the transistors they used to make are giving way to others. They simply can't bear to think that something manufactured at the cost of so much toil is now valueless; they hate to see it go. And this, mind you, is no exaggeration. It is the literal truth, which tells us much about the true nature of human beings.

It all makes me realize keenly how cruelly the traditional work system has been oppressing human beings. Modern industry, since the nineteenth century, has indeed paved the way toward despoiling the important resource we call humanity. Against this background, how can we fail to appreciate the true causes of the labor shortages and the absence of needed skills from which we suffer in modern times? We have had plenty of human beings, but human beings are beginning to show less and less capacity for work and for creation.

The situation at the present moment, to repeat, is such that workers are expected to work exactly as ordered. Their function is exactly identical with those of machines; so let's call this *meaningless labor*. Etymologically, the word "labor" implies "slavelike work." Although no buying or selling of labor is involved in present-day industrial relations, labor contracts sever human capacity for labor from human beings; they are based on buying and selling this human capacity. And the only difference between *slave labor* and *slavelike labor* is a matter of the little suffix "-like" added to the first word.

Three basic laws in our country stipulate work by human beings in the context of this meaningless labor and negate any other interpretation of the term. Up until recently, we thought that such stipulation was indeed progressive and modern. Many people still believe so. However, when we try to free human beings from slavelike labor, these laws which deny any other interpretation of labor but their own interfere with us. I can't help but think that such laws are far from progressive and that, on the contrary, they tend to be reactionary at the present time.

Labor in the context of buying and selling is regarded as only one source of energy for production. The movement of human beings is equated with that of electrical or mechanical power. The unit by which labor is measured is so much per hour, and the unit price varies depending on the quality of the energy. Labor unions are considered to be organizations which deal in this kind of buying and selling, and employers try to buy needed labor resources as cheaply as possible from them. Companies are convinced that effective management amounts to effective utilization of such resources.

It is impossible for us, in practice, to separate human beings from labor resources. When we buy labor resources, human beings accompany them to complicate matters. I venture to use the phrase "complicate matters" because I think it expresses the true sentiments of traditional management people. When labor resources are to be used just like machines, the human beings who inevitably come with them will eventually cause trouble. Many plans, methods, and procedures have been devised to placate burdensome human beings or even to pacify them when they rebel against their treatment.

I have been extremely candid and blunt about this subject of labor and may have incurred the resentment of many people. But a fact is a fact, and we can't help recognizing that employers use human beings in place of machines when mechanization seems to be unfeasible. A certain satirist in the United States once said, "The ideal aspired to in industrial relations is to eliminate human beings. The way to more and better work lies in the elimination of workers." What the United States now faces is the fact that employers are increasingly in need of workers—workers who are capable of performing people-oriented work. And the same thing can be said about Japan.

Work That Sets Its Own Goals

We have a concept which is the antithesis of meaningless labor. Let us call it *meaningful work*.

What is this meaningful work? It is comparable to the kind which prevented Beethoven from committing suicide and made him continue his composition. It is analogous to children's playing in the pasture or to mothers' rearing of their children. Meaningful work represents responsible and challenging assignments in which, driven by their inevitable urge to live, people set their own goals, establish plans of action to achieve their goals, implement their plans, and coordinate the results. This is the true form of work for human beings, and there are no others. When human beings are forced to engage in meaningless labor, the end result is their own self-destruction.

For human beings to live does not mean that they are to live without any purpose. To live is to engage in meaningful work. Meaningless labor is vice; meaningful work is virtue. It is an act of virtue to shorten the hours of meaningless labor, but it is not necessarily an act of virtue to shorten the hours of meaningful work. On the one hand, meaningless labor is something that human beings cannot stand; on the other, they have the urge to engage in meaningful work.

The real solution to the problem faced both by mankind in general and by industrial companies in particular will never be found if we let meaningless labor remain as is. We have no alternative but to transform labor into work. In view of my past experiences, I am convinced that we can do this. The choice before us transcends the question of whether we have a socialistic or a capitalistic system.

Drastic Change Needed in Our Concept of Work

For those people who are unable to rid themselves of the meaningless-labor concept, the need expressed in the heading above is hard to understand. When I explain to these people the importance of orientation toward human beings, they in turn put people and work in a dichotomous relationship and ask me how I propose to coordinate conflicts between orientation toward human beings and orientation toward production.

I get tired of being asked this kind of question by this kind of people. Men and work cannot be regarded in terms of a dichotomous relationship. Men and work are one entity; neither cannot be separated from the other. Orientation toward human beings is the same as orientation toward work. There can be no orientation toward human beings without work, and there can be no work without orientation toward human beings. The conditions of meaningless labor prevailing in modern times are the manifestation of a momentary sickness, and those modern people who spend their lives only under the prevailing conditions become insensitive to this sickness. They can think of human beings only after working hours. They all look forward to enjoying their leisure time with money they have earned by meaningless labor reluctantly performed. How can they possibly find any worthwhileness in this kind of living?

The only key left for us to use in solving this problem is to overcome meaningless labor and to rediscover and regain meaningful work in our jobs. This, rather than specific management techniques in themselves, is what is fundamentally important.

Such management innovations as goal setting and the zero defects movement probably are intended to restore meaningful work to our jobs. Should we lose sight of their true intent and implement them as mere techniques to gain a certain effect, we will end in disaster. During the initial period of implementation, bells, trumpets, and banners may conceivably contribute by their very novelty to producing the desired effect. When the novelty subsides, however, the net effect becomes negligible. And the more impatient managers become with the dwindling results of their efforts, the more pronounced their inclination is to employ such management techniques as they would the old carrot and stick. This merely results in fortifying the meaningless-labor factors in jobs and expediting their own self-destruction.

Conversely, Taylor's scientific management techniques were the principal agents in establishing the so-called meaningless-labor system, although we must give due credit to the time and motion studies originated by Taylor and his followers as a great benefit to mankind. Time and motion studies can and should be gainfully utilized as effective management weapons under the meaningful-work system. The evil in the Taylor techniques lies in the fact that staff specialists were designated to establish efficient procedures by these means and that the workers were expected only to follow the orders given them. It would be wonderful if we could ask the workers themselves to utilize time and motion studies, so that they could devise ways of improving the efficiency of their work and implement them of their own volition.

That a combination of time and motion studies and similar devices with the meaningful-work system achieves far better results than the old Taylor system by itself is shown by the experience of Texas Instruments. Dr. M. Scott Myers, who was then with the company, has reported that a certain work-simplification process proved to be the first successful step taken in the effort to change labor into meaningful work. Other examples as well indicate clearly that it is not the techniques involved that are important; rather, it is the thinking of the managers concerned that is significant. The drastic change that has occurred in this thinking—with managers abandoning the twin assumptions that workers can hardly be expected to improve their efficiency on their own and that they are incapable of thinking out the necessary plans by themselves—has enabled us to make the vital switch successfully. Meaningless labor is yielding to meaningful work, but management is still applying the same effective techniques and, simultaneously, promoting a series of brilliant innovations.

Unlimited Capacity of Human Beings

When meaningless labor is transformed into meaningful work, human beings begin to show a potential for growth that is almost unimaginable. It is not too much to say that the possibilities for growth are unlimited.

This makes me wonder why we have to establish standards stipulating how often a worker's hands must be moved within a prescribed period of time in order to increase productivity. All we should have to do in this regard is to inform the worker of the past efficiency record for his job. No emancipated human being will ever be satisfied if he can't exceed this record—in fact, make continuous progress. The results to be obtained from meaningful work must, in short, be seen to be believed. The rate at which work-speeds increase trends steadily upward; defects are reduced to infinitesimal percentages.

When we develop a new transistor and new techniques for producing it in our plant, our engineers estimate the probable efficiency of the operation. These engineers never fail to be embarrassed by the fact that their estimates of efficiency invariably are left far behind by actual performance. There is nothing mysterious about this. For instance, let us go back to our example of the 100-meter dash, which calls for running in a straight line from start to goal. This is the simplest possible form of labor. Now, the making of transistors may sometimes call for simple tasks to be done, but these are highly complex when we compare them with the 100-meter dash. Yet, simple though it might be, human beings have continued for centuries to compete in this type of race; new records are being made even to this day, and they never stop. Why are there so many eager contestants, and why do spectators clap their hands for them? It is because, for sportsmen, this 100-meter dash is not meaningless labor but meaningful work. They are not competing because they have been whipped into running or are running for a reward called an hourly wage. Should they be forced to run under such conditions, the 100-meter dash would be just like labor in hell.

It is, therefore, not simplicity or complexity as manifest in outside appearance that distinguishes labor from work. The difference lies in the attitudes of the workers.

To state the facts objectively—when people are faced with the drudgery of meaningless labor, either they become self-destructive or they still go on looking for the satisfaction of doing a good job and being treated like human beings. This is clearly explained by Dr. Frederick Herzberg's research findings (see Part Four, Chapter 3): The admirable desire to achieve dignity through work persists in the minds of the employees.

This is true of managers as well. They too are members of organizations; but, regardless of their situation, they are still searching for dignity and worth in their jobs. And, if managers are searching for dignity and worth, can we say less about their subordinates? Managers must recognize it as a fact that their subordinates are motivated by the same desires that they themselves feel. When they do recognize this, they will begin to trust their subordinates, and it is only through this sense of trust in people that they will really be able to transform the meaningless labor of slaves into the meaningful work of human beings. Superficial changes may also be necessary, but these are by no means a basic requirement.

Make a Courageous Effort

When we think about jobs as they are, we can make no clear distinctions as to which parts of them are meaningless labor and which are meaningful work. There is an infinite variety of shadings between these two extremes; the labor-versus-work dichotomy is simply a matter of relativity.

As soon as everybody's job approaches the status of meaningful work, we can say, figuratively, everybody will be thinking and feeling like the company president himself.

To go back to the subject of trust, however, we have no alternative initially but to trust human beings even under the prevailing meaningless-labor conditions, and naturally this involves some risk. But we can't implement the meaningful-work concept in the first place without trust. Meaningful work is possible only when people are trusted to do their jobs properly. And such a managerial attitude prevails as will trust people only when everyone is highly motivated to work or everyone is in a frame of mind amenable to the logic of meaningful work.

My own experience bears witness to the importance of trust. Our plant was in a wretched plight, and I felt considerable pity for all our young employees with most of their lives still ahead of them. It was, in fact, because of my concern for the future of these young people, and because of my desire to do something for them, that I decided I must trust them—feeling as I did so that I was about to become a martyr. I couldn't possibly have found the courage to do what I did if I hadn't been feeling the way I did then. Even if the workers betrayed me, I told myself, it would be none the worse for them. I was only thinking about the inconvenience it would cause the company if my innovations should fail. I was only thinking about the trust placed in me by Mr. Ibuka—who, at the very beginning, had urged, "Feel free to do what you like." So, in the end, I decided to take him at his word and proceed boldly.

I was surprised, later, to notice how people were responding to my trust in them as their jobs slowly changed from meaningless labor to meaningful work. I was inspired, too, and able to fortify my sense of trust still further—which expedited the progress of my plans for change.

To make progress is to try—to make a courageous effort. Without this effort, management can't hope for improvement. Something very close to self-sacrifice is demanded. It takes nerve on our part to commit ourselves to trusting others in spite of our fears. We think, imagine, dread, suffer, and anticipate as, step by step, we advance in our chosen direction. There is no other way.

Motivated Women

Women are generally said, in Japan, to make less highly motivated workers than men. The same thinking seems to prevail in the United States; Dr. Myers says, for example, that "women in general are not motivation seekers, but maintenance seekers." Others declare that women can be positively motivated only as mothers.

Here let us consider, specifically, women at work. In this sphere it is generally accepted—at Sony as in other companies before our recent success with housewife workers—that housewives are mainly concerned with their homes. Therefore, they are less interested in their work, have high absenteeism rates, and can be placed only in supplementary jobs. Housewife teachers are cited as a good example of the validity of this thinking.

I believe such notions about women are wrong. They are derived from static observation of people, and people change depending on given conditions. In general, women are not assigned to worthwhile, challenging jobs, and this may make them look like "maintenance seekers." If, on the other hand, they are assigned to jobs in which they can find dignity and worth and can take pride in their work, they will become "motivation seekers." At least, that has been my own experience in the plant.

We used to take the customary negative attitude toward women workers, using as justification their supposed lack of motivation. We deliberately changed our attitude, however, and started to look at them from a dynamic viewpoint. We provided adequate growth opportunities in the plant for any girl or woman as long as she had the will to work and her family situation would permit her to do so. We placed women on our plant teams so that they would be motivated to work on their own, not as mere helping hands. What surprised us as a result was the fact that one housewife after another wanted to learn more about transistors. Their attendance rates improved, and so did their morale. Moreover, there seems to be no evidence that they have neglected their duties at home in making this improvement.

The 1,200-odd housewife workers in our plant account for about half the total number of our women workers. The reason for this large percentage is that the housewives are indeed magnificent workers, and the fact that they continue to commute to the plant with bright, lively faces every day can be attributed to improvement of their management of household matters. My personal feeling is that they may well be advised to resign from their work at Sony in case their employment with us should give rise to problems at home and that their family life should never be disturbed for the sake of a relatively meager sum of money.

At one of our plant study meetings this year, a group of housewife workers presented a candid case study dealing with the effect their jobs had upon their home situation. Professor Jiro Kawakita, of the Tokyo Institute of Technology, happened to be present, and at the end of the presentation he commented on it briefly. "I envy you all," he said. These housewives were able to sublimate at the workplace all the pent-up domestic frustrations they would have accumulated by staying at home in small houses. This, I believe, refutes the idea that housewives can't concentrate wholeheartedly on the job because they are home-oriented or, simply, because women are different. No "meaningful work" can be created on the basis of such static observation.

Pride of Women Sweepers Dumbfounds Intellectuals

Meaningful work can, of course, exist in all kinds of jobs. It is commonly assumed, for instance, that floor sweeping is a degrading job which is not worthy of anyone's best efforts. This is an outrageous idea, but too often it is spontaneously accepted as fact. In our plant, however, the women sweepers have their own teams and leaders, as at any other work stations, and they have a great deal of autonomy in their work. Their determination and morale are among the highest in the plant—and in this connection I should like to cite an example.

Since the outset of our existence as a plant, we had not had any scribblings on the walls of the toilets. Then, three or four years ago, for the first time in our history someone began scribbling on the walls. It must have been someone smart because the messages were full of humor and they encouraged others. We naturally had no means of controlling this growing vandalism, since the toilets were private. A factory newspaper denounced the culprits: "This is a disgraceful situation. Whoever you are, we urge you to stop." But that didn't deter these smart alecks—their only answer was further scribblings. One scribbling led to another.

I had reached the point where I shook my head, lamenting that our plant had become a place, like any other, for scribblers. But suddenly, one day, the scribblings stopped. I became curious about this and checked into the matter. I found that the women sweepers, who used to take pride in keeping the walls shining, had been doing their best to erase the scribblings. Finally, though, they got fed up and decided to display posters on the walls. "This is our place of work," the posters read. "Please don't stain our walls." The vandalism stopped immediately.

I was tremendously moved when I heard this story. If these women's sweeping had been meaningless labor, calling for them only to sweep, they would not have reacted the way they did. The spontaneous action they took dumbfounded those long-haired humorists—which was something even the plant manager hadn't been able to do despite his appeals to reason. The scribblers couldn't fight back any more. In short, the women sweepers in our plant did indeed give every indication of feeling that their jobs were meaningful work.

Floor sweepers elsewhere are, in general, treated differently. To me, this is nonsense. In our plant we provide orientation for everybody as a matter of course, and we talk about transistors with everybody. We even take new employees to visit other plants. "Respect human beings" is a fashionable slogan nowadays, and many plant managers may, as a matter of routine, bow to workers as a token of "respect" and thank them for their work. Mere lip service, however, will not work. Like every other aspect of plant management, clean toilets are a contributing factor in the production of high-quality transistors. Similarly, every team member is indispensable and, as such, must be treated with the same fairness. So, when we establish our plans for the next six-month period, plans by the sweepers' groups are included. They determine, for example, how they can achieve a high degree of cleanliness with fewer people and what kind of equipment or detergents may be desirable. And the women frequently express their ideas about such topics.

This, then, is how our sweepers are performing their meaningful work. Each has her territory to cover, and the territories are rotated. The goal is always to maintain the assigned area spankingly clean at less cost, and they are proud to achieve it. In their meetings they discuss how they should rotate their territories, how they can effectively clean areas where expanded facilities are under construction, how and where they should keep their equipment, and so on.

Every employee, under this kind of system, becomes the master of his job and, as I have said, begins to feel that he is his own president. The only difference between the woman sweeper and the real company president is that the woman sweeps floors and the president steers the company. As Peter F. Drucker aptly puts it, the fact that we now have an emerging system in which each employee is an employer himself deserves to be called a management revolution.

3

Work Can't Be Purchased with Wages

ONE of the biggest problems we face at the present time is that of creating a management which will be capable of understanding correctly the relationship between men and their work and which can motivate people to work. This is exactly the theme of this book and exactly the area that we are exploring in our plant.

Satisfaction Through Work

The basis of our exploration derives from the fact that it is the job itself that motivates human beings. To believe in this fact is to place trust in human beings. "Trust"—to recapitulate—is not here used in the context of the ethical doctrine which holds that

213

man's inborn nature is basically good. "Trust" in the sense we use the word is based on our recognition that human beings are bound to look to their jobs as their reason for living.

When, occasionally, we glance at the ranks of our employees lined up in front of us, we may have the impression that they are devoid of any desire to work, that they are trying to slow down their work, that they are interested only in money and won't try hard enough despite our offers of assistance. Indeed, they sometimes do look that way—the facts seem to confirm such an attitude on their part. This, however, is not the way human beings really are. Their true nature is somehow hidden, and for one reason or another we see only its surface manifestations.

In my briefing on the management philosophy and policies of Texas Instruments Incorporated, I learned a great deal. At the same time, I was surprised, as I think I have already pointed out, to notice the striking similarity that exists between their thinking and ours. Their philosophy, like ours, goes back to their views on human beings and the nature of human beings. And the philosophies of AT&T (to which I have also alluded), of IBM, and of Idemitsu Kosan in Japan, are all similarly based.

All Human Beings Are Motivated Workers

In 1960, under the guidance of Dr. Frederick Herzberg of Case Western Reserve University, Texas Instruments started its six-year research on employee motivation. Subjects were selected from three salaried job categories (scientist, engineer, and manufacturing supervisors) and two hourly-paid classifications (technician and assembler). There were 282 in all. The following conclusions were reached, with minor discrepancies in details depending on job categories.*

What motivates employees to work effectively?

A challenging job which allows a feeling of achievement, responsibility, growth, advancement, enjoyment of work itself, and earned recognition.

---

* M. Scott Myers, "Who Are Your Motivated Workers?" *Harvard Business Review*, Vol. 42, No. 1 (January/February 1964), pp. 73–88.

What dissatisfies workers?

Mostly factors which are peripheral to the job—work rules, lighting, coffee breaks, titles, seniority rights, wages, fringe benefits, and the like.

When do workers become dissatisfied?

When opportunities for meaningful achievement are eliminated and they become sensitized to their environment and begin to find fault.

The company's findings are further explained as follows:

. . . The potency of any of the job factors mentioned, as a motivator or dissatisfier, is not solely a function of the nature of the factor itself. It is also related to the personality of the individual.

For most individuals, the greatest satisfaction and the strongest motivation are derived from achievement, responsibility, growth, advancement, work itself, and earned recognition. People like this, whom Herzberg terms "motivation seekers," are motivated primarily by the nature of the task and have high tolerance for poor environmental factors.

"Maintenance seekers," on the other hand, are motivated primarily by the nature of their environment and tend to avoid motivation opportunities. They are chronically preoccupied and dissatisfied with maintenance factors surrounding the job, such as pay, supplemental benefits, supervision, working conditions, status, job security, company policy and administration, and fellow employees.

Although an individual's orientation as a motivation seeker or a maintenance seeker is fairly permanent, it can be influenced by the characteristics of his various roles. For example, maintenance seekers in an environment of achievement, responsibility, growth, and earned recognition tend to behave like and acquire the values of motivation seekers. On the other hand, the absence of motivators causes many motivation seekers to behave like maintenance seekers, and to become preoccupied with the maintenance factors in their environment.

All of the five occupational groups discussed below, *except female assemblers,* seemed to be largely comprised of actual or potential motivation seekers. Scientists are the group most strongly oriented as motivation seekers, and female assemblers those most strongly oriented as maintenance seekers. Maintenance seeking among female assemblers probably stems from the tradition of circumscribed and dependent roles of women in industry as well as from their supervisors' failure to provide them with motivation opportunities.

I agree. The majority of the present girl workers in our plant, unlike the female workers of the past, compare favorably with the male workers—if indeed they do not excel their male colleagues—from the standpoint of being motivation seekers. I believe this is the result of our giving them opportunities for both motivation and autonomy.

The Reward of Work Is Work Itself

We did not conduct any research in our plant like that of Texas Instruments. Rather, we concentrated our efforts in areas where we intuitively felt problems existed and, by our efforts, were able to produce certain results. In fact, I can say on the basis of what I know now that we arrived at similar conclusions.

To put it briefly—I do not believe that wages are everything work offers—that is, its sole reward. We management personnel are obligated to offer every one of our employees a reward for his work in terms of both wages and something that is far more valuable than wages themselves. I refer to a feeling of dignity and worth and to the satisfaction of doing a competent job. As far as wages are concerned, we have enough problems as we are. But what bothers us even more—what should bother us even more—is how we can create this sense of satisfaction and sheer pleasure to be had from work. We are exerting our best efforts to this end.

The supreme reward of working is work itself. Granted that wages also are significant, they are still only a small part of the reward, ranking second or third in terms of importance.

Without waiting for any findings by Dr. Herzberg, we can understand the true nature of human beings if we will just consider ourselves. For instance, I think I would accept an offer from a company for less money if the job would give me something that was lacking in my present job; that is, something to live for. I don't say I would go for any amount of money; and conversely, I would never accept any job I didn't much care about even for more money. I don't want to think at all in terms of selling my efforts to a company. It is quite idiotic to talk in terms of selling or buying something which is close to man's soul for a certain price and to settle the account then and there once the deal is made. At least, this is how I feel, and I believe I am not so very different from other people in my attitude. Certainly this belief of mine, which amounted to an intuition, triggered the start of management innovation in our plant.

So it is, too, with technological development. No company in the world which tries to hook engineers with money as bait and no engineer in the world who is willing to be hooked with money can engage in successful developmental work. Creation is possible only when we are attempting to overcome insurmountable difficulties. We achieve a breakthrough only when we approach a problem with all we have—as if we were risking our lives on it. We can't talk about those lives and about monetary rewards in the same breath. In reality, companies are being supported by something which can't be bought with money.

Many intellectuals have heads full of labor regulations and laws. And many professionals think privately that the proper reward for their studious research in the past is money. These people may someday, however, become slightly touched in the head—perpetually frustrated by the fact that they are selling the fruits of their learning and the harvest of the research into which they have poured their efforts and affections for a price. The reason why I feel so grateful for being at Sony is that I have been assigned a job by Sony in which I can find dignity and worth and that I am being paid on that basis. I have been assigned work to which I can devote all I have and from which I am able to derive the supreme reward. We want to make all the people in our plant feel this same way.

In the zero defects program, recognition is often stressed. Its sponsors say it is important for the company to recognize the achievement of a certain zero defects goal. Thus the reward under the zero defects program is not money or position. It is recognition. In the same context, Dr. Herzberg describes recognition as one of the important elements of motivating human beings, and he further stipulates that recognition is by no means any sort of coaxing.

Revolution in Our Thinking About Wages

If all this is true, what *are* wages? Professor Tadao Umezawa, of the Research Institute for Cultural Science of the University of Kyoto, has an interesting comment on this. "Wages in the future," he says, "will come to be like alms." Alms, it will be recalled, are usually given to a priest from a Buddhist temple, as a form of respect, after he has come to a home and recited a sutra for a deceased member or friend of the family.

We would not buy a memorial service offered by a priest by giving him wages. Naturally, there is a difference in the amount of alms given—a difference which comes from the relative rank of the priest and his supporters. But, although this concept of alms may not be able to solve all our problems regarding the matter of wages, we can say with certainty that we are beginning to see wages interpreted in such a context.

For instance, I had occasion to meet with a certain American employer. "We are not paying salaries and wages to our employees in consideration of their services and work," he said. "We are paying them so that we may keep these employees in our company." This, I feel, represents a sincere and honest confession on the part of managers and employers everywhere amid today's extreme labor shortages. We can sense in this remark a lament to the effect that "we wouldn't be paying out such high amounts in salaries and wages just as compensation for services and work. We are forced to pay so that we can prevent people from changing their jobs and going to other companies."

These employers' viewpoints signal a change of still greater significance. It means that the concept of equating the price of recruiting and maintaining labor resources with wages no longer is valid. Nor are labor shortages the only reason for this. Professor Umezawa backs up his alms theory by saying, "Modern industries are rapidly moving from the phase of simple production of goods and energy to the phase of producing information (in the broader sense of functioning like a brain)." What is needed in the new phase is not mechanical labor but creative (human) work. Such creative work cannot be measured in terms of money, nor can it be sold or bought for money. The fact that "we are paying them so that we can keep them in our company" is heralding the abandonment by management of the old, evil concept of separating labor resources from human beings. Wages being paid under the new concept are closely akin to alms.

The American employer might casually have said what he did without any deep thought. However, should he start thinking seriously about his plight and searching for a solution to it, I am sure that the coming revolution in the relationship between labor and wages will recommend itself to his attention and that he will try to make it a reality.

Wages Are an Honorarium:
Girl Workers Prefer Pay Based on Seniority

My basic philosophy—to put it a little differently—is that wages are meant as an honorarium for human beings, not as compensation for labor. We can't explain the wage system developing in the majority of companies solely in terms of compensation for labor. Some companies, true, are now moving toward "modernizing" their pay system along the lines of the old concept of wages; but this modernization, to me, is retrogression. These companies are thinking of what they are doing in terms of further stressing this old idea of compensatory wages for labor and in terms of devising means of enticing workers to work so that they can draw a veil over the difference between what they are actually paying to their workers and what those workers are entitled to. They are entirely wrong.

It is because we in our plant aspire to a newer concept of wages that we are applying a system which is totally unrelated to merit or incentive pay to girl workers in jobs which are traditionally considered most suited to incentive-type wages. We allow the same amount of seniority-based pay across the board to all workers who were employed at the same time. We apply this system, not because it is adequate, but because it simply makes for better results. Visitors often ask girl workers, "Is it fair for you to work hard for the same amount of money that everyone else gets?" And they are always puzzled to hear the girls answer, "It's better that way, because everybody is working hard, anyhow."

The gist of such questions from visitors appears to be the conviction that it ought to be necessary for us to treat these girls differently, depending on their performance, because workers won't be motivated to work hard unless they are recognized for their achievement by the people surrounding them. Such visitors believe in the superstition that wages are one of the most important, if not the only, means of giving recognition. Workers, on the other hand, are encouraged by the fact that they have done their best. Of course, when we talk about doing one's best, our words may convey different meanings depending on the variables in both companies and people. Thus, if we chose to recognize performance through wages, we might end up creating, not satisfaction, but dissatisfaction. This conclusion is endorsed by many research projects in the area of the behavioral sciences, particularly those conducted by Dr. Herzberg and Dr. Myers.

Too many self-appointed specialists in personnel and industrial relations do not understand the fundamental basis of human satisfaction. They assume that they are ministering to the employees. What they are actually doing is to meddle with the wage system, which they call a reward for labor. They are meddling with it as though they were seriously endeavoring to create the dissatisfying factors to which Dr. Herzberg refers.

The gifts that we hand out once every month to sections in the plant which have achieved outstanding production records are not meant as rewards or citations; they are purely a form of congratulation. They cost only 50 yen (approximately 13 cents) apiece. Yet the workers in each section draw lots eagerly to decide who will be their representative and receive the gift from the plant manager. I feel and they feel a tremendous thrill on every such occasion.

Sometimes, too, they have their own private gatherings to congratulate themselves for achieving their goals. They display their records in graphs going back several years, or they have parties, or they take snapshots of the entire group to commemorate their success. Some of them send these pictures to their mothers. The mothers may not understand what it's all about, but to these girls the pictures mean a lot.

Assuming, however, that wages are now considered a kind of honorarium, we still need to have some difference in the amount of honorarium to be paid to different people, just as the alms offered vary from one priest to another. The reason for honorarium differentials is nothing like the reason for pay differentials under the concept of compensatory wages for labor. Such differentials are never based on the carrot-and-stick philosophy of labor and compensation. Instead, they are based on differences in ranking from one person to another.

What kind of ranking are we talking about? It's easy to sense the differences in rank among people, but these are nothing that can be clearly identified or logically explained. The determining factor may be seniority, age, ability, or personality. Depending on circumstances, seniority may be the chief consideration in some cases and ability in others. The emphasis seems to vary in accordance with who is to receive the honorarium and what the prevailing conditions are. But this change in emphasis is necessary—otherwise things will not work out well.

Wages under the new concept also take hours worked into account. Hours worked, however, should not be broken down to the extent they are under the old concept of labor compensation —as though we were tabulating the cost of electricity, for example. For this reason I have serious doubts about overtime payments in compliance with the current labor-standards law. Frankly speaking, I am not impressed with this system. It is nothing but a remnant of the dehumanizing labor system encouraged by our former philosophy. Japanese labor laws, moreover, force this system upon almost all job categories, and it is because of this enforcement across the board that we are beginning to have all sorts of problems.

Fringe Benefits Not Meant to Be Bait

Like wages, fringe benefits also tend to be considered one of the most important media for motivating employees. Improvement of benefits based on this concept, however, will create factors of dissatisfaction contrary to management's original intentions. For the truth of the matter is that bait of this kind will not motivate human beings.

The basic question here is whether people are finding satisfaction and even joy in their jobs. As long as they are, inadequacy of benefits despite the company's best efforts to the contrary will not result in a disastrous reaction on the part of employees. Provided they can continue to feel pleasure in working as human beings, they will accept this inadequacy for the moment and, meanwhile, do their best to help the company prosper in order that it may grant them better benefits in the future. And I'm talking, not about dreamland, but about reality. I recognize the need for employee benefits as a means of assisting in the autonomous development of human beings and increasing their enjoyment of life. I believe, in fact, that we have failed in this respect. Managers must consider whether they may not have provided employee benefits without any real sincerity.

Our job is not just to provide employees, for example, with luxurious buildings. There are some data indicating that employees prefer inexpensively built wooden housing to reinforced concrete buildings painted a shining white. And another company's experience leads to the same conclusion: Employees in a certain firm which provided its employees with reinforced concrete buildings changed en masse to another employer who provided them only with wooden housing. The reason, I suspect, is that the reinforced concrete buildings for employees turned into prisons without bars. The wooden dormitories, on the other hand, were warm places full of human touches. It is no wonder that the employees in this case preferred the simpler facilities.

While many dormitory buildings have been built since I came to the plant, Sony already had many that predated these. Even in the early days, however, employees complained that they were sick and tired of their living quarters. In view of the fact that they really had very nice buildings, management undoubtedly thought there was no end to the luxury demanded by employees.

One specific problem we had concerned the entrances to the dormitory buildings, which faced away from the main gate so that the residents had to take the long way around to go in or out. I was at a loss to understand why in the world those in charge could have been so mean as to put the entrances on the wrong side. Naturally, this made the workers take shortcuts—which encouraged management to declare that they had no morals. Talk about nonsense! The managers would no doubt have understood the situation better if they'd had to live in the dormitories themselves. The workers, of course, made it a habit to arrive in the plant at the very last moment before work was due to start. Why shouldn't they take shortcuts? The trouble was that the buildings had been planned with supreme indifference to the prospective residents' convenience and with the typical bureaucratic concern for precedent.

The bureaucratic staff specialists of those days might have said, "What? You're building dormitories, eh? Well, then, build them in accordance with the established plan." Those who would have to live in the buildings were the last thing they would think about. Neither did they have any sense of affection or obligation toward the residents. So thoroughly bureaucratic were they in planning every detail that they supplied curtains which looked as though they had been dipped in mud, making an ugly contrast to the gleaming white walls around them. It wouldn't have cost much to change those curtains for flower-printed ones; but the bureaucrats, left to themselves, had no intentions whatsoever of replacing them.

With the space surrounding the buildings transformed from barren land into a veritable garden, visitors who now see the dorms may be pardoned for feeling that they look a little luxurious. And the change was all engineered by the girls living there. I helped them, I might add, carrying a straw basket full of dirt over my shoulder. In fact, I believe it is important for managers to cultivate a state of mind that will enable them to help the workers in the way I spontaneously helped those girls—without any underlying motive. I hope I will not give the impression here that I am preaching on the subject of mental training for human beings. I think it is a matter, rather, of the mental *habits* of human beings.

I simply couldn't stand the way this dormitory-entrance prob-

lem persisted. True, conversion of the reinforced concrete buildings called for considerable construction work and a sizable
investment, too. But I was determined: I saw to it that the
entrances were changed. Determination and thoughtfulness of this
kind on the part of management can influence the success or failure of dorms. They can also encourage employees to trust management.

At any rate, the situation has certainly changed since then.
The girls themselves started claiming that their dorms were much
too luxurious for them. For instance, the bathing facilities were
extremely well arranged and convenient. "We should have to
suffer a little by having to take care of ourselves. Otherwise, we'll
be acting like a bunch of contented hogs. So please make our
dormitories simpler." This, then, was the genesis of our so-called
"home dormitory" which was designed for autonomous, family-
like living.

Assistance in Realizing Individual Goals

If there is any way in which our plant dormitories differ from
others, it may be the fact that ours are full of "heart." We have
done everything possible to make the dorms pleasant places for
everybody living in them.

If we were to build a solid four-story building with reinforced
concrete, it would cost us, at the present level of construction
expense, somewhere between 700,000 and 800,000 yen per employee. This is indeed expensive. The girls, on the other hand,
wanted to suffer a little by having to take care of themselves; so
we conceived the idea of the home dormitory, consisting of a
basic two-story prefabricated house. The whole setup occupied
just about the same space as would have been required if we had
built four-story buildings instead. The complete cost per employee was 400,000 yen. Each house faced a different direction,
and we deliberately created undulations of the land surface and
paid similar attention to other details. Now everybody wants to
live in the home dormitories, and visitors envy the residents. The
visitors, of course, should go back to their plants and build home

dormitories of their own—and they should be able to build these at much less cost than their traditional dormitories.

As far as the expense of running the dormitories is concerned, we are not so very different from other companies. Our dorms are well maintained and clean—the results of our efforts. In the case of the home dorms, however, residents have to pay for room, electricity, city gas, water, and what-not. They have to heat their own baths and cook their own meals in their kitchens. They do everything for themselves, in other words, but that's the way they wanted it. And the expense of running such a home dorm, naturally, is far less than the cost of operating a regular dormitory.

But there is another point relating to the administration of the home dorms that is more important than the relatively modest expense itself. We now have 45 home dorms; six to ten persons live in each of them, and the residents form their own assembly and live autonomously. The company is involved in no expense for this kind of activity. The residents also sponsor a series of lectures to enhance their knowledge of general arts and sciences, and the company does not subsidize this, either. Everything is financed by the workers. They plan their activities, and they share the resulting expense, including that of many special events and gatherings. Certain basic costs—for example, those of facilities— are financed by the plant; subsequent expenses, however, are generally borne by the participants.

The same pattern holds good for the cafeterias which are an important employee benefit. The company makes it a practice to finance all the costs involved in cooking the meals. The workers share the costs of all materials. In other words, fixed-cost items are taken care of by the company; direct costs are shared by the employees.

So far as the lectures on general arts and sciences are concerned, we take the position that the participants in such programs should finance them because they themselves are the ones who will benefit. The same principle is applied to recreational and all other activities. The two exceptions are the company's annual field day and annual spring tour. These two programs are entirely financed by the company as reminders of past practice.

Some of the girls in the dormitories entered the plant's professional School of Technology so that they could someday become engineers. They have their own plan, and they are making progress toward attaining their goal. Teachers, dormitory mothers, various managers are always ready with warm, kindly counsel, so that personal burdens are lifted from the girls' shoulders and they are able to devote themselves to their work. No benefit program intended as heartless, insincere bait to employees could produce this kind of result.

The Same Human Beings

Neither wages nor fringe benefits, I have said, are motivators of human beings. But now I should like to return to the point I made some pages back about employees who give the impression that they are devoid of the desire to work and are interested only in money.

Why is it that they give us this impression? I have insisted so far that basic human nature is contrary to what it appears to be, so how does it happen that this basic nature becomes the antithesis of outer appearance? Because the jobs and environment to which employees are subjected are dehumanized by machine-orientation, organization-orientation, work segmentation, and bureaucracy-mindedness. The effect such negative factors have upon human beings can never really be understood until we experience it by ourselves in the lowest stratum in the organization, where these factors prevail in the worst form. Those people who belong to the ranks of the elite, for whom the way is paved, may understand the plight of this lowest stratum in their minds, but they can never feel it in their hearts. Unless managers truly understand the predicament of human beings placed in really desperate conditions, they won't be able to reflect upon their own motives and conduct before accusing their employees of what appears to be a lack of proper motivation and effective performance. They won't be able to understand the true, undistorted nature of human beings.

Those managers who are incapable of understanding human nature usually are conceited in that they believe they themselves are human beings but that their subordinates are inferiors, to be looked down upon. Such conceit would disappear quickly if they were placed in the lowest stratum of their company and made to experience personally what it is like. Some people start at the bottom and succeed eventually in getting to the top; but by that time, unfortunately, many of them have forgotten how it feels down below. The Bible describes an episode in which Jesus Christ reprimanded certain people who were stoning a harlot. This story illustrates a deplorable trait of human beings—we all tend to forget ourselves and to point the finger at others. Also, the situation becomes worse when the finger pointers are promoted to management and start thinking they are somebody. Herein lies one principal cause of managers' misunderstanding of their people; and it is, of course, the source of much mutual distrust.

What is fundamentally important for managers to know is that, when we trust ourselves, we can equally well start trusting others. We must try our best to give others what we want most for ourselves; that is, give them something to live for in their jobs, give them stability from day to day and from year to year. Managers who think it is their prerogative to let people who are different do jobs which the managers themselves would not like to do and who think that it should be possible to lure employees into working by means of money because they want money anyway will end in self-destruction.

The man who spits into the sky will get his spittle back in his own face. And, for somebody up in heaven, what a sad yet humorous scene it will be when all the managers who have gotten a dose of their own spittle cry out that their men are a bunch of good-for-nothings and that society is rotten, unknowingly cursing themselves as they curse others.

4

Establishment of Relationships Based on Trust

THE true dignity of any human being lies in the satisfaction of having a challenging job, in being able to grow in that job, and in finding what he is doing worthwhile. To understand this is to endow human beings with their real nature and worth; that is, to trust them. To use Mr. Halpin's phrase once again—this understanding of human nature is the basis for molding the "proper attitude of employees." I should like here to review the facts briefly.

Mr. Halpin told me that when he summoned his QC staff specialists, asking whether it would be possible to reduce defects in missile systems to zero, they declared it was out of the question. He persisted, saying, "Human beings are *capable* of eliminating defects to zero." The staff specialists retorted, "You're an engineer, but you don't know much about quality control," and they advised him to read a few books on the subject. Mr. Halpin therefore had no alternative but to turn to the employees. He summoned all who were engaged in manufacturing missile systems and said, in effect, what a shame it was that the situation with regard to defects wasn't good enough; that what was wanted was perfect systems; that those who refused to believe they could achieve zero defects might leave and those who did believe they could achieve zero defects might stay and try to realize that goal. As a result, everybody stayed—joined in the common effort. And they made perfect systems. Mr. Halpin described the incomparable delight they all felt at this achievement in such vivid terms that I could understand it just as if I had been one of them.

The World of Trust

"The zero defects program is not magic," Mr. Halpin continued, "nor is it a tactic. It is a way of life. This way of life, grounded in the basic nature of humanity, was being lost by industrial companies—a fact which, given a hint or two, our imagination enabled us to discover. We then set about organizing in a systematic way what our hard work had taught us.

"Human beings are imperfect. Thus it follows that we managers should not look down upon our men for their imperfections. What we can do is to appreciate their efforts to be perfect and to encourage them. This is the basis of our zero defects program, and no ZD program will succeed unless managers who really understand this are placed in charge of it."

There is real insight in these words; Mr. Halpin penetrates to the very heart of the question. Trust as I see it is something quite close to what he describes—trust as the antithesis of the human emotion that feeds on contempt and loathing for those who are imperfect.

In our industrial society, not only are companies and their employees living in the world of distrust in which their management seems to be rooted. Companies, on the one hand, tend to view their employees as inscrutable human beings who want to get more and more money from them for less and less work while, on the other hand, these same employees view their companies as hard-driving tyrants which want to give less and less and think only about profiteering.

This sense of distrust is not restricted to companies and labor unions only. As we can easily detect in the sad faces around us, each and every worker has a deep-rooted sense of distrust whose strength is unimaginable. Once they are out on strike, these workers will line up in a scrumlike formation and fight together, but they are not in this scrumlike formation out of trust for their fellow men. Rather, they have already lost their humanity in the industrial organizations where they work, and it can hardly be expected that they will march hand in hand with their fellow workers in a warm glow of mutual trust. They have become egoistic and lonely. If by chance any of their number dared to offer a suggestion to management—for example, to reduce waste or otherwise improve productivity—such a person would be accused of trying to soft-soap the company. This is the kind of world they live in.

Destruction Caused by Distrust

Once labor unrest emerges, companies rush to take steps against the unions that are the equivalent of allopathy in medicine. These steps, however, are utterly meaningless—except in cases of a very serious nature. Sometimes, too, management finds it necessary to cope with this labor unrest by providing better fringe benefits, which, by themselves, will never solve any basic problems. No amount of money can buy people's affection or souls.

Wages and fringe benefits, whatever form they may take, are bound to dissatisfy employees. We can install the best wage system in the world and still have complaints about, say, the amount of the scheduled annual increase in base wages and salaries— simply because we are earthly human beings. This should not drive us to despair, however. It is just because we human beings complain and give of ourselves grudgingly that we make progress and transform ourselves into superior, even wonderful, human beings. So the question is whether dissatisfaction and complaints will have destructive or self-destructive results or lead to constructive action. The direction we take at this crossroads is influenced by whether our human relations are based on trust or on distrust.

Dissatisfaction arising out of human relations based on trust becomes a motivating factor in further improvement. Managers' tours of their departments under this kind of prevailing climate will be accepted by their people as a gesture of encouragement. When, however, such visits are paid by managers in a climate of distrust, they will be taken by the workers as an attempt at surveillance.

As long as we are human beings, we will naturally be dissatisfied about many things. This constant dissatisfaction is our greatest hope for improvement. That's why it is wrong always to be afraid of arousing dissatisfaction among employees and to feel it must invariably be eliminated. What is more important than anything else is that we managers build human relations based on trust—in other words, trust people, not wait until we are sure they are trustworthy. Managers who demand that their subordinates trust them on the one hand yet who do not trust their subordinates on the other are absurd, to say the least.

At the time when I assumed my post as plant manager, I could discern several self-destructive phenomena among the employees. The famous anniversary-day strike and certain Communistic labor-union activities were examples, and so were the signs of the small-pebble complex that was deeply imbedded in the minds of our young girls and, of course, the delinquent behavior that resulted.

I was, however, opposed to attempting any coaxing or taking allopathic measures against these phenomena. If we had turned our dormitory mothers into prison guards to tighten our surveillance on the grounds of the girls' moral laxity, we would have made matters worse. And no steps against the labor unions based on pressure tactics or coaxing would have improved the situation in the slightest. I believed then that we must first eliminate all negative factors, such as the fundamental problems growing out of our organizational structure and the deep-rooted sense of distrust prevailing in the relations not only between management and employees but among the employees themselves.

Let me cite one symbolic example. We were then having problems with the girls' period leave. Since 75 percent of the employees in our plant were girls, this constituted a major problem. The labor union insisted that the privilege of taking leave during her monthly period is one of the rights of every woman; therefore, the girls should be able to avail themselves of it freely. Management, however, was trying to reduce it to a minimum. As is clearly indicated in the Labor Standards Act, the period-leave privilege amounts to the right to take leave whenever one finds it rather painful to work at a certain time during the month. Management contended that the girls were abusing this right, that they were deliberately taking leave even when they were not in pain. The labor union counterattacked by making inflammatory speeches on the subject to the girls. Management then resorted to implementing a rule which stipulated that a doctor's certificate was required in order for girls to take period leave.

All this, again, is sheer nonsense so far as I am concerned. No doctor in a first-aid room has any means of certifying that a girl is in pain; the kind of checking specified was impossible in actual practice. Girls who wanted to take period leave had to visit the medical office each time they applied for it—a fact which increased their embarrassment and their distrust of the company which was treating them as if they were criminals. I immediately terminated the checking requirement. What was involved here was a simple question of human rights.

We Must Discard Our Authority Orientation

Very well: Companies do not trust their employees, and vice versa. This makes both take defensive action, which further deepens their distrust of one another. We have a vicious cycle here of the sort that too often results from the posture commonly assumed by management in general. If we think about it, we realize that the word "company" (or "companies") is inappropriate in this context. A particular organization or person or thing is arousing this sense of distrust in people, and the sum of these people's distrust comprises the distrust of the whole.

For instance, the following episode took place in our plant. A worker found a tabulating mistake in his pay slip, and he visited the Personnel Department to have it straightened out. Now, human beings can occasionally be despicable, and the man in charge made it known that he felt the worker was deliberately making trouble, trying to pin the mistake on the man himself. A slightly more sophisticated man might have said, "I'm sorry. We've already finished processing this payroll, but we will make sure that your account is properly adjusted for this mistake next month." In short, he should have put himself in the worker's position instead of taking the defensive and, by his attitude, denying any trace of sincere concern. The worker immediately filed a complaint with higher management. I told the man from the Personnel Department to go to company headquarters at once and get the money for him. The mistake in tabulation had inconvenienced this worker, and the least the man responsible could have done was to give him the money due him on the spot—if necessary from the man's own pocket.

This petty bureaucrat's failure to do just that might have implanted the seed of distrust in the worker; in fact, it is often the heartless acts of those bureaucrats who surround management at its various levels, not the companies themselves, that contribute most to the prevailing sense of distrust. We can find many such hidden seeds in companies, and all of them encourage the growth of distrust. Nobody, obviously, has any right whatsoever to denounce employees for being distrustful when they are often subjected to treatment like this.

Another, similar case had to do with the personnel evaluation program in our plant. Again, a mistake was made in tabulation; in recording the results of an appraisal, a Class 8 status was assigned a person who had actually been evaluated as Class 9. This person was not aware of the fact that the mistake in tabulation had been made, but he filed a complaint on the grounds that he was given a smaller pay increase than certain of his colleagues. The man in charge looked into the case and found out that the employee had been accidentally downgraded while the information about him was being transferred onto a graph. So the employee in question found himself brushed aside with an unfeeling "Hold this till you get another increase. I'll take care of it then." The reason for this absurd reaction by the man in charge was that he had to haggle with company headquarters to increase wages and salaries and he didn't have the nerve to go back and ask headquarters for more money on the grounds that he had miscalculated. His primary concern was his own standing with headquarters and nothing else, an attitude which was outrageous.

The wronged employee finally persuaded him to get instructions from the plant manager. I then said to the man in charge, "Why is it that you have to consult with me over a matter which should be obvious to anyone? If you erred, you erred. You should run to company headquarters and say, 'I'm sorry, but I made a mistake. Please give me some more money!' They may call you all kinds of bad names, but you must correct your mistake right now, as of this month."

Thoughtfulness toward people need not take the form of exaggerated sympathy or grandiose humanism. It should be the expression of the natural concern felt by one human being toward his fellow men. Any failure on the part of management to express this thoughtfulness will definitely contribute to building up any lurking distrust of the company.

Staff specialists in personnel or industrial relations departments, because of the very nature of their work, should be doubly careful in this area. I am given to understand that bank clerks who handle voluminous amounts of money come to look at it in a different way than the general public—as a mere "thing," in fact. Likewise, employees and managers in personnel departments come to treat people like unimportant "things." The new type of personnel department must discard this penchant for handling men and women impersonally, for managing by dint of power and authority. It is vitally important that old attitudes give way to the new mission of providing assistance on personnel matters to everyone from line managers to crew members.

Learning the Joy of Trusting

When I came to work at Atsugi Plant, my initial task was to eliminate the omnipresent sense of distrust. This I saw as the root of all our problems. These people had never experienced the joy in living in a climate of universal trust. To them, my reasoning that it should be possible to achieve an atmosphere of mutual trust, and that nothing could be compared to the good feeling one got from working in such an atmosphere, made little sense. They had to experience it by themselves. Even I had no clear-cut idea at that time as to what was involved in this sort of trust. I was too absorbed in other matters. This may sound like a slight exaggeration, but I had no alternative but to devote my body and soul to this problem, tackle it squarely, and implement several plans accordingly.

For instance, there was my plan for a cafeteria without any attendants at its service counter. When I first proposed this plan, every one of my managers opposed me, contending that it would be impossible to implement. They were justified in opposing me in view of the prevailing realities of employee attitudes at the time; but it was, of course, these prevailing realities that were forcing us to regain people's trust. We would therefore proceed with our plan slowly but steadily; however, our campaign needed the initial stimulus of an official kick-off. I was determined that, right at the start, every employee should see for himself that mutual trust is indeed possible and should experience for himself how enjoyable it is to trust others and have others, in turn, trust him.

The introduction of the cafeteria without counter attendants was the best method we could possibly have used at that time to make everybody experience the joy of trusting and being trusted that is the birthright of every man and women. It was followed by the abolition of controls over period leave and by the removal of our time clocks. I don't believe that this method would be applicable to all companies, but I believed then, as I do now, that for us it was absolutely necessary. We had to take these steps in our plant under the existing conditions, and we threw everything we had into the effort. It was our first desperate attempt to demonstrate our wish to pave even a foot or two of the road leading toward the establishment of a society in which we can all trust each other.

We were lucky enough to succeed in all these undertakings. People responded to our trust in them beautifully. You can imagine how exuberant not only I but all the other managers were at that time. It was pure joy that we felt—exceeded only by our pride as human beings.

It may be interesting to compare our experience here at Sony and the process by which Mr. Halpin realized his goal of zero defects in the production of missile systems. Managers' initial opposition to the idea . . . a general appeal . . . implementation . . . success . . . pride and joy universal. The sequence is identical; and the secret of its success, in the case of both Mr. Halpin and me, is similarly identical though less apparent. In a nutshell, it is the fact that neither of us believed he had a right to denounce or despise other people for their imperfections. Nobody—and that includes Mr. Halpin and me—is perfect. We also believed sincerely that people want in their hearts to be good, worthy human beings. It was because the management posture assumed in both companies was one of encouragement, not punishment or contempt, that zero defects were attained in the production of missiles and the cafeteria without attendants paid off.

This management posture is our only "trick." If it should be lost, zero defects, cafeteria without attendants, leave without controls, time keeping without time clocks—all would immediately begin to disintegrate.

Challenging the Future

The trust which people ought to have for the company they work for can never be developed by a company that is devoid of any real entity. It is only possible as aggregates of the trust which people come to feel for one another when they are closely associated. That's what gives the examples I have cited thus far so much significance. The vertically enriched job in which workers are entrusted, say, to assemble a complete product by themselves is another good example. For a true sense of trust on the part of top management vis-à-vis their employees is expressed in their actions, not in forms or words. In the minds of junior and senior workers, their leaders, and other managers, this trust is created when all participate in activities initiated by top management. Through this process, trust in a company is literally built from the beginning.

Visitors to our plant often say something like this: "When I pass a work station, people are so obviously preoccupied that they don't even take notice of me. Yet, once they leave their station, they are all smiles, and the climate of your plant reflects their cheerfulness. You must be a happy man. You don't have any problems, do you?" I would be lying if I were to say I am not happy, but I always counter this kind of remark by saying, "No problems? Far from it! We always have many of them."

It is true; we do have many problems. "Ordeal" would be an appropriate word to describe what I am going through. But I am not the only one here who has problems; all our smiling people have them to a greater or lesser degree. We have plenty of dissatisfaction and discontent, too—a feeling which is shared even by the plant manager. However, it is just because we do have problems and we do have dissatisfaction that we are so full of vitality, that we are finding life worth living, that we are challenging the future, and that we are happy and cheerful. I am still wondering how to explain this to visitors, who are likely to pose rather simple questions about complex problems. Yet this mentality of ours may have something to do with the secret of building human relations on the basis of mutual trust.

Once I had an opportunity to talk with a company president who is well known for his unique management of his firm and also for its success. I had always held him in respect, but his conversation was so full of his beliefs and principles that I was bold enough to ask him the following questions. "Do you think that your company is perfect? Do your employees have any gripes about wages and salaries?" I was surprised to hear him say in answer to the second question, "No, I don't believe so. I don't think they have any gripes." So then I said to him, "In our plant, I and everybody else are continually complaining about salaries and wages." He looked at me with pity in his face, but a few minutes later he apparently had second thoughts about what he'd said. "We don't have such problems, do we?" he asked the secretary who was sitting beside him. I was amused by this sudden doubt on his part; and at the same time, as I recall now, I felt a sense of relief.

Probably I would respectfully decline an offer to work for this kind of company. That's because I would have nothing to do there. I believe that arteriosclerosis is a dangerous sickness for any good system or organization. And I believe an open climate of mutual trust can be maintained only by constant effort and soul searching amid the ordeal of problem solving and brinkmanship coupled with discontent and dissatisfaction. We cannot possibly hope to establish an atmosphere of trust if we fear betrayal of our trust by others—this I have said repeatedly. Trust can be established only upon the basis of unconditional self-abandonment. Normal, worldly human beings that we are, we can bring ourselves to trust people for the first time only when we see a crisis ahead and there exists no other alternative but to face it together.

The introduction of cafeteria service counters without attendants, the abolition of time clocks, the elimination of controls over period leave, and all our other improvements made me feel as though I were walking a tightrope as the newly appointed plant manager. I didn't know how I could ever account for my actions to Mr. Ibuka if I should fail. In other words, it was my awareness of the crisis I faced and my indomitable sense of responsibility that made me take the steps I have described.

I once expounded my empirical principles of self-abandonment to Mr. Sohgen Ohmori, senior mentor of the Tesshu Society.[1] He told me, "The same principles hold good in the mysteries of Japanese fencing. It is through this self-abandonment that a man finds his life again."

[1] Tesshu Yamaoka (1836–1888) was a master of Japanese swordsmanship. Active during the mid-nineteenth-century, Meiji Restoration period, he was noted for his deep understanding and practice of Zen. In 1941, the head priest of Tenryuzi Temple built the Kohoin Temple on the site of Tesshu's home and founded the Tesshu Society, in his memory, to cultivate Zen and swordsmanship. Sohgen Ohmori became the resident high priest of Kohoin in 1948. The society, at present, has 1,000 members.

5

The New Industrial Relations

THE reader will recall that our current concept of work is based on the notion of its being labor. This means that work is equivalent to work—that is, labor—purchased.

People claim that, while the purchase of human beings amounts to slavery, the purchase of the capacity for labor does not. However, it can't really be said that the latter isn't tantamount to slavery. Human beings and the capacity for labor are as inseparable as the relationship between an electricity-generating plant and electric power. This fact notwithstanding, it is generally assumed that labor in the traditional sense is not to be regarded as slavelike labor. Moreover, those who hold that human beings and the capacity for labor should be separated are regarded as quite progressive. Which leads us, I believe, to one of the biggest problems of modern times. Especially here in Japan, we have a strange situation in that schoolteachers consider themselves to be

offering their capacity for labor and that they even have their
own labor union.

Profit Is a Symbol of the Worthwhile Life

The capacity for labor is regarded as being in the same class
with such forms of physical energy as electricity, and it is sold
and purchased at such and such a cost per hour. Those managers
who can buy the capacity for labor at the lowest possible cost
and who can maximize profit by effectively utilizing that capacity are considered to be competent. It follows, then, that this
capacity for labor is expended in the same manner that physical
energy is expended. And why not, since, as I have already explained, it is viewed by such managers as so-called meaningless
labor?

Human beings, however, cannot be separated from their capacity for labor, and they are incapable of withstanding meaningless labor. They don't find it interesting, they can't feel they
are doing a worthwhile job if they engage in it, and—what's worse
—they come to harbor uncontrollable indignation and anger over
what they are doing. But, although these are the sentiments commonly held by workers in modern times, those who feel them
are not aware of the true cause of their surging emotions. On the
contrary, they may even think that labor is the fashionable, up-to-
date way of work. Thus they are naturally led to search for the
cause of their emotions in the environment surrounding them.
Sooner or later, management and company profits become the
targets of their distorted hatred and resentment.

An emotional word like "exploitation" does a good job of describing the circumstances under which too many workers must
function today. Of course we have plausible academic theories to
justify this exploitation, and the use of the very term is somewhat
justified in that modern management in the majority of cases
handles people who work rather inhumanly and makes a profit
from it. No problems will be solved, however, by improving working conditions while keeping meaningless labor as it is. Nor will
any problems be solved by establishing production cooperatives

or by nationalizing private industry through government action, because in either case the workers' attitude toward their jobs will remain essentially unchanged.

Occasionally, voices are raised to the effect that workers' ignorance is beyond help. If workers weren't ignorant, people say, they wouldn't ignore prevailing conditions and ask management for increased wages at a time when companies are unable to earn any profit. Some people say, also, that workers in Socialist countries won't produce unless quotas are forced on them and that this, too, is indicative of immaturity. I shall not defend these workers—on the grounds that anyone who is living from hand to mouth has no alternative but to accept whatever is made available to him. Rather, I believe we should interpret this apparent ignorance and immaturity as evidences of self-destruction by human beings under the rigors of meaningless-labor systems.

At any rate, profit and management are the targets of workers' hatred, and the cry of "exploitation" expresses the prevalent feeling toward both. Giving vent to their emotions, people cry out against what they are pleased to call profiteering. Karl Marx tried to prove the exploitative nature of profit by using the phrase "excess value," but I believe that in any kind of economic organization we have to have profit. This is clearly indicated by the fact that even in the Soviet Union the question has been debated and the concept of profit has been introduced into the country's economy and industrial organizations. Profit is a symbol of the economic value of production activities.

According to the managerial accounting system we use in our plant, profit and loss are tabulated for each departmental unit. This enables everyone in the unit to evaluate his own functions and activities in a very direct way. When we fail to earn a profit, this means that we are engaged in activities which have little or no value. When we do earn a profit, we are correspondingly reassured. In fact, people in the plant get a great deal of pleasure out of making a profit for the units they belong to, and this pleasure encourages them to find life worth living. Far from being a target for hatred, profit under this system is turned into an occasion for rejoicing.

Where does this change come from? It comes from the fact

that people's jobs have turned into meaningful work and that they are now the masters of those jobs. Meaningless labor is gone; in its place there is the sheer joy of making a profit. For profit is a target for hatred or a symbol of the worthwhile life depending solely upon whether management offers meaningless labor or meaningful work.

No words can fully convince people that what I have just said is true. In order to get them to understand, we must teach them about work as it should be, enable them to work joyfully and realize that life *is* worth living. Once they have this basic understanding, they will naturally come to realize that they enjoy making a profit and are proud of their contribution to it. This not only gives them satisfaction but results in material progress as well. Meaningless labor only provides material progress at the expense of human beings.

Who Holds the Key to the Future?

Texas Instruments (the reader will have realized by now that this is a company I admire tremendously) is aware of the basic nature of human beings. Human beings have their reason for existence, and so has Texas Instruments. The company declares, "Our reason for existence is to provide our worldwide customers with our capacity for developing, producing, and marketing useful services and goods. Profit is the indispensable means of achieving this purpose." This represents a new concept of a corporate entity.

Since its earliest days, Texas Instruments has had a management philosophy which says that "the best way to achieve company goals is see to it that employees can achieve their own goals." This statement can be better understood if it is related to the declaration I cited previously. The true goal of the individual employee is to find dignity and worth through his job. The reason for the company's existence is business itself. Texas Instruments has no labor unions. Dr. Myers explains this as follows: †

† Earl R. Gomersall and M. Scott Myers, "Breakthrough in On-the-Job Training," *Harvard Business Review*, Vol. 44, No. 4 (July/August 1966) p. 72.

People in jobs which offer opportunity for growth, for achievement, responsibility, and recognition, have little incentive to get sidetracked with peripheral issues and feel no need to seek the intervention of a labor union to "police" management. In fact, on a properly designed and delegated job in a suitable organizational climate, the employee is in a real sense a manager himself. His proprietary interest in managing his job gives him a sense of company identification that causes him to see unionism as a deterrent to his effectiveness. Hence, meaningful work eliminates the wastefulness of uninspired and reactive behavior and the cost of elaborate systems for dealing with dissatisfaction.

Dr. Myers is an industrial psychologist whose comments are candid and to the point. My own experiences tell me he is right.

I am told that the number of union members in the United States is decreasing gradually and that the labor-union movement as a whole is on the decline. Young workers do not seem to care to join unions. I suspect that this trend can be attributed to lack of creativity on the part of the labor unions themselves, their resistance to technological innovations, and the emergence of an apparent conservatism which makes them seem chiefly concerned with protecting their professional prerogatives. I feel, moreover, that the same situation may well prevail both in England and in other Western European nations.

Another psychologist at Texas Instruments, Dr. Charles L. Hughes, offers a particularly lucid explanation of recent tendencies in labor unionism.‡

> . . . There is just one conclusion we can reach: that unions can serve only maintenance needs and cannot serve motivation needs. Unions—to repeat—cannot help people set or achieve personal goals; they cannot assist the company in setting or achieving its goals; in fact, they are evidence that motivation opportunities are severely lacking or were lacking sometime in the past.
>
> . . . As a matter of fact, they often operate in a way which results in subdividing jobs and reducing their importance till

‡ Charles L. Hughes, *Goal Setting: Key to Individual and Organizational Effectiveness* (New York: American Management Association, 1965), pp. 75–76, 77.

the workers are mere automatons—interchangeable people making interchangeable parts for interchangeable machines. The presence of a union can also inhibit proper planning and setting of company goals, and it certainly can create conditions that do not encourage the achievement of personal goals. And the time is long past in most companies when attention needed to focus on such maintenance factors as physical working conditions, job security, fringe benefits, and equitably determined pay.

Can labor unions improve and play their part in the development and progress of society by turning labor into work? I have my doubts about this. As to Dr. Hughes, he says:

> The future belongs to whichever group is the first to provide significant opportunities for people to satisfy their needs for growth, recognition, responsibility, and achievement. If history has taught us anything, we can predict that should unions be the leaders, there will be just as much industrial conflict over motivation opportunities as there has been over maintenance factors. And again, if history is any indicator, we can assume that should the unions take the initiative, we will have people seeking personal goals which have been set by a process that did not involve company goals. A time may then come when personal goals are being met through collective bargaining efforts but company goals are not being met at all.

I do not think that labor unions are evil and unnecessary. They have played a historically important role in our progress in the past, and even in modern times they are playing an innovative role, objectively viewed, in some cases against reactionary managements.

My views are, in fact, well summarized by Dr. Myers when he says that the pleasure which employees can get from seeing the giant called a company picked on by their labor unions is a poor substitute for the pleasure they could get from confirming that they are whole men by engaging in meaningful work. My past experience as an underdog makes me agree with him. The relationship between union and management at the present time, based as it is on the catalyst called labor, will not produce any means of opening up the future. Disillusionment with the possibilities of the welfare society that we once thought might be based on this kind of relationship can be observed clearly in some of the Western European countries.

At the risk of being redundant, I should like to say that the only way left for us to build our future is to turn meaningless labor into meaningful work. The management that is directly responsible for technological innovation will, I believe, lead the way toward management innovation as well. I am apprehensive about the possibility that traditional labor unions may play a reactionary role, opposing this latter kind of innovation. And this reaction by the unions would run counter to the progress of society and true well-being for the workers. Should they increase their wages and enhance the sophistication of their way of life, filling their leisure hours with hobbies while still keeping the concept of meaningless labor intact, further destruction of humanity could only result. I would hope that if matters reached this danger point, the workers would then, for their own sake, desert their unions.

What is important is human beings. Labor unions and ideologies are mere means of achieving the status of a true human being for every worker. When that has been done, it will be time for the historical role of the unions to come to an end.

My Concern About Labor Unions

Why do I discuss labor unions at such length? Not because I am now a member of management and, therefore, labor unions are a nuisance to me. That is definitely not the case. Rather, I am thinking seriously about the welfare of human beings. Specifically, I have two reasons for being concerned.

One reason—to put it very frankly—arises from my anxiety over the activities of Japanese teachers' unions. For instance, during a recent television program someone argued against annual field trips for students on the grounds that night work by women teachers during such excursions violates the Labor Standards Law. If the program participants had been talking about these annual school excursions from the educational viewpoint, the discussion might have been worthwhile. Instead, to my consternation, they were approaching the subject from the standpoint of preserving the rights of workers.

No parents should ever think of sending their children to this kind of teacher. What we see here is an absence of education itself and of proper teacher-pupil relations.

Japanese labor law, as I have explained, defines educational work as labor. And, to make the situation worse, the teachers' unions are among those who regard this concept as progressive. Yet educational labor has to be meaningful work to be effective. I am wondering what will happen to future generations if the situation remains as it is now. The humanity of young people could even be eroded away during the process of education. This is a subject, of course, which keenly interests industrial managers who are continually receiving newly graduated children in their plants. It is urgently to be hoped that school management above all will feel the impact of innovation.

In Japan, because of our backward notions, working people in general are treated as laborers. The workers themselves are apprehensive about this designation, but they meekly convince themselves, obedient to the teaching of progressive intellectuals, that this concept is the correct, modern one. In Western European countries, however, people clearly distinguish laborers from workers. Industrial employees have no illusions about not being laborers, whereas white-collar people—government workers, teachers, engineers, salesmen, and so on—do not doubt that their jobs constitute meaningful work. The two groups have diametrically different views on working conditions. As for the United States, the rapid increase in the meaningful-work portion of industrial jobs may just account for the recent decline in union membership and influence.

The second reason for my concern about labor unions is—and again I speak frankly—the fact that the situation in our local plant troubles me in a certain way. Sony, like any other firm, used to have a companywide union which gradually became extremely aggressive and communistic. All the employees in the plant were members. However, the number of members has since declined steadily, and at present the union represents only a small percentage of the 3,000 employees. Since the 1960 strike, an organization called the Sony New Labor Union has been formed, but none of us in the plant are members. Then, in 1964 or thereabouts, the Sony Atsugi Labor Union was formed, and it has a membership of 500 workers at the present moment. The majority of the workers do not belong to any labor union.

I was opposed from the beginning to management's becoming preoccupied with measures against labor unions. I absolutely forbade management personnel to interfere with employees' union activities because of my belief that such activities should be strictly voluntary.

What we were trying to do was to relieve human beings of meaningless labor, which we aimed to turn into meaningful work. This goal, of course, was totally unrelated to labor-union matters. Collective bargaining between unions and management was proceeding at company headquarters, but our plant had virtually nothing to do with it. Much the same thing, moreover, could be said about the Sony Atsugi Labor Union. All problems were being solved democratically in the process of day-to-day management, chiefly by the teams to which I have referred in earlier chapters. With labor changed to work, it was inevitable that no collective bargaining would be required. This, plus other basic management innovations, without any doubt contributed to the relative inertia of labor unions in our plant.

I used to be plagued with doubts as to whether our ongoing management policy of keeping union activity to the minimum is justified or not in our present capitalistic society. The officers of the Sony Atsugi Labor Union are proving instrumental in creating meaningful-work conditions in their jobs. These officers, however, have to assume the so-called labor-union posture in order to maintain their union standing, and as a result they seem to be troubled by a certain sense of contradiction. At one time, therefore, I felt both compassion and sympathy for them. I asked myself whether the situation in the plant could be tolerated, reflecting on its social significance, with something akin to a guilty conscience, over and over again. Gradually, however, I came to feel easier in my mind. In light of the unions' significance in the stream of history, I began to feel there was no other course for us but to let nature have its way.

The important thing, let me say in conclusion, is still human beings. Management should concern itself solely with what it can do for the benefit of human beings, and it should march forward steadfastly toward that goal.

Index

Abilities Inc., 59
ability, evaluation of, 181
ability-oriented staffing, 180–182
absenteeism, 27, 34–36, 42–44
accounting, managerial, 113–115
accounting department, 114
address, form of, 40
allopathy
    distrust and, 230
    organization and, 128
American Telephone and Telegraph
    Co., 201, 214
analytical approach, vs. oriental
    mind, 69
anti-organization principles, organi-
    zation through, 125–138
Atsugi High School, 48–51
Atsugi Plant (Sony, Inc.)
    current problems of, 237
    dormitories at, 21–37
    English titles used in, 134
    Guide to Dormitory Life at, 26–29
    interconnecting cells in, 38–39
    managerial accounting system in,
        113–115
    "revolution" at, 10–17
    safety and hygiene committee of,
        108–109

second phase of educational devel-
    opment at, 51–52
    working hours at, 47–48
Atsugi Topics, 36, 163
attendance
    autonomy in recording of, 34–36
    checking of, 42–44
authoritarian organization, 22–23
    communication in, 157–161
    immobility in, 167
    leadership qualities in, 175
authority
    absence of in leader, 175–183
    power structure and, 130
    responsibility and, 137
    short-circuiting of, 166
authority orientation, discarding of,
    232–234
autonomy
    crisis avoided through, 36–37
    in dormitories, 23–32, 224
    in recording attendance, 34–36

Beethoven, Ludwig van, 203
Bible, 227
boss
    communication with, 160
    dislike of, 131–132

249

About the Author

SHIGERU KOBAYASHI has been Managing Director of the Sony Corporation since 1969. He is also Chairman of the Sony Manpower Committee and Board Chairman and Principal of Sony High School. Previously he was Managing Director of Sanseido, Ltd., Managing Director of Kyodo Printing Company, Ltd., and Manager of Sony's Atsugi Plant.

Mr. Kobayashi is a graduate of the Tokyo Advanced Industrial Arts School. He serves as a member of the Science Education and Industrial Education Council of the Japanese Ministry of Education and is a regular lecturer at many top management seminars.